STARS OF THE OLYMPICS

STARS OF THE OLYMPICS

Bill Libby

HAWTHORN BOOKS, INC.
Publishers
New York

STARS OF THE OLYMPICS

Copyright © 1975 by Bill Libby. Copyright under International and Pan-American Copyright Conventions. All rights reserved, including the right to reproduce this book or portions thereof in any form, except for the inclusion of brief quotations in a review. All inquiries should be addressed to Hawthorn Books, Inc., 260 Madison Avenue, New York, New York 10016. This book was manufactured in the United States of America and published simultaneously in Canada by Prentice-Hall of Canada, Limited, 1870 Birchmount Road, Scarborough, Ontario.

Library of Congress Catalog Card Number: 72-21313

ISBN: 0-8015-7120-0

2 3 4 5 6 7 8 9 10

For Allyson, a beautiful bonus

CONTENTS

PREFACE	xi

ACKNOWLEDGMENTS	xii

1
TOOMEY THE TYPICAL	1

2
THE FIRST MODERN OLYMPIC GAMES, 1896
America's First Hero	12

3
THE EARLY OLYMPIADS
A Standing Jumper	19

4
STOCKHOLM, 1912
The Immortal Indian	27

5
THE 1920s
A Tarzan Is Born — 36

6
LOS ANGELES AND LAKE PLACID, 1932
The Babe Leads the Ladies — 49

7
NAZI GERMANY, 1936
The American, Jesse Owens — 60

8
ST. MORITZ AND LONDON, 1948
A Young Man Named Mathias — 70

9
OSLO AND HELSINKI, 1952
Boxers Strike Gold — 83

10
CORTINA AND MELBOURNE, 1956
One from the Shadows — 93

11
SQUAW VALLEY AND ROME, 1960
Rafer and Wilma — 103

12
INNSBRUCK AND TOKYO, 1964
Schollander, the Superswimmer — 115

13
GRENOBLE AND MEXICO CITY, 1968
Peggy and Debbie   *125*

14
SAPPORO AND MUNICH, 1972
Another Superswimmer, Spitz   *140*

15
INNSBRUCK AND MONTREAL, 1976
Stars to Be Born   *159*

OLYMPIC GAMES SUMMARIES   *167*

INDEX   *181*

PREFACE

THE MOST SPECTACULAR sporting event in the world is the Olympic games. It has been held every four years since 1896 in cities all over the world. Originally conceived as a summer celebration, a winter pageant was added in 1924, and its renewals have been divided between summer and winter sites and sports ever since. Originally it was mainly for men; women became a more prominent part of the program in 1928. At first, 285 athletes from 13 nations competed in 10 games. By the 1970s, between 7,000 and 8,000 athletes from more than 100 nations were competing in more than two dozen different games.

The Olympic games has become the sporting world's greatest gathering ground of men and women, who come from all around the world to meet in friendship and the most intense competition in amateur athletics. The medals they win, and especially the gold medals that represent triumph in each event, are the most coveted prizes of their kind. While the spotlight shines brightest on the men who go for the gold in track and field, this book highlights the stars, women as well as men, in winter as well as summer games, in all sports on the Olympic program. While the emphasis here is on the outstanding American athletes of the last 40 years, the superior performances of athletes from all over the world throughout all the olympiads leading to the 1976 games are covered on these pages.

ACKNOWLEDGMENTS

The author wishes to thank the athletes themselves most of all, for many interviews over many years. He wishes also to thank the organizers, promoters, and public relations men from all countries who made it possible for him to follow the many sports. And, finally, he wishes to express his gratitude to E. D. Lacey of England, Jon Hendershott and the staff of *Track & Field News,* and to the many other photographers whose work appears on these pages and the journalists whose writing contributed so critically to the author's accumulation of knowledge of the athletes and events portrayed in this volume.

1
TOOMEY THE TYPICAL

HE HAD MISSED his first two attempts, and now he stood at the end of the runway preparing for his third and last chance to clear the first height of the pole vault, the eighth event of the ten events of the decathlon competition. He could see a dozen years of dedication and determination, of sweat and sacrifice, of practice and pain, of injuries and frustration coming to nothing if he failed. "It is not possible to be more nervous," he recalls. "I could feel my heart pounding. My arms and legs were shaking. I could barely breathe. I was scared half to death."

This was the Olympic games in Mexico City in 1968, the 19th Olympiad, and this was Bill Toomey, a 29-year-old part-time schoolteacher from Philadelphia, Pennsylvania, and Santa Barbara, California, who was at the crossroads of his sporting career. He had dreamed of winning an Olympic decathlon title—and with it the coveted gold medal—all his adult life. He had put everything else aside in his quest. And now, suddenly, unexpectedly, it all came down to a single effort.

It was one of the most dramatic moments in sports history.

Contestants in the decathlon sprint 100 meters, long jump, put the shot, high jump, and run 400 meters on one day, then run the 100-meter high hurdles, throw the discus, pole-vault, throw the javelin, and run 1,500 meters on the following day, in that order. They compete side by side, but against stopwatches and tape measures, their performances translated into points from a scale devised by experts and added up to produce a winner.

Because each of the events requires different techniques and timing and each requires the use of different sets of muscles, the competitor in the decathlon must divide his training time among them and may put in more time and be more vulnerable to injuries than those practicing for a single specialty.

Some decathlon men are outstanding in one or two events and build on that base, but most, as Toomey was, are jacks of all trades and masters of none. Yet, because it is such a demanding test of speed, strength, and stamina, the gold-medal winner from the decathlon in each Olympiad is regarded as the greatest all-around athlete in the world.

This was what Toomey wanted more than anything else in his life. This was what he had worked for a great part of his life. At thirty-one he was older than any man who ever had won an Olympic gold medal in the decathlon before. Most other men gave up if they did not get the gold before they reached their thirties. He was young as most men measure age, but old as all-around athletes are regarded. There was no real money in it and little glory, except in Olympic years. He was driven on by his dream, the rest of his life left waiting.

The Estadio, the enormous soccer stadium converted into a track and field arena for this glamorous international competition, was packed with more than 80,000 tourists who had traveled from all over the world and residents of the host city and capital of Mexico. Millions more watched on television. The press box was packed with correspondents who would report the event in newspapers and magazines of all countries. And all eyes were riveted on the husky, handsome American who led Hans-Joachim Walde and Kurt Bendlin of West Germany, Joachim Kirst of East Germany, and Nikolay Avilov of the Soviet Union late on this second and last day of the decathlon.

The bar in the pole vault was set at approximately 11 feet, 9 inches. The great pole vaulters can clear six feet greater heights. Toomey was not a great pole-vaulter, but he regularly cleared two feet higher. This, then, was but a modest test of his talent. Yet, almost torn apart by the pressure which pounded at him, he had missed twice. And now he had only one more opportunity to clear this modest height. To miss would mean he would miss out on a medal. He did not have to be at his best in every event to win. He could run a little slower in one event, throw something less far than usual in another event, and make it up in others, but failure to complete any event would finish him.

"I had done so many things wrong on my first two jumps, I couldn't figure out how to correct anything," Toomey sighs. "All my friends were yelling advice to me and there wasn't time to sort it all out. Everything was closing in on me—the people in that huge arena, the people watching on television back home, my whole life, all those years of working and waiting for this moment. If I missed, it would be like dying. It was as though I was holding a gun and had to pull the trigger with life or death at stake. It was horrible."

He had the 30 seconds permitted him to make the most meaningful effort of his career. He made up his mind to close his mind to everything, to just go all out. Suddenly he pulled the trigger. In the growing darkness of that great arena he ran down the runway, jammed his pole into the slot, arched up awkwardly, cleared the bar clumsily, and fell into the foam rubber below as he and everyone else in that place, except for his foes, roared with relief. A broad smile broke out on his dark face and he did a little dance as he bounced away, ready to resume his search for the ultimate prize in his sport.

"I stole a look at the bar, just to make sure it was still in place, just to make sure I hadn't knocked it loose somehow," he recalls. "It was there, all right. Suddenly it didn't look so high up. A few moments before it had seemed a mile into the sky. I had gotten over it somehow.

"All the technique I had learned and practiced, the hundreds of vaults I had made had been forgotten in the fear and frustration I felt. I was like a beginner, clumsy and uncertain. But I had made that jump on sheer determination. I'm not even sure I needed my pole. And now I had it all together again. I was back on the right road again. I was on my way again. The gold medal was within my reach again."

If one athlete can be considered typical of those who go for the gold, Bill Toomey may be the one. He worked long and hard to attain his goal, overcoming enormous obstacles along the way. He had handicaps which he would not let stop him. He did not begin as the best. He made the most of himself. He may have wanted it more than others wanted it. If he needed a little luck along the way, he got it.

He was born in Philadelphia of Irish Catholic parents with some money. His father was vice-president of a winery and his job required moving the family from one part of the country to another several times. Bill went to grade school in Long Island, New York, to high school in Connecticut and Massachusetts, and to college at Colorado University and at Stanford. He earned master's degrees in English and education. But he wasn't sure what he wanted to do in life, except that he knew he wanted to make a mark in sports.

He had run short races in track with mediocre results and regretted that he was not good enough to go further with it. He preferred track to other sports, however, and had some all-around ability, so he tried a decathlon in 1959 with discouraging results. He tried again three years later with a more promising performance that persuaded him to pursue it seriously.

Two years after that, he finished fourth in the trials and thus was barely beaten out of a place on the three-man U.S. decathlon entry for the 1964 Olympics in Japan. In frustration he followed the team to Tokyo, where he watched from the stands enviously.

Among those he observed was Mary Rand, a pretty Englishwoman, who won a gold medal in the long jump, a silver medal in the pentathlon (which is a sort of miniature decathlon), and a bronze medal in the 400-meter sprint relay for women.

After Bill watched Willi Holdorf of Germany win the decathlon, he turned to a German tutor, Friedel Schirmer, who trained him in the 10 events. Toomey taught English in a Cologne school to support himself.

Stricken with mononucleosis and hepatitis, Toomey returned to his parents' home in Newport Beach, California, where he fought for five months to regain his strength.

He recalls, "On my first day out of bed, I walked down the hill in front of our house. When I got to the bottom, I started back up. But I couldn't make it. I sat down and cried because I thought I was through."

Three months later, he won his first national title. With it he broke the world record for the event with 8,234 points, but the record was not recognized because it turned out the hurdles were not the correct size. Frustrated, he was to seek the record six more years before getting it.

This was at Salina, Kansas. Toomey pointed out, "The hurdles weren't the only things wrong there. The track was like a pasture, the bugs big as cows. The heat was 100 degrees, and the corn was popping in the field. I was like a slab of half-eaten, dried-out meat when the event was over."

Sadly, he observed, "Decathlon championships often have been held in tiny towns like Walnut, Tulare, and Salina, where about sixty people turned out to watch us each day. None of these were reporters, and the results were telephoned into the newspapers, which might or might not run them the next day, depending on how many baseball games there were.

"It's funny, but in Olympic years the decathlon champion is celebrated as some sort of superman. Every other year he's ignored. Unless you have a specialty, you can't even get invited to compete in any of the big meets. I offered to pay my own way to enter a meet once in Baltimore and was rejected. I was invited to another meet in New York another time and then the invitation was withdrawn when they found a glamour guy they could buy with the travel money.

"Let's face it, ours is not a glamour event, so I'm not a glamour guy. I didn't go into this thing for glory, but the lack of recognition I have gotten for it has depressed me."

Wistfully, he wondered about it. He said, "All your life, you think about doing something special, getting something you couldn't buy. Then you do it and nothing happens. And you find you're disappointed. And you begin to wonder about yourself. At my age, I could have made money, built up a business, found a future for myself, started a family. Instead, I'm a track bum, roaming the world looking for a little medal.

"It's hard to explain the glamour of an Olympic gold medal. So many seek it from all over the world and so few get it. You have to give up so much to get it. You need so much good luck. Some of the greatest never get it. So you find yourself going for it when you should be retiring from track and trying for something else in life."

He and his best buddy and fiercest rival, Russ Hodge, chose to establish a decathlon hermitage in Goleta, just beyond Santa Barbara. The track coach at the University of California at Santa Barbara was willing to help and let them use the school's facilities. It was an area without a lot of distractions and with a climate suited to year-round training. And Toomey found work teaching at a local junior high school. Soon other decathlon hopefuls moved into the area to train with them.

In 1967, as another Olympiad neared, Toomey repeated as national champion and captured the Pan-American Games title but lost a big meet that meant more to him. In the process, however, he met the woman who later became his wife. In midsummer, Russia withdrew from its scheduled annual track meet against the United States and other countries were invited to compete instead at the Coliseum in Los Angeles. Among those who came from Great Britain was Mary Rand, and it was at this time that she and Toomey met.

A decathlon was included and Toomey and Hodge fought to the finish within reach of the world record. Entering the last event on the last day Hodge led, but he had to finish within 21 seconds of the faster Toomey in the 1,500-meter run to protect his advantage. It was twilight and some 60,000 persons, a much larger crowd than they were accustomed to, cheered them on.

Exhausted, they struggled around the oval with the leaner Toomey forcing himself further and further ahead. Finally he finished, after 4 minutes and 20 seconds. Collapsing in the grass, he raised himself on one elbow to watch the burly Hodge labor on. With a last lunge, the big man crossed the finish line just in time to retain his lead and land the record. As others stood to applaud Hodge, Toomey fell back in disappointment.

Toomey and Hodge became estranged after that and Hodge moved to Los Angeles. Toomey later said, "We got to be so competitive, we stopped being compatible. Other people spoiled things for us. They kept asking us if we were jealous of each other. They put things in our minds that weren't there." Bill went back to work in Santa Barbara, where he was making less than $10,000 a year. Asked about him, a fellow decathlon man, Dave Thoreson, said, "He's thirty years old and doesn't have a decent job. That explains him about as well as anything."

At that time Toomey said, "My parents have money, but I try to make it on my own. I'm capable of doing something else in my life, but it will have to wait until I do this thing first. There are always girls around and we have dates and parties and I want to get married, but I don't have time for much else besides track.

"It's tougher to train for the decathlon than for any other event because there's so much to learn. There are 34 separate movements to the pole vault, for example, 14 to the hurdles, 12 to the high jump, and so forth. The pole vault is the toughest. If a man knew nothing, he could put the shot, even if it was only a foot in front of him. But if he knew nothing about it, all he could do with the pole was impale himself on it. The first time I tried the pole vault I went about as high as I could high jump. Our biggest fear is looking bad out there.

"Actually, we train for nine events and 'gut' the tenth. There is no way we could take the time to prepare properly for the last event, the 1,500 meters, which is called the metric mile and is only a little shorter than the mile. We practice as many hours as any athlete, but distance runners run 15 to 25 miles a day and we don't have the time for that. So I lay down on the grass after nine events and wait for them to call the tenth event and wonder how the heck I ever let myself go into this damn business because I know it's going to hurt like hell. Then they call it and I just get up and do it."

This spring day in 1968 was his day for practicing the high jump and high hurdles, and he worked all that day under a hot sun, trying and failing, and trying and failing, and trying and succeeding, skinning his shins, continuing until he was exhausted. Later he sat in the dressing room in a hot whirlpool bath easing a sore rear end. "There are times when there is not a muscle in my body that doesn't ache," he admitted.

Standing 6 foot 1 and weighing 195 pounds—having built himself up from 165 pounds with weight lifting—he looked a marvel of fitness, but he was in some ways a physical wreck.

All his life he had worn eyeglasses to compensate for poor vision, but he was in the process of converting to contact lenses, which were irritating his eyes. As a boy, he suffered a slashed arm when a friend tossed him a pop bottle and it broke on him, severing some nerves. He was left with only a fifth of normal feeling in his left hand, but he learned to live with it. He wears special innersoles and shoes to compensate for a left leg that is a quarter of an inch shorter than his right leg, and for the shin-splints and heel-spurs from which he suffers.

He has pulled and torn muscles in his legs, his groin, his arms, and his shoulders. He battled back from his bout with mononucleosis and hepatitis in 1966. He suffered from bone chips in his knee joint for years until he had to have an operation in April, 1967. Two months later he won his second straight national title.

Now he nervously fingered the scar on his knee and said, "I can't sleep good for weeks before and after big meets. I doze off, wake up, toss and turn. The tension builds up until it twists me all out of shape. Normally, I'm an outgoing guy. I like people. I like to kid around. I laugh a lot. But on the days of meets, I can't stand to speak to anyone. And it takes a long time later to unwind.

"Now, in an Olympic year, the thing that scares me is that one injury could throw all the working and waiting right out the window. And even if I get to Mexico City, I may not win. If Hodge makes it, he may win. Or one of the Germans may win. I think I'm the best, but I have to be the best on those two days. I don't have to win the ten events, but if I mess up too much in any one of them I'll lose."

Hodge did not make it. He suffered an injury that finished his hopes forever. Kurt Bendlin, the best German, made it, but with an injury that hurt his hopes. Toomey made it, healthy and hoping for the best. "The Olympic Games! Games! The Olympics are no games!" he said later. "I had such headaches in Mexico City, you couldn't believe it. I couldn't sleep and I could hardly eat anything at all."

The first day, the first event started at 10 A.M. There were 33 finalists. In practice, Toomey pulled a leg muscle a little, but he ignored it and sprinted 10.4 in the 100 meters, the fastest of the contenders, and within a tenth of a second of his fastest time ever. An hour later he had the longest long jump of his career and of the competition, just under 25 feet 10 inches.

Later in the afternoon Toomey put the shot a little past 45 feet 1 inch, but bigger men did better, and the brawny Joachim Kirst of East Germany did so much better, 53-11, that he took the overall lead in points. About an hour later Nikolay Avilov of Russia led the high jumpers at 6-9, but Kirst remained in front at 6-6, while Toomey settled for a bit beneath 6-5.

It was late in the evening when the day's final decathlon test, the 400 meters, was staged. Toomey put everything he had into it. He was sensational, running the route in 45.6 seconds, by far his fastest ever and the fastest of the contenders. The 1,021 points he earned later turned out to be the most taken in any of the 10 events. This regained the lead for him at the halfway mark. "It gave me the big boost I needed psychologically," he recalled later.

Then he suffered a slight setback. Randomly selected Olympic athletes were tested to prove they had not taken any illegal drugs to improve their performance, and Toomey was one of two chosen to be tested at that point.

He remembers, "I was out there at 8 A.M., we didn't finish until 9 P.M., and then I had to take that test. Did you ever try to go to the bathroom with 15 Mexican officials looking on? I had to drink about 40 cups of water before I could urinate. This was while the competitors were back in their rooms resting. I passed the test, but I didn't get to go to bed until after midnight. Then I couldn't sleep. I was up at 6 A.M. I was so nervous, I was sick to my stomach."

He arrived at the track early in the final day of the decathlon

Toomey the Typical

with a sore shoulder and a sore leg. He and a teammate turned their vaulting poles over to an attendant to take to the main stadium while they worked out on other events in the practice stadium nearby. Then they went to the main stadium to start the final five events.

The first test was the 110-meter high hurdles at 10 A.M. Ten competitors, hopelessly beaten and discouraged, had dropped out, reducing the final field to 23 men. The fastest hurdler was Eduard de Noorlander from Holland, but he was not among the overall leaders. Afraid of falling, Toomey skimmed the barriers cautiously in 14.9 seconds, which was far from his fastest but good enough to maintain his lead over the Germans, Kirst and Walde.

Throwing the discus, Toomey stretched a muscle in his groin and it hurt horribly, but he ignored it and went on to get off a heave of 143 feet 5 inches. He had spun one 12 feet further in practice, but was satisfied with this one, since he'd suffered an injury but still held his edge over his foes.

There was a bit of a break before the next event, the pole vault, but Toomey and his teammate found their poles missing and spent the time searching frantically for them. Desperately, they returned to the practice stadium to look there without luck. They could not find the attendant who had taken them. They asked about them but, unable to speak Spanish, had difficulty making themselves understood by the Mexican officials.

On an impulse, Toomey pointed to a storage room and indicated he wanted to look in there. It was unlocked. There were their poles. As they ran with them the half mile back to the main stadium, they could hear the crowd roaring. Had they missed their starting times and been disqualified? "It was a nightmare," Toomey remembers.

They were just in time to start. But then Toomey, tired, out of breath, and shaken, missed his first vault. And his second. He was left with his last effort in front of him. A miss would have meant elimination from the meet and missing out on that medal he wanted so much.

He did not miss. Somehow, he made it and the next five heights as well, despite a sprained thumb, regaining confidence as he went. Others went as much as two feet higher. Bendlin went more than a foot higher. Walde went a couple of inches higher. But Toomey bettered 13 feet 9 inches to hang on to a lead which was diminishing now.

Two events remained. The javelin throw started late in the afternoon, as heavy black clouds blotted out the sun and cold winds swept across the cement saucer and the grass surface. Despite a sore elbow which bent him in agony on each throw, Bendlin hurled the spear more than 247 feet to shoot into second place past Walde, whose best throw went just under 235 feet. This was not Toomey's best event, and his 206-foot toss reduced his lead to a mere 56 points. A man could make up more than a hundred points easily in the final event, the metric mile.

The 1,500 meters went off at 6:45 P.M. as a chill, light rain started to fall through the gloom. It had been 33 hours since the start of this grueling competition, and almost all were close to collapse. Toomey's uniform was soaked, his muscles were sore, and his bones ached. His face seemed drawn, as though he had aged. "I have never been so scared and tired in my life," he later recalled. The pressure had sapped his strength and stamina.

He did what he could do. He gave what he had left. The race was run in heats with the leaders in the same heat, and Toomey led all the way. He would not permit his rivals past him. Lap after lap he held them off, and on the fourth and final lap, with pain knifing his side and his breath coming in agonized gasps, he gave the last of himself to break the tape in just over 4 minutes 57 seconds. Less than 2 seconds later, Walde struggled home. In 10 more seconds, Bendlin labored across the finish line, so spent he collapsed and had to be carried off on a stretcher.

"I didn't care about the time. I knew if I finished in front, I protected my lead in the meet," Toomey said later. He stood for a second as though stunned, trying to realize he really had won this greatest of his goals at last. Walde, who had risen to the runner-up spot in the last event, went to him, and the two warriors embraced. A little later the top three mounted the victory stand, Toomey standing the highest, while the Mexican musicians played "The Star Spangled Banner" in his honor, and the gold medal on a colored ribbon was draped around his neck.

"It was," he says, "the one moment in my life I will never forget. In that one moment, all I had worked for was worth while."

He returned to his country a hero, a celebrity, an immortal of sports, heir to a legend created by Jim Thorpe early in the century.

Bill Toomey went on in competition long enough to land that elusive world record in 1969. However, he says, "it was something I wanted, but not something which will last. Records are broken. A gold medal is forever." He retired and married Mary Rand. They had a daughter, Samantha. The offspring of a decathlon gold medalist and a pentathlon silver medalist, she seems destined to become a superathlete.

Bill taught English in college for awhile, worked in marketing for a major product manufacturer, did some acting, served as a sports commentator on television, but when the chance came to get back into track as coach of the team of the University of California at Irvine, he took it.

Declared a professional because of a television commercial he cut and so no longer eligible for amateur competition, he nevertheless continued to practice and kept a track suit and shoes in the trunk of his car. Asked what he would do if he were ruled eligible again, he smiled and admitted, "I'd probably go into training to try to make the Olympics."

2
THE FIRST MODERN OLYMPIC GAMES, 1896
America's First Hero

THE OLYMPIC GAMES grew out of the athletic ideals of ancient Greece, and according to tradition the first Olympiad was held in 776 B.C. on the grassy plain of Olympia. Greece revered physical fitness in its citizens as much as it did intellectual attainment. In the sixth century B.C. frequent competitions were staged between representatives of rival cities and even of neighboring countries. Running, wrestling, and lifting tests were regularly held, as well as dramatic, oratorical, and musical events. By the fourth century B.C., outstanding athletes were concentrating on specialties full time. Their daily practice sessions, their dietary habits, their sleeping periods were strictly controlled by state trainers. The leading scholars of the day, such as Socrates and Plato, complained that these men neglected their minds so they could glorify their bodies.

By the time the Romans conquered Greece in the second century B.C., professional athletes dominated sporting competition. The Romans gave the games form and introduced a life-and-death element by bringing in boxing, in which the foes wore deadly metal studs on their hands. With Emperor Nero came corruption. One year he bribed the judges and his rivals so he could be declared the best musician, the best singer, the best orator, and the best chariot driver. When he fell from his chariot during his race, his rivals paused and waited to resume until he was back in business and whipping his way to victory.

The prestige of the events started to pale, which is not so surprising. These festivals had lasted nearly 1,200 years before they were abolished by the Christian Emperor Theodosius after the

The First Modern Olympic Games, 1896

290th Olympiad in A.D. 390. The sacred site of the festival at Olympia subsequently was all but destroyed by barbarian invaders. For 15 centuries there were no more such sporting celebrations in the spirit of Greece although there were some awesome spectacles staged. Life-and-death struggles were witnessed in the Circus Maximus by as many as 350,000 persons in a single afternoon. At the opening of the Colosseum, thousands of men—Christians, prisoners of war, and criminals—and some 10,000 animals were slain in battles staged to entertain the crowd. This scarcely could be considered sport.

In the middle 1800s, the Greeks, led by Evangelios Zappas, staged some sporting contests similar to Olympic Games, but these were unstructured, drew few competitors, and stirred little interest. They can be considered as minor international competitions. It was not until the late 1800s that a Frenchman, Baron Pierre de Coubertin, a scholar who admired ancient Greece's sporting ideals, pushed a movement toward a modern Olympic celebration. He was an educator, not an athlete, but he believed athletics were as essential as education to the development of well-rounded young men. In 1896 he met with sportsmen in Paris and outlined a plan for regular revivals of the old Olympic Games in which amateur athletes of all nations would meet in friendly competition in sport. Another meeting two years later drew warm response from representatives of many countries. Another two years later, the first modern Olympiad was staged, appropriately enough, at Athens.

The baron stressed that the Games should feature friendly competition among individuals, not between nations, and among amateurs who competed for prizes, not pay. His idealistic spirit was typified by this statement: "The main issue in life is not the victory, but the fight; the essential is not to have won, but to have fought well." This became the creed of the Olympics. Participating athletes pledged the following oath: "We swear that we will take part in these Olympic Games in the true spirit of sportsmanship and that we will respect and abide by the rules which govern them, for the glory of sport and the honor of our country."

By the fourth Olympiad in 1908, a system was devised of awarding gold, silver, and bronze medals for first, second, and third places in each event. The Olympic flag was not conceived and did not appear at the Games until 1920 at Antwerp, Belgium. It consists of a series of five interlocking rings of blue, yellow, black, green, and red on a field of white. The rings represent the five major continents, and their colors are those that appear in most of the flags of the various nations. They are linked to symbolize friendship and togetherness. The words "Citius, Altius, Fortius," which frequently appear within the rings, are defined as "Swifter, Higher, Stronger." The symbolic bearing by relay runners of a lit torch from Olympia, Greece, to the site of the Games each four years was begun in Berlin in 1936.

Baron de Coubertin became the first president of the International Olympic Committee, which governs the Games, although the athletes of the individual nations are ruled and selected by the amateur groups that rule within each country. Most members of the IOC are wealthy sportsmen who have the time, interest, and finances to serve without pay. They are aristocrats who are criticized constantly for their dictatorial tactics and for their reluctance to change with changing times. One such was the American, Avery Brundage, who served for two decades until after the 1972 Games, who served into his eighties, who refused to alter the original concept of amateurism as modernists would have it. But the Brundages insist the true spirit of the Olympics must be maintained as originally intended or else the Games themselves must be ended.

In the 1970s this magnificent meeting of men and women in friendly athletic competition is endangered. Commercialism has crept in. Competitors say it is impossible to sustain themselves without the support of sponsors. Skiers say they cannot continue without financial backing. The companies that back them say they cannot afford to do so without being allowed to advertise on the skiers' uniforms and skis. Brundage and his successor, Lord Killanin of Ireland, hint they then must be barred. There are countless such cases.

So many attractive competitors in so many "amateur" sports are paid "under the table" that declaring all athletes professional may be the only answer, but Olympic leaders prefer to avoid any taint of professionalism. Yet many Olympic competitors are supported by their countries, which frees them to concentrate on their specialties and gives them an unfair advantage over athletes not receiving such benefits.

Presumably politics have no place in the Olympics, yet the system fosters it by continuing to raise the flags and play the national anthems of the winners' countries after each event. And, more and more in recent years, partisans have been pursuing politics with a

The First Modern Olympic Games, 1896

passion. Before the 1968 Olympics at Mexico City, students demonstrated against the use of funds that they felt might be put to better use by the needy. Demonstrations turned into riots as the government police used force to put them down. Many were imprisoned, and many killed. During the competition, black athletes, who had threatened to boycott the Games as a protest against racial injustice in America, dramatized their feelings as the first two finishers in the 200-meter run, Tommie Smith and John Carlos, raised black-gloved fists and lowered their heads while the U.S. anthem was played. During the 1972 Games in Munich, Arab terrorists invaded the Olympic village and took as hostages a number of Israeli athletes, killing many before the horror was done.

Yet anyone who has attended an Olympics, who has mixed with men and women of the world's many nations, who has heard the music of a dozen languages being spoken at once, who has witnessed the intense competition between superb performers in dozens of sports, who has observed the joy of victory and the despair of defeat, who has seen the flag-bearing representatives of the countries of the world marching into a great stadium in the opening ceremonies, and who has seen them dissolve into a delightful, dancing, handholding frenzy of friendship in closing ceremonies that encircle the great stadiums has to have felt the greatness of these Games and has to hope that the original spirit of this sports spectacular somehow can be preserved.

From the first it was settled that the Olympics, if successful, would be staged every four years, although in 1906 an attempt was made to renew them every two years. Dramatic contests and other such theatrical events were included in the original programs but soon abandoned in favor of pure athletic competition. Many sporting events that were on the early schedules, such as standing jumps, soon were discontinued, but over the years other games have been added. Some winter sports were included in the original games, which were designed as summer celebrations, but a separate Winter Olympics was not added until 1924. Some which may be considered winter games, such as basketball, remain on the summer calendar. Women competed in the Olympics as far back as 1912, but it was not until 1924 that they were given a major place in the proceedings and their participation has been increasing ever since.

Ten times as many nations send forty times as many athletes to the Olympic Games today as they did when the modern Games were begun back in 1896. At that time Greek officials raised about half a million dollars and constructed a 60,000-seat stadium, 13 countries sent 285 athletes, and on a drizzly spring morning the king of Greece declared the Olympics open. The hills above and beyond the stadium were crowded. In all, an estimated 100,000 spectators were in attendance as the five-day program commenced.

The Americans had a small team on hand, yet won nine of the twelve track and field events. Princeton University and the Boston Athletic Association were the only groups who sponsored entrants. Most of the competitors had to pay their own way. They went by sea, switching ships twice and winding up on a train for the last lap of their journey. They had scheduled the trip so they would arrive with a week or more to regain their "land legs" and prepare, but they had received incorrect information and on their arrival learned they had to commence competition on the following day.

Refused time off from Harvard, James Connolly had quit college and paid his own way to Athens. He won the first event of the first day—the hop, step, and jump, later renamed the triple jump. He went more than 45 feet to win by more than 3 feet. They did not give gold medals in those days. He got a silver medal and an olive wreath. As an American flag was hoisted to the top of the staff, a 200-member band beneath it played the winner's national anthem to start the tradition that endures to this day.

"It was a great moment in a young man's life," he later recalled. "I thought the folks back home would be thrilled when I returned." He returned with 12 cents in change in his pocket, and no one was waiting for him at the station. He celebrated with a soda, which he drank alone. That took care of one of his nickels. With his two pennies, which he called "coppers," he bought a newspaper to see if his name was in it. It wasn't. With his last nickel, he took a trolley home. The conductor helped him off with his suitcases, and the bundles of trophies presented him, and the souvenirs he had collected. "I brought the news of my victory with me," he recalled. "No one knew what had happened far across the ocean."

He never returned to school but became a celebrated writer of sea stories. He died in 1957 at the age of eighty-eight, a few years after being presented an honorary Harvard letter sweater at ceremonies during a reunion of his original class.

Connolly also was second in the high jump and third in the long jump, which was called the broad jump until recent years. And he returned to the Olympics in 1900 to take second in the triple jump.

The First Modern Olympic Games, 1896 17

Ellery Clark of the United States won both the high jump and the long jump in 1896. His high jump was just above 5 feet 11 inches, his long jump 20 feet 10 inches. Bob Garrett, Princeton's track captain, won both the discus throw and the shot put with tosses of 95 feet 7 inches and 36 feet 9 inches.

Garrett never had seen a discus before he picked one up, tried to throw it the day before the competition commenced, and decided to enter. An outgrowth of the throwing of stones and rocks in ancient times, the discus and shot events were traditional Greek events but were not contested often in the United States at the time. The local fans despaired when their champions, Miltiades Gouscos and Panagiotis Paraskevopoulos, were conquered. Garrett also was second in the long jump and third in the high jump.

Tommy Curtis of the United States captured the 110-meter high hurdles in 17.6 seconds. Thomas Burke of the United States doubled by winning the 100-meter dash in 12 seconds flat and the 400-meter run in 54.2 seconds. The American domination ended when Teddy Flack, the Australian champion, who was working as an accountant in London and who had gone to Greece on his own, swept the two middle-distance races, winning the 800 meters in 2 minutes 11 seconds, and the 1,500 meters in 4 minutes 33.2 seconds.

The Greek fans had all but given up hope of a victory in the featured sport on the program when one of their own won the featured event, the marathon. This was Spiridion Loues, a water carrier from the poor village of Amarousion. At that time many poor villages had no water supplies of their own and carriers had to travel to the nearest depot to fetch containersful. Twice daily, Loues rode to the depot on a mule, loaded water containers on the animal, and jogged alongside the long nine miles back. On the day of the marathon, Loues was a superbly conditioned young man who covered the 25-mile distance in just under three hours, finishing 7 minutes in front of his nearest rival. This remains the widest margin any marathon has produced in the Olympics.

The event was named and the distance set because, as legend has it, this was approximately how far a messenger, Philippides, ran in 490 B.C. when carrying news of the victory of the Greeks over the Persians from Marathon to Athens, falling dead on his arrival. Now a water boy, Loues, was a hero in his homeland. He was offered riches but asked only for a cart and horse so he would not have to run alongside a mule in the future when he fetched water. The king granted his request and the runner never ran another race. His fame is marred by the fact that no two of many reference works on the Olympics spell either of his names the same, or even put them in the same order.

There were other sports contested at Athens in 1896 and the Greeks did well in these, taking nine first places, including three in shooting and two in fencing, to tie the U.S. with a total of 10 winning medals.

Hungary won two swimming events, and Great Britain two tennis events. Germany won four of the seven gymnastics tests, and France four of the six cycling tests. Masson of France was the lone triple winner of the Olympiad, capturing three events in cycling, a sport which always has been more popular in Europe than in America.

The United States got its other winning medal in shooting. It did not have a winner in swimming, a sport in which it was later to dominate. The American champion, Gardner Williams, traveled 5,000 miles to compete in the 100-meter freestyle sprint, dove in at the start of the race, found the water icy cold, was heard to curse in his discomfort, and promptly climbed right back out.

And so it had begun.

3
THE EARLY OLYMPIADS
A Standing Jumper

FOLLOWING THE FIRST of the modern Olympics in 1896, it was not clear that the Games would continue. The Greeks wished them to be held in Athens permanently, and many sportsmen around the world agreed this was as it should be, but Baron de Coubertin insisted they should be moved around among the great cities of the world and he succeeded in locating the 1900 renewal in Paris in his honor.

However, it was not much of an honor. The French refused to recognize the competition as an Olympiad. They staged an "International Meet of Champions" strictly as a sideshow to the 1900 Paris Exposition, which was a sort of world's fair. The word *Olympics* did not appear on the medals, in the programs, or in any publicity. The events did not get much newspaper coverage, and it was not until later that this was recognized as a renewal of the Olympics.

The competitors outnumbered the spectators. More than 1,000 participants arrived from 20 nations, but attendance any single day never exceeded 1,000 spectators. Most of the American participants came from colleges or from the New York Athletic Club, and again many paid their own way. The famous football coach Amos Alonzo Stagg borrowed $2,500 from friends to cover expenses for some competitors from the University of Chicago. And he was one of many who were outraged to learn some events were scheduled for Sundays. Many threatened to withdraw, but few did.

The events were spread over a five-month period. The track and field events were staged on the grounds of the Racing Club de

France. The French refused to disturb the grass by installing a cinder track. In the throwing competitions, the javelins or discuses often disappeared into the bushes or trees surrounding the grounds. Yet there were some outstanding performances, notably by two Americans, Alvin Kraenzlein and Ray Ewry.

The Americans won 17 of the 23 track and field contests. Kraenzlein was from Princeton and was the pioneer of modern hurdling form, devising the technique of tucking his trailing leg back. Until he came along, some runners actually jumped over each hurdle with both feet at the same time. At one time he held every world record in the hurdles at various heights and distances, as well as the world record in the long jump. In 1898 he set a world record for the 200-meter high hurdles of 23.6 seconds, which was equalled but not lowered for a quarter of a century.

In 1900, in Paris, he won both the 110-meter and 200-meter hurdles, as well as the 60-meter dash and the long jump. To this day he remains the only track and field competitor ever to win four individual first places in a single Olympiad. He was twenty-three years old at the time.

Improvements in techniques, training conditions, competitive conditions, and living conditions have been so great from year to year that it is unfair to judge athletes of the past by the present standards. A great athlete of one era probably would have been equally great in a later era. Those who dominated their eras and whose records endured awhile must be regarded favorably alongside those who later bettered their records. Thus, there are those who regard the inventive, swift, and strong Kraenzlein as the greatest hurdler of all time.

Similarly, while the standing jumps were discontinued after World War I, many recognized Ray Ewry as one of the most remarkable athletes America has produced. He also was a remarkable man. Born in Lafayette, Indiana, in 1873, Ewry as a boy was paralyzed by an unknown ailment and confined to a wheelchair. Doctors told him he never would walk again. However, he devised his own exercises and worked many hours a day for weeks, months, and years until he not only was able to walk but could generate the explosive power in his legs that enabled him to leap enormous distances from a standing position.

At the Paris Games in 1900, at the age of twenty-seven, Ewry won three events—the standing high jump, the long jump, and the triple jump. To illustrate his skill and strength, he high-jumped 5

The Early Olympiads

feet 5 inches and long-jumped 10 feet 6 inches from a standing position. Later, he long-jumped 11 feet 4 inches this way. As a bonus, the former Purdue athlete threw in an unofficial leap of 9 feet 5 inches—backwards.

This was only the start of his Olympic heroics. He won the same three events in the 1904 renewal in St. Louis. Then, at the age of thirty-five, he went on to win the only two standing events—the high jump and the long jump—that were contested in the 1908 Games in London to give him eight victories in eight Olympic events, which remains a record. And he is one of the few to spread triumphs over three Olympics.

Additionally, he won the standing high jump and long jump in the unofficial Olympics that were contested at Athens in 1906, so by stretching a point he could be credited with 10 for 10 over four sets of Games.

Another American standout was Myer Prinstein, a versatile and durable performer. Prinstein was first in the triple jump and second in the long jump in 1900. The world record holder in the long jump, he might have won this event but refused to compete on a Sunday in the finals when Kraenzlein captured the honors. Prinstein returned in the 1904 Olympiad to win both the triple jump and the long jump and won the long jump in the unofficial Olympiad of 1906. He also sprinted, though without Olympic success.

Still another athlete of unusual versatility was Richard Sheldon, who won the shot put and was third in both the running triple jump and the standing high jump. And then there was John J. Flanagan, one of many remarkable weight men from the Irish-American Athletic Club, who won the hammer throw in the 1900, 1904, and 1908 Games. Only Al Oerter, who later won the discus in four consecutive Games, also defended an Olympic crown in a track and field event more than twice.

Flanagan, born in County Limerick, Ireland, but an emigrant to the United States, was a massive man who competed at a time when the hammer really resembled a hammer, with a head and handle, unlike the chained ball that later came into use. He held the world record in this event.

He also set records in the 56-pound weight throw, won six National AAU titles in the event, and set a championship meet record that endured for 35 years, until shortly before his death in 1938 at the age of sixty-one. By then he had returned to Ireland, where he coached a two-time Olympic hammer-throw champion, Dr. Patrick O'Callaghan.

Among other double winners in 1900 were John Tewksbury, who won the 200-meter dash and the 400-meter low hurdles and was second in the 60-meter and 100-meter sprints and third in the 200-meter low hurdles; and Irving Baxter, who won the high jump and pole vault and was second to Ewry in the standing high jump, long jump, and triple jump. Both Baxter and Tewksbury were from Pennsylvania University.

The Paris marathon was memorable. The French, eager for a track and field triumph, altered the route shortly before the race was run and after all the visiting athletes had learned the original course. Not surprisingly, Frenchmen finished first, second, and third, led by Michel Teato, a baker's aide, who was running over a route he ran daily delivering fresh bread. What did surprise some of the others was that, although the course covered long stretches of muddy ground, the Frenchmen were the only ones who arrived at the finish line unsoiled. They were not seen to pass the others on the route, and there were those who suspected they had taken shortcuts through familiar back alleys. Nevertheless, their names remain atop the Olympic listings for 1900.

There were other events aside from track and field, of course, including tug of war, lawn bowling, pigeon flying, and fishing. Great Britain dominated the swimming events as her Johnny Jarvis won the 100-meter and 400-meter freestyle races. The English also dominated the tennis events, while the Swiss shone in shooting. The French hosts were the pacemakers in rowing, cycling, and fencing.

The 1904 Olympiad was not unlike the 1900 Games. It was staged in St. Louis in conjunction with the Exposition and was overshadowed again by a world's fair. Less than 500 athletes from 11 nations participated, and the percentage of Americans was so high that U.S. domination was deceptive. Montreal policeman Etienne Desmarteau was the only track and field winner who was not an American, beating out the great Irish-American John J. Flanagan in the 56-pound weight throw.

James Lightbody won four first-place medals, capturing the individual 800 and 1,500, and the 2,500-meter steeplechase, and running a leg on the four-man metric mile relay championship team. Archie Hahn won all three sprints. Harry Hillman won the 400 and both hurdle races. The Texan Ray Ewry swept the three standing jumps. Prinstein won the running long jump and triple jump. Another policeman from the Irish-American AC, Martin Sheridan, won his first of two straight Olympic discus titles. He also won the unofficial Olympic discus and shot put in 1906. Ralph Rose won his first of two straight Olympic shot put titles, and he came back in 1920 to win the odd right-handed and left-handed weight throws.

Again the marathon created controversy. The American Fred Lorz finished first, but after the president's daughter, Alice Roosevelt, had draped a laurel wreath around his neck and presented him with the bronze medal, which represented triumph at that time, he was found to be a fraud. The early leader, Lorz, had collapsed at about the halfway point from cramps suffered in the stifling heat of the 102-degree day. A passing motorist picked him up and was driving him back when his car overheated and stopped a few miles from the finish. Rested and refreshed, Lorz leaped out and resumed his run. Having been driven far in front, he had no trouble hitting the tape well ahead of the rest. When this was discovered, he was disqualified.

Almost as memorable a marathoner was a Cuban mailman, Felix Carvajal, who showed up at the starting line in full uniform, including the bulky boots he wore when delivering mail in Havana. Running, the heavy heat oppressed him and he started to shed his clothing. To restore his strength he picked peaches and apples off the trees he passed en route and at one point suffered such stomach pains that he had to lie awhile alongside the road. He got up to finish an astonishing fourth—in his underwear. Some revere him as more heroic than the man eventually declared the winner, Thomas Hicks of Boston, who had a doctor administer painkilling drugs and shots to him and who drank brandy along the way to ease his tortured route.

The Germans dominated the swimming events, led by Emil Rausch, who won three races. The American Charles Daniels won two races, was second in another, and third in another. The Cubans dominated the fencing events, led by Ramon Fonst, who won three events. But the Americans, with far the most entries, dominated boxing, wrestling, rowing, cycling, gymnastics, tennis, and archery, among the many sports contested.

The most unfortunate sporting events were the special Anthropology Day games, in which American Indians, African pygmies, South Pacific giants, and tribesmen from other remote areas were brought in to demonstrate their legendary prowess. What they demonstrated was lack of training. Observers reported deep disappointment with the poor performances put forth by these fellows, who, sadly, were spotlighted like freaks in a sideshow.

Two years later, the Greeks staged their own "Olympics" in Athens. While these were unofficial and the results are not included in the records of the Games, they were so smoothly conducted, so well contested among more than 900 athletes, and so well attended—by as many as 60,000 spectators in a single day—that they did much to remove the sideshow atmosphere which obscured the Olympics of 1900 and 1904 and to restore international interest for the fourth Olympiad in 1908 in London.

These Games originally were scheduled for Rome, but the eruption of the volcano Vesuvius two years before they were to start was so destructive to several Italian towns and so drained the country's financial resources that the Olympics were relocated in England. It was a turning point, in which the Games were established as a permanent fixture on the world sporting scene. They were an enormous success—the entry rolls doubled as more than 2,000 athletes representing 22 nations participated. And crowds of up to 100,000 spectators packed the main arena.

One controversy was created when the English did not have the flags of the United States, Finland, and Sweden arrayed with the others around White City Stadium. Sweden withdrew in a rage. The United States and Finland remained, but the United States protested the slight: As the national teams marched into the arena during the opening ceremonies, the athlete chosen to carry the flag at the head of each group dipped it in the traditional gesture of respect as he passed the head of state, in this case King Edward. Shot-putter Martin Sheridan, leading the Americans, declined to do so. Since then, the U.S. team never has dipped its flag in such ceremonies. At Mexico City 60 years later Harold Connolly was honored by being offered the role of U.S. flag bearer, but when he warned officials he would dip his flag the offer was withdrawn.

Mel Sheppard was the star of the American track team. The tiny New Jersey runner swept the two middle-distance races, setting new world records of 1:52.8 at 800 meters and 4:03.4 at 1,500 meters. It was the second straight and last such sweep for an American runner. He also ran a leg on the winning 1,600-meter relay team to get his third gold medal. The system of gold, silver, and bronze medals was introduced in this Olympiad. Ray Ewry got

The Early Olympiads

the golds in the two standing jumps, and Marty Sheridan got the golds in both the freestyle and the Greek style discus throws. Eric Lemming of Sweden got the gold in the Greek style javelin throw. He repeated in the freestyle javelin four years later, getting the Greek style javelin then as well.

An American divinity student, Foster Smithson, protested the Sunday scheduling of his event, the 110-meter high hurdles, by running with a Bible in one hand. Nevertheless, he won in world record time. It might also be noted that a young Yale man, A. C. Gilbert, tied an Ohioan, Ed Cook, for first in the pole vault at a world record 12 feet 2½ inches. Gilbert, who was working his way through college as a magician, later coached another Yale man, Sabin Carr, to an Olympic pole-vaulting victory. Still later, Gilbert found fame as the inventor of the Erector Set, maybe the top seller among toys of all time.

There were two controversial events: In the 400-meter, the four finalists were three Americans and a lone Englishman. Rumors swept London that the Americans would set up one of their number for the victory by ganging up to block out the Englishman. As the quartet broke in a bunch down the stretch, an English judge rushed onto the track and pulled an American runner off amid cries of foul. As the two remaining Americans neared the finish in front, another English judge snapped the tape before they could get to it. Although impartial observers did not observe any illegalities, one American was disqualified and it was declared the race would have to be rerun. The remaining Americans withdrew, and the Englishman circled the oval alone to win his tainted gold medal.

Perhaps the most famous of all Olympic races occurred in the marathon that year. In searing heat, the runners set out from Windsor Castle for White City Stadium. South Africa's Charles Hefferon led much of the way but faded near the finish as first Dorando Pietri of Italy and then Johnny Hayes of the United States passed him. As they entered the stadium, the Italian had a good lead, but he had little left. Dazed by exhaustion, he turned the wrong way around the track. Although it was illegal, a sympathetic official thoughtlessly grabbed him and turned him in the right direction. But after a few faltering steps, Dorando, as he came to be called because his name was incorrectly listed as "Pietri Dorando" in the program, collapsed onto the track. Other officials rushed out to help him up. They held him erect as he struggled through his last steps, practically carrying him across the finish line.

One of these officials was Sir Arthur Conan Doyle, the writer of the famous Sherlock Holmes detective stories and a track enthusiast.

Dorando finished first but had to be disqualified. Hayes finished second shortly thereafter and was awarded the gold medal. Publicized as a shipping clerk at Bloomingdale's department store in New York City, Hayes really was not working there but was sponsored by the store for publicity purposes. However, it was not the winner but the loser who became the most famous name in Olympic annals.

Dorando, who almost died on the track after the race but recovered in a few hours, received a gold cup from Queen Alexandra who had sympathetically observed the event from her royal box. He was immortalized in a song titled "Dorando," written by an unknown young American, Irving Berlin.

Dorando, a pastry cook, turned pro and earned a lot of money running before crowds who never again paid such handsome sums to see a marathon runner. He moved to England and operated a restaurant there, forever a famous figure.

Ironically, this was the first marathon run at 26 miles 385 yards and a few inches, which became from then on the traditional distance for this event. Had it been run at around 25 miles as in prior marathons, Dorando probably would have won. And swiftly been forgotten.

Outside of track and field, the United States won only seven gold medals for a total of 22. Charles Daniels, who had won two events in swimming at St. Louis, won another one in London. But Henry Taylor of Great Britain was the star in swimming with three gold medals, winning the 400- and 1,500-meter freestyle races and anchoring the winning 800-meter freestyle relay team. As was usually the case in the early Olympiads, the host nation had a deeper team than the visitors and a great advantage. At London, the English won 57 gold medals.

The most noteworthy visitor was Paul Anspach of Belgium, a fencer who started a string of two gold, two silver, and two bronze medals that stretched over four Olympiads.

However, the most memorable hero of the early Olympiads was Ray Ewry of Texas, who jumped long and high from a standing start.

4
STOCKHOLM, 1912
The Immortal Indian

SWEDEN WAS SELECTED to host the 1912 Olympiad, which was to become one of the most controversial of all time. The Games in Stockholm lured more than 2,500 participants, who contested more than 100 events. One of the events was the military pentathlon, which consisted of five riding, running, swimming, and shooting events. An army man, Lt. George Patton, was the favorite after winning the cross-country race but fared so poorly in target shooting he finished fifth, behind four Swedes. This was the same "ol' blood and guts" Patton who became famous as a general in World War II.

Women had been competing in the Olympics since the second Games in 1900, when six took part in tennis. They participated in figure skating in 1908, but this then was discontinued until 1920. Women joined in the swimming and diving contests in 1912, but the stars of this competition were George Hodgson of Canada and Walter Bathe of Germany, who won two individual gold medals each.

A Hawaiian representing the U.S., Duke Kahanamoku, won the 100-meter freestyle title and returned to successfully defend it eight years later, in 1920, before finally losing it to Johnny Weissmuller in 1924. A powerful figure, Kahanamoku popularized the crawl stroke, which remains in use today. He introduced it to Americans when he came to California for the trials in 1912.

Born in Honolulu in 1890, the Duke later was a wonderful water polo player and a pioneer surfer who, more than any other person, was responsible for the popularity of this sport that surged into prominence in the 1960s. He was the sheriff of Honolulu before he died in 1968 at the age of seventy-seven.

Among other standouts in the Stockholm Olympics were the Italian Alberto Braglia, who won his second straight gold medal as the outstanding all-around gymnast, and the Hungarian fencer Jeno Fuchs, who won his second straight gold in the saber.

In track and field, the leading gold medalist was the first of the "Flying Finns," Hannes Kolehmainen, who won three with triumphs in the 5,000- and 10,000-meter runs and the 8,000-meter cross-country event.

A small, slender twenty-two-year-old, the durable distance runner ran and won four grueling races, including a trial and heat each in the 5,000 and 10,000, in four days then, after a day's rest, returned to set a world record at 3,000 meters in a four-man relay. His teammates failed him, and the Finns did not attain the finals of this event. Undiscouraged, Kolehmainen returned a few days later to win the 8,000-meter cross-country race the only year it was held. Eight years later he won the gold medal in the marathon at the Olympics in Antwerp.

Arnold Jackson of Great Britain became the first man to break four minutes for the "metric mile" with a run of 3:56.8 in the 1,500-meter. Relays were run for the first time, and Great Britain won the 400. However, the U.S. won the 1,600. The U.S. again dominated track and field. Ralph Craig swept the sprints. Chuck Reidpath and Teddy Meredith set world records in winning the 400 and 800 respectively. Pat McDonald brought America its fifth straight gold medal in the shot put. Matty McGrath, whose Olympic efforts spanned 16 years, won the hammer throw. It was his only gold medal, although he won silver medals for second-place finishes in these events in 1908 and 1924.

However, the hero of the 1912 Games in Stockholm, and possibly of all of the early Olympiads, was an American Indian, Jim Thorpe, whose star was clouded by scandal.

Black Hawk, one of Thorpe's forebears, was the best runner, the best jumper, the best wrestler, and the best swimmer of the combined Sac and Fox American Indian tribes. He became their greatest chief. At seventeen, he led a war party against the Osage and took his first scalp. At nineteen, he led his people to victory over the Cherokee in bloody battle. He led his people against the white men, too, but the whites outnumbered the Indians and overcame them, tribe by tribe, taking their land and restricting them to reservations. In 1832, Black Hawk, an old man by then, retired to the reservation set up near Fort Des Moines in Iowa.

An Irishman named Thorpe came to live on the plains at that time, settled near the fort, met and married Chief Black Hawk's granddaughter. They had a son, Hiram Thorpe, who grew to look more Indian than Irish. He was a 6 foot 230-pounder, powerful, and the greatest athlete among the men who grew up around the reservation.

He married, but his wife died. Leaving his two children there, he left to settle in Oklahoma where he married again. His second wife, Charlotte View, was three-fourths Sac and Fox and one-fourth French. In a cabin by the North Canadian River near the Oklahoma Indian Reservation, on May 28, 1888, she gave birth to twin sons, one christened James, the other Charles. Jim's Indian name was "Wa-Tho-Huck," which translates into "Bright Path." Jim Thorpe's twin brother, Charles, died of pneumonia at the age of eight.

Although he was not a purebred Indian, Jim Thorpe was regarded as an Indian, as was anyone who had more Indian than white blood in his veins. Accordingly, he suffered from public prejudice. The United States government controlled his life. His opportunities to escape a reservation life were limited. He grew up on a ranch. The chores he liked best were roping, riding, and breaking young colts. He also liked to hunt and fish with his father. He worshipped his powerful father. They often walked 20 to 30 miles on trips through the woods.

During school periods Jim was boarded at the reservation school 23 miles away. He didn't like school, and he was lonely for his family. Once he just left and walked the 23 miles home. His father immediately walked him back. After his father left, Jim left again, running cross-country over a shorter but rougher route. When his father got home, his son was waiting for him. Determined that his son should get schooling, the father sent him far away to the Haskell Institute, a government school for Indians in Lawrence, Kansas. Here there were sports, such as football. Jim found out he was good at such games and was happier than he had been at the other school.

However, when he received a letter that his father had been shot in a hunting accident, Jim walked home, from Kansas to Oklahoma. It took him two weeks. By the time he got there, his father was recovering, but his mother was sick. Within two weeks she was dead of blood poisoning. Jim, who was 12 then, ran away from home to Texas, where he worked as a cowboy. After a year, he had earned enough money to return home with a team of horses. His father accepted him back, and Jim was enrolled at a nearby school this time. There were no sports, and he disliked it; but he stayed with it.

A representative recruiting promising lads for the Carlisle Indian School in Pennsylvania visited the reservation in Oklahoma and offered Jim an opportunity to learn a trade at his institution. Encouraged by his father, the boy accepted. He was fifteen when he arrived at Carlisle. He was 5 foot 3 in height and 115 pounds in weight, but he went out for football and he tried so hard he was permitted to remain on the team as a reserve, though he seldom played. Two months after he arrived, blood poisoning killed his father as it had his mother. Jim did not go home. After his first term, he quit school to work on farms in the area. Two years later, at nineteen, he returned to the school, aware by then that he needed an education.

By this time he stood 5 foot 11 and weighed 180 pounds. He went out for football, baseball, and track, and developed quickly in all of these sports. He was a natural athlete, swift, strong, and with great reflexes. Everything came easy to him. He was regarded as lazy. He hated to practice. But he enjoyed playing the games. He loved competition. He was proud of his ability to do better than others. It brought him the first real recognition he'd ever had in his life.

At twenty he was maturing rapidly. In 1908 he starred as a runner, punter, and drop-kicker on the football team from this tiny school of 500 boys, which astonished the nation by beating Penn, Pitt, Navy, Nebraska, and Syracuse. He also led his baseball team in hitting and was seldom beaten in track in the sprints, hurdles, and high jump.

However, he still had not settled down. In those years, many college players picked up a little money by playing summer semipro baseball under assumed names. Jim was invited to accompany some teammates to a tryout with the Rocky Mount team in North Carolina. When he found out it paid $60 a month, he stayed. Instead of returning to school after the season, he returned to Oklahoma, then went back to bush-league baseball at Rocky Mount and also at Fayetteville, North Carolina, the following year. Naïve about such things, he never changed his name. He played under his own name. He was a superb pitcher but

Stockholm, 1912

was used so much his arm grew sore and he had to switch to playing first base and the outfield.

His coach at Carlisle, "Pop" Warner, who became one of the most famous football coaches of all time, regretted losing Thorpe, a prize prospect, and wrote him a letter asking him to return to school with the thought of going out for the Olympic track team, which would be going to Stockholm in 1912. Intrigued by the idea, Thorpe again went back to college. He was now 6 foot 1 and 185 pounds, a homely young man who was built like a bull.

He was a sensation in football, running wildly with speed and power, drop-kicking field goals of up to 50 yards, punting up to 70 yards. He scored all of Carlisle's points in an 18-15 upset of mighty Harvard. He scored 17 points in 17 minutes of another game. With only 16 men, Carlisle was the most colorful team of the time, and Walter Camp, who selected the All-Americans of those years, put Thorpe at the top of his list in 1911.

Thorpe was equally effective in track. Most noteworthy was a meet against Lafayette at Easton, Pennsylvania, in May, 1912. When the Lafayette coach, Harold Bruce, met the Carlisle visitors at the train station, he was surprised to see that their coach, Warner, had only seven young men with him. Bruce asked where Warner's track team was. Warner said this was it.

"But we have 48 men and we're undefeated," Bruce said.

Pointing to Thorpe, Warner said, "That one man will be enough to defeat you."

The Lafayette coach figured him for a fool until the meet.

Tewanima, who was to win the silver medal in the 10,000 meters in the Olympics, won two distance races. And Thorpe, who was to win two gold medals at Stockholm, won six events—the 120-yard hurdles, the 220-yard hurdles, the shot put, the discus throw, the high jump, and the long jump—and was third in a seventh event—the 100-yard dash. He won more first places than the entire Lafayette team, and Carlisle won the meet.

Thorpe tried out for the U.S. Olympic team at the Polo Grounds in New York City that summer, and his all-around ability was so awesome he was selected to compete in both of the tests of track and field versatility of that time—the one-day, five-event pentathlon and the two-day, ten-event decathlon. The track pentathlon was merely a miniature decathlon and soon discontinued, so no other athlete ever will match Jim Thorpe's feat of sweeping the two in one meet.

The pentathlon came first in Stockholm. Thorpe led all

competitors in the long jump with leap of more than 23 feet 2 inches and in the discus throw with a heave of around 116 feet 8 inches. He was third in the javelin at 153 feet 2 inches. But then he was first with a 200-meter sprint of 22.9 seconds and first with a 1,500-meter run of 4 minutes 40.8 seconds. With four firsts and a third, he finished far in front of Ferdinand Bie of Norway, the runner-up.

Then came the decathlon. Again Thorpe led in four events with a high jump above 6 feet 1 inch, a shot put of 42 feet 5 inches, a run of 15.6 in the 110-meter high hurdles and one of 4:40.1 in the 1,500 meters. And he was third in four events with a pole vault of 10 feet 7 inches, a long jump of 22 feet 2 inches, a discus throw of 121 feet 3 inches, and a 100-meter sprint of 11.2 seconds. And he was fourth with a 400-meter run of 52.2 seconds and a javelin throw of 149 feet 11 inches. Again he finished far ahead of the runner-up, Hugo Wieslander of Sweden.

Fifth in the pentathlon and fifteenth in the decathlon, incidentally, was Avery Brundage, a powerful, erect twenty-four-year-old, who later became three-time American all-around champion, winner of a super decathlon in which contestants had to contest ten events in one day with no more than five minutes between events. He never entered another Olympiad as an athlete, but became president of the International Olympic Committee after he founded a construction company that made him a millionaire. And he ruled the Olympics with an iron hand.

But as an athlete he was beaten badly by poor Jim Thorpe, who never had a hundred dollars in his pocket a day of his life. Thorpe's point total of 8,412 for that 1912 decathlon was almost twice that of any of his rivals and was not topped for 36 years. Yet you will not find that total, nor his individual performances, nor even his name in any of the Olympic record books. And Avery Brundage, who might have restored them, refused to do so.

At the time, Jim Thorpe was hailed as the most heroic of heroes. Along with his gold medals, King Gustav V of Sweden presented Thorpe with a bronze bust of himself and a jeweled medal of a Viking ship. "You, sir," said the king, "are the greatest athlete in the world."

"Thank you, King," grinned the athlete.

National AAU official James Sullivan said, "Thorpe is the greatest athlete the world has had."

On his return to the United States, Thorpe was given a victory

Stockholm, 1912

parade up Broadway as hundreds of thousands of New Yorkers cheered him. President Taft told him, "You are the highest type of citizen this country can produce and we are proud of you."

Thorpe was offered as much as $1,500 a week to tour the vaudeville circuit, but he preferred to return to Carlisle to captain the football team for his senior season. Again, although all foes were pointing for the now-famous Indian, Thorpe was almost unstoppable.

Against an Army team that included a young player named Dwight David Eisenhower, who was to become a general and a president, Thorpe returned one kickoff 90 yards for a touchdown, but it was recalled because of a penalty. Army kicked off again, and the Carlisle comet returned this one 95 yards for a touchdown. He scored 22 of 27 points in the defeat of Army, 28 of 34 points in an upset of Pitt.

He was amazing, an All-American again. He scored 198 points in his senior season. He concluded his college career with eight scoring runs of 50 yards or more. He was the most celebrated sportsman in the world.

But early the following year, in January, 1938, a sports writer who had pitched for Jim's Rocky Mount semipro team wrote in a Worcester, Massachusetts, newspaper that the Olympic champion had been paid to play baseball a few years earlier and so had not been an amateur, as Olympic rules require. The story was reprinted in the *New York Evening Mail*, where it was called to the attention of officials of the National Amateur Athletic Union. The AAU's Sullivan, whose name was to become immortalized with the Sullivan Award, a trophy that is given annually to the outstanding amateur athlete in America, contacted the coach, Warner, at Carlisle, who contacted Thorpe.

A letter was composed and sent to the AAU. It said, in part, "I did not play for the money. I was not very wise in the ways of the world. I hope I will be partly excused by the fact that I was simply an Indian school boy and did not know that I was doing wrong because I was doing what many other college men had done, except that they did not use their own names."

He could not be excused. The rules then were very rigid. An athlete cannot be paid to play one sport and remain an amateur in another according to Olympic standards, though he can now by the standards of some other amateur groups. Maybe many cheat, but this one had been caught. And despite public sympathy for the

Indian, the AAU had to act even as the International Olympic Committee would. AAU officials met and declared Thorpe had become a professional and so had not been eligible for Olympic competition. He was ordered to return his prizes. He was stunned. "I am guilty, I guess," he said sadly. He left school. He left the returning of his trophies to his coach, who packed them and shipped them back to Sweden.

The IOC ordered his name and records removed from the rolls and the medals for first place sent on to the runners-up, Wieslander and Bie. Both protested that Thorpe had earned the medals, but they accepted them. Bie, who became Norway's first gold-medal winner, never tried to return his medal to Thorpe. And Wieslander, who said he tried to make contact with Thorpe to return his medal in the late 1960s, said he was unable to do so. The fact was, Thorpe already had died.

After the scandal, Thorpe was offered a pro baseball contract by the New York Giants and accepted. But his pitching arm was ruined; he had to play the outfield, and he was too inconsistent a hitter ever to earn a regular's role. Still, he lasted six years in the majors with the Giants, Cincinnati Reds, and Boston Braves, as a reserve who averaged batting around .250 for his career. Although he hit .327 in 60 games in 1919, that was his final season in baseball.

He had started to play pro football winters. Offered an opportunity to become player-coach of the Canton Bulldogs when the National Football League was organized in 1919, he returned to his first love. At season's end, he kicked the field goal that beat Massillon 3-0 in the league's first championship game. But by then the bounce was gone from his step. He served as president of the league strictly as window dressing in 1920. He returned to action the next year and drifted from team to team until 1925. At one point he organized his own team, the Oorang Indians, which included former Carlisle players, but the team did not succeed. Thorpe tried a comeback with the Chicago Cardinals in 1929 at the age of forty-one, but he was finished.

He had neglected his education and had nothing to fall back on. His name brought him minor opportunities, but his fame was faded. He was given bit parts in movies on and off. He was invited to sit in the box of Vice-President Charles Curtis, a part-Indian, when it was learned Thorpe could not afford to attend the 1932 Olympics in Los Angeles, but he dropped from prominence again immediately after that. During the depression he was found working with pick and shovel as a day laborer for $4 a day, digging out the site of what is now Los Angeles County Hospital. He drifted from job to job, through several marriages, and began to drink heavily. For awhile he toured with a troupe of Indian dancers as narrator, but then cancer of the lip silenced him. He was an alcoholic and penniless, living in a trailer near Lomita, California, when he collapsed and died of a heart attack in March, 1953, at the age of sixty-four.

Three years earlier, an Associated Press poll of experts had named him the outstanding college football player and the outstanding all-around athlete of the first half of the twentieth century. He is the only athlete ever to win Olympic gold medals in track and field, win All-American honors in college football, play big-time professional football, and play big-league baseball. It was not merely his decathlon and pentathlon triumphs of all-around ability that earned him his recognitions as the greatest. Over the years many efforts were made to have Thorpe's Olympic laurels restored and his medals returned to him, but they never succeeded. In 1973, National AAU spokesman Larry Hanneman said that there was agreement that Thorpe had been punished beyond reason originally and that his honors should be reestablished. A formal request was made for a review of the ancient affair by the IOC. But the Indian had been dead 20 years by then.

He may have been the outstanding Olympian of all time, but his name is not in the record books of these great Games.

5
THE 1920s
A Tarzan Is Born

THE SIXTH OLYMPIAD was scheduled for Berlin, Germany, in 1916, but canceled because of World War I. Eighteen months after the armistice, the Games were resumed. During the 1920s the Olympics grew enormously in prestige and popularity with the renewals staged at Antwerp, Belgium, in 1920; Paris, France, in 1924; and Amsterdam, Holland, in 1928.

Although Germany and Austria were not admitted back into eligibility until 1928, the entry rolls swelled to more than 3,000 athletes participating from more than 40 countries during this decade.

Additionally, the Winter Olympics were begun in 1924 at Chamonix, France, and continued in 1928 at St. Moritz, Switzerland, by which time nearly 500 more athletes from 25 nations were involved. This was when the Olympics truly came of age.

Beyond doubt, the outstanding Olympic track and field performer of the 1920s, if not of all time, was Paavo Nurmi.

Nurmi was born in June, 1897, in Turku, Finland. His father died when Paavo was twelve, and his mother became a laundress to support her family of five children. They lived in one room. Paavo, the eldest child, quit school and became an errand boy who pushed a wheelbarrow through the streets making deliveries. He also became bitter, parted from boyhood buddies who spent their days in school. He was poorer than they. He resented their easier lives. He became a loner, whose only pleasure came from running alone through the black pine forests outside of town. At fifteen, he apprenticed as a mechanic. He disliked the inside work but had little opportunity to do anything else.

That year, however, Hannes Kolehmainen returned from the Olympics in Stockholm the winner of three gold medals in the distance races, acclaimed as a national hero. Inspired, Paavo, who felt he had the ability to run long and fast, determined to be a great runner, too. It was the first time it had occurred to him that he could make something of himself.

He spent all of his spare time in training, usually in the forest, though he chased streetcars and mail trains to provide competition for himself. He became a vegetarian because he believed it was healthy. He gave up coffee and tea and refused any harder drinks. He denied himself sweets and refused to smoke cigarettes. He went to bed early to get rest. He did not go out with friends. He had no friends. He did not date. He trained and trained and did not even have a race until he was seventeen, when he joined a local track club, entered a 3,000-meter national championship event for juniors, and won it. After that, he was given help, including some coaching, but he guided his own destiny.

When he had to serve a hitch in the army, assigned as a mechanic, he got up at 5 A.M. so he could run, often over icy roads, before his workday began. When it ended, he ran some more. Evenings he spent alone in the barracks figuring out how to win races, scribbling on scraps of paper the best times it would take for each lap if he was to break records at various distances.

He spent his savings on a stopwatch and from then on often ran with it strapped to one wrist so he could keep track of his own pace. He studied the records of prominent runners of the time to determine the paces they favored and which of them won most often by leading early or by coming from behind. Eventually he became a great tactician who could win any way, by leading or rallying, depending on the distance and the nature of the competition.

It was as if ice water ran through his veins. He was cold, calculating, determined almost beyond reason. With most great runners, running was the central part of their lives; with Paavo Nurmi it was his life.

Slim, smooth, an apparently effortless runner, he exploded into prominence at Antwerp in the 1920 Olympics. His first race was the 5,000 meters. He led almost all the way, but was passed by Joseph Guillemot of France at the finish and had to settle for the second-place silver medal.

Then came the 10,000 meters. Altering his tactics, Nurmi hung back behind Guillemot and did not make a move on him until the start of the last lap. At the bell, Paavo sped past and won going away for his first gold medal.

He followed the same form, running an even pace, then pulling away at the finish to win the 10,000-meter cross-country race for his third medal and second gold.

This time it was Nurmi who returned to Finland a hero. But he despised publicity and shunned interviews. Not that he was without a big ego. On the contrary, he was vain. He boasted in advance of the times he would run in races, much as Muhammad Ali did years later when the heavyweight boxing champion would attempt to predict in poems the rounds in which he would knock out opponents.

Nurmi was no poet, but he was accurate with his predictions. This was what he was ready to run, he would say; if someone can run faster, I will lose. He seldom lost. He was like a machine. He set higher and higher goals for himself, stretched and reached them.

He set world records in distance races until eventually he held at one time or another every one from 1,500 to 10,000 meters, from one to six miles. Among others, he lowered the world records for 1,500 meters to 3:53.0 and for one mile to 4:10.4. He was world famous but remained almost a recluse who emerged only to race.

At his peak at twenty-seven, he determined to sweep the major distance races in the 1924 Olympics at Paris but appeared stymied by the schedule which placed the 1,500 and 5,000 only 55 minutes apart on the same day. A protest by Finn officials failed.

In April, in an Easter cross-country race, Nurmi slipped on the icy road and injured his knee. He could not straighten it for almost a month. He recovered sufficiently to gain a place for himself on the Finnish team at the country's Olympic trials late in May, but he was overshadowed by Willie Ritola. Ritola was a Finn who had been living in the United States but returned to win the 5,000 and 10,000 so he could represent his native country at Paris.

By mid-June, however, Nurmi was fully recovered, as he showed in Helsinki when he won and lowered the world records in both the 1,500 and 5,000 within an hour to prove he could double in these events. Finnish officials agreed to let him try at Paris but refused him permission to try to win the 10,000 meters.

While Nurmi ran a faster time on a practice track nearby, Ritola won this one. But Nurmi won the 1,500, then trimmed Ritola in the 5,000, setting Olympic records in both, within about an hour the following day. And two days later, he won the 10,000-meter cross-country race on an afternoon so hot over a course so rough that more than half the field failed to finish. Ritola was second. Finally, the next day, Nurmi won the 3,000-meter cross-country race in Olympic record time with Ritola again second.

Nurmi had won four gold medals in individual races, which only one other man ever has done—the American Alvin Kranzlein, in 1900, but in far less demanding events. Most felt the Flying Finn could have won five. And he had won two more golds as a member of the winning team in the cross-country relay.

Nurmi made a triumphal tour of the United States in 1925, losing only one race—a short one of a half-mile—in 55 meets, breaking 40 records. Along the way, he became the first man to run two miles in less than nine minutes, a feat comparable to the later conquest of the four-minute mile.

Reportedly, he received considerable money from American promoters who wanted this great foreign runner who filled arenas and stadiums across the country. He would not admit it and it was not proven at the time. He continued to run despite charges of professionalism which dogged his steps and further drove him into his shell.

By the 1928 Olympics at Amsterdam, Nurmi was close to thirty and slowing some, but he worked hard to go for more gold. In his hard way, he said he did not run for Finland or for fame, but for himself. "I am the best and I want to be the best as long as I can be," he once observed. He still was close to the best at Amsterdam. He won the 10,000, beating Ritola, was second to Ritola in the 5,000, and second to another Finn, Toivo Loukola, in the 3,000-meter steeplechase.

He continued to run and was training to win the one major distance race he had not won in the Olympics, the marathon, in Los Angeles in 1932. However, shortly before the Games a Swedish protest led to an investigation that resulted in Nurmi being declared a professional by the IOC. Most feel that even at the age of thirty-five Nurmi would have won the marathon. The Finns were so furious they refused to run meets against the Swedes for many years, canceled trade agreements, and almost went to war.

Thus, Nurmi's incomparable career concluded with 7 individual gold medals over three Olympiads, an incomparable accomplishment, and 20 world records. If he was furious, he refused to comment. It was his way.

At twenty-six, a statue of Nurmi was placed in a prominent public park in Helsinki, but he scorned the spotlight and the public. He made a lot of money with a sporting goods store and investments in real estate, but he lived a reclusive life. He married once, but it lasted only one year and he never remarried. He had a son but late in his life seldom saw him. He was sullen, stoical, uncommunicative.

Nurmi surprised everyone by reappearing in public when Helsinki hosted the Olympics in 1952. Invited to run the final lap, carrying the torch into the stadium, he accepted. He trained hard and at fifty-four was surprisingly slim and smooth as he strode through his symbolic lap. He never smiled or showed any emotion whatsoever as he received a thunderous, standing ovation.

Nurmi returned to the shadows, living a Spartan life, seldom spending any of his money. Many were amazed when word got out that he was permitting one of his expensive apartments to be rented at half price. The tenant was the aging, sickly Ritola, who had returned to spend his last days in his homeland and had little money.

Nurmi was aging and sickly, too. He died in October 1973 at the age of seventy-six, and was given a state funeral. Six gold-medal winners were pallbearers. Flags throughout the nation flew at half-mast. The nation's president and 2,000 citizens stood in the snow in bitter cold to observe the ceremonies. Nurmi was not loved, but he was respected.

The success of Kolehmainen and then of Nurmi especially inspired men from this tiny country to a flurry of dedication to long-distance running, which resulted in a domination of these events that endured through several Olympiads. Had not Nurmi been exceptional, Ritola would have gained additional glory. As it was, he won three gold medals and three silver medals in three Olympiads. And other Finns won seven gold medals in long-distance races from the 1924 through the 1936 Olympics. One Finn, Volmari Iso-Rollo, won in both 1932 and 1936 in the 3,000-meter steeplechase, which Finns won in four straight Olympiads. There was a carry-over in other events as well. Finns won the triple jump, shot, discus, and javelin in 1920, the javelin and pentathlon in 1924, and the decathlon in 1928. John Myrrha took the javelin in both 1920 and 1924, and Eric Lehtonen the pentathlon both years. Mati Jarvinen was second in the decathlon in both 1928 and 1932 and first in the javelin in 1932.

The most surprising winner in this time probably was Albert Hill of Great Britain, who made his Olympic debut at Antwerp in 1920 at the age of thirty-six and proceeded to sweep both the 800 and 1,500, upsetting the injured American immortal Joie Ray in the latter event.

The only other double gold-medal winner in track and field that year was walker Ugo Frigerio of Italy, who gave the stadium band a list of tunes he wanted played while he walked and paused to insist they pick it up several times when he felt they were not playing loudly enough.

"The world's fastest human" at that time, Charlie Paddock won the 100 for the United States in 1920 but lost it in 1924 to Harold Abrahams of Great Britain, who bragged that he trained on beer and cigars and became boss of Britain's amateur athletics later.

Bud Houser of the U.S. won the shot put and the discus in 1924, but another American, Harold Osborn, scored a more remarkable double, winning the decathlon and the high jump—the only man in any Olympics ever to win a single event as well as the 10-event decathlon. He became an osteopath in Champaign, Illinois, but continued to compete into his forties, high-jumped better than 6 feet when he was close to fifty, and coached at the University of Illinois for awhile.

On the fiftieth anniversary of his outstanding double, he observed, "I wasn't gifted, I was a worker. Competition is more intense today because the winners receive greater recognition. I wasn't a celebrity in my day, but I got self-satisfaction from my achievements."

United States runners dropped to their all-time Olympic low in 1928 when Ray Barbuti in the 400 was the only one to win a gold medal. However, Americans did win five gold medals in the field events. The track star that year was Percy Williams of Canada, who swept the sprints.

America triumphed in other sports, too. The eight-man crew contest is the featured rowing event, and in 1920 the United States started a streak of victories in eight straight Olympiads in this event. Usually the college crew which won the trials represented the United States as a unit. Navy crews won in 1920 and 1952, Yale in 1924 and 1956, California in 1928, 1932, and 1948 and Washington in 1936.

A member of Yale's eight in 1924 was one Benjamin Spock, who became a doctor, the author of a best-selling baby care book, and a public crusader for controversial causes. A gold medalist in both the single and double sculls rowing event in 1924 was Jack Kelly of Philadelphia, who became the father of the movie actress who became Princess Grace of Monaco.

The division of the Olympics into Winter and Summer Games in 1924 brought gold and glory to performers in many new sports, though winter events had been included on and off over the early years of these international gatherings.

The star of the first Winter Olympics at Chamonix in 1924 was Norway's Thorleif Haug, who won three cross-country skiing races, a feat that still has not been matched. These endurance races are classified as "Nordic Events." The speed skiing races are considered "Alpine Events," but these were not added until 1936.

Speed in 1924 was reserved for ice skating and a Finn, Clas Thunberg, won three golds. The United States has not won many golds in speed skating, but Charles Jewtraw did win at 500 meters in that first Winter Olympiad. Jacob Thams brought Norway its first of six straight golds in the 70-meter ski jump. And Canada's hockey team won its second of five straight golds.

An oddity occurred in 1974 when Anders Haugen, a Norwegian-born American member of the Lake Tahoe Ski Club was invited to Oslo at the age of eighty-six to receive a silver medal fifty years late. An error had been discovered in the original results in Nordic skiing in the 1924 Games. It has been corrected and Haugen has been moved up from fourth to third place in the standings in his event, belatedly bringing to this country the only medal ever won by a member of the U.S. team in this Olympic class.

At St. Moritz in 1928, Johan Grottumsbraaten of Norway won two golds in Nordic skiing, and added another in 1932. The U.S. scored a big upset in the five-man bobsled in 1928 and repeated it in 1932. The U.S. two-man team also won in 1932. Clas Thunberg of Finland captured two speed-skating golds. And one went to the American Irving Jaffee at 10,000 meters.

In figure skating, Gillis Grafstrom of Sweden won his third straight men's title, a feat as yet unmatched. Yet the show was stolen by a sixteen-year-old Norwegian, Sonja Henie, who won her first of three straight golds in the women's competition.

As young as Sonja Henie was, she was not the youngest winner in the Olympics of the 1920s. That honor went to a twelve-year-old American lass, Aileen Riggin, who won the springboard diving event, belatedly bringing to this country the only medal ever won by a member of the U.S. team in this Olympic class.

The 1920s

Females, young and older, were coming to the forefront. Ethelda Bleibtrey of the United States won gold medals in the 100-meter and 300-meter freestyle races and the 400-meter relay in swimming competition in 1920. Elizabeth Becker swept the springboard and fancy diving events as the U.S. won seven of the eight women's swimming and diving contests in 1924. Gertrude Ederle, a member of the winning 400-meter freestyle relay team, later became famous as the first woman to conquer the English Channel. Martha Norelius of the United States won her second straight gold medal in the 400-meter freestyle event in 1928. More than 40 years later she admitted, "Tears still come to my eyes when I think about it."

Women's track and field competition was added to the Olympic summer program in 1928, and Elizabeth Robinson had the distinction of becoming the first American woman to land a gold medal in this prestigious sport as she won the 100-meter dash in the world record time of 12.2 seconds.

In men's swimming, the standout in 1920 was Norman Ross, who swept the 400-meter and 1,500-meter freestyle events. Louis Kuehn won the first of what was to be 11 straight gold medals for Americans in springboard diving, a dynasty that was to span 50 years. In 1928, Ulysses J. "Pete" Desjardins swept both the low springboard and high platform diving titles, the only time this has been accomplished.

In 1924, Warren Kealoha won his second straight gold medal in the 100-meter backstroke. He followed in the footsteps of Duke Kahanomoku as a Hawaiian who swam to Olympic gold-medal glory for the U.S. However, after having won his second straight gold in the 100-meter freestyle sprint in 1920, the aging Duke was defeated by Johnny Weissmuller in the event in 1924.

It was no disgrace. Weissmuller won the 100 and 400 and led off the winning 800 relay. World records were set in all three. He returned to win the 100 and anchor the winning 800 relay in 1928 for his fourth and fifth gold medals.

Weissmuller was the Olympic swimming star of the 1920s and one of the great American Olympians of all times. His feats were not surpassed for 44 years, and many still consider him the greatest swimmer of all time.

Born in Windber, Pennsylvania, in June, 1904, and reared in Chicago, Weissmuller, the son of a brewery worker, was a skinny, sickly lad. At fourteen he stood 6 feet tall but weighed only 135 pounds. A doctor put him on a special diet and suggested swimming as a sporting exercise to build him up. Johnny didn't know how to swim, but, encouraged by his father, he gave it a go.

Free lessons were not available, nor did the family have money to pay for any. Johnny went to the west side and tried the river. He floundered around, trying to copy the other kids. He was so bad, the other guys laughed at him. "This made me determined," he recalled years later. "It made me work much harder at it than I otherwise would have. It made me want to be a champion to prove I could be as good as the best."

When winter came, he joined a YMCA so he could keep swimming in an indoor pool. As he got good, he tried out for the Chicago Athletic Club team, but barged into an official, was bawled out, and bowed out. Undiscouraged, he tried out for the Illinois Athletic Club team. He had grown an inch and filled out to 170 pounds. He was without form, but not without talent and determination.

The coach, a cigar-smoking 300-pounder, Bill Bachrach, recognized the lad's potential and offered to make him a good swimmer if he'd agree to work hard. Johnny agreed. The better he became, the harder he was worked. Bachrach was something of a tyrant, who once kicked the kid in the stomach when he did not do something the way the coach wanted.

Driven on, the youngster added the coach as one of many he wanted to show how good he could be.

He became Bachrach's prime project. Through this youngster, the coach put pet theories into practice. Weissmuller was taught to swim higher in the water than any other swimmer before or since. While other freestyle sprinters swim flat in the water with their head under the water most of the way, Weissmuller held his head and chest high, aquaplaning over the surface. The use of his feet was fundamental to his form. He was forced to swim for hours with both hands on a board, propelled only by his kick, to develop a powerful kick.

Forty years later, Weissmuller's successor as a superswimmer, Don Schollander, employed a modern style in which his kick was incidental and at times nonexistent. Possibly, any style will work if you do well enough with it. Weissmuller's way worked with him. But he worked for almost two years in secrecy before Bachrach was ready to spring him on an unsuspecting public.

Shortly after the Antwerp Olympics, Weissmuller was unveiled in the National AAU Championships of 1921. At nineteen, Johnny won four sprints and broke world records in each. It was one of the most amazing debuts any athlete ever has made. The great swimmers of the day could not believe the boy's ability. They went back to work with new, higher standards. But later that year, at the Brighton Beach Baths in Brooklyn, the boy broke two more world records and all were convinced.

Except Kahanamoku. The Duke refused to come to the mainland to race, so Bachrach took Weissmuller to Honolulu. The Duke taunted the youngster when they met before a meet. Weissmuller did not know what to say. Bachrach said, simply, "See for yourself." He handed Kahanamoku a stopwatch and invited him to a practice performance. The coach told his pupil privately to pour it on. Weissmuller went out as if it were for a world championship. Kahanamoku clocked him. Psyched out, the Duke suddenly was taken sick and scratched from the meet. Weissmuller wiped out the rest.

All that was left was to wait for the 1924 Games at Paris. While waiting, Weissmuller swept all prizes in his sport. He not only was the dominant swimmer of the day, but became a top water polo player.

In the National Championships indoors in 1923, Weissmuller won four first place awards. Still feeling fresh, he asked if there was another event he could enter. "Only the 150-yard backstroke," an official laughed, adding, "and thank goodness that's not one of your events." Johnny laughed, too. Although strictly a freestyler until that time, he entered the event and won it—in world record time. "He may be the greatest athlete of all time," admired Bob Kiputh, one of the outstanding swimming coaches. Bachrach beamed.

At Paris, Weissmuller proved himself. Confident to the point of cockiness, the Chicagoan finally caught up to Kahanamoku, cut him down in the final few feet, and won one of the most memorable 100-meter sprints of all time. Then Johnny beat the supposedly unbeatable Arne Borg, the "Swedish Sturgeon," in the 400. Both were won in world record time. Finally he helped the U.S. 800 meter relay team home first to garner his third gold medal. Then he went to work with the U.S. water polo team and helped the club capture third place in that rough competition to add a bronze medal to his bag. At nineteen, he was tops in his sport.

Between 1924 and 1928, Weissmuller was the most outstanding swimmer in the world. His father had died and he had to support himself. But when he got work as an elevator boy and bellhop in a hotel, Bachrach talked him out of it. To enable his protege to devote himself to swimming, Bachrach demanded and was paid $100 fees for each of Johnny's appearances. By spending the money for "expenses" and not giving the young man anything for himself, the coach protected Weissmuller's amateur standing. He did not want Weissmuller running around with girls or partying, anyway.

By the Olympics at Amsterdam in 1928, Weissmuller was wearying of the rigid life he was leading, but he maintained his status by winning two more gold medals—in the 100-meter freestyle and 800-meter freestyle relays.

Weissmuller had set 50 international records and was in training for the 1932 Olympics in Los Angeles when he received an offer of $500 a week for five years to promote a new line of swimming suits being marketed by the BVD underwear people and to model them in ads. "I had been a bum too long," he laughs. "I went to Bachrach and told him I had a chance to make some money and he agreed I should grab it."

Shortly thereafter, however, a movie man spotted his muscular physique in an advertising photo and suggested he try out for the part of Tarzan in a new movie based on the famous fictional jungle character. Johnny went for it and won.

They wanted him to change his name. When it was pointed out to them it was the name of the most famous swimmer in the world, they decided to keep his name and add swimming scenes to their film. "Just that easy and that fast a fella's life turns around," Weissmuller has sighed.

He became the most famous Tarzan, playing the lead in 12 ape-man movies between 1932 and 1948. He was not, however, the only Olympian to play the role.

Herman Brix, who was national champion in the shot put four times and a silver medalist in the Olympics of 1928, became movie star Bruce Bennett. He proved himself a fine actor in some forty-four films, including a Tarzan serial in 1935.

Buster Crabbe, a bitter swimming rival of Weissmuller's, who never got ahead of him but did succeed him as an Olympic gold medalist in 1932, beat out a lanky cowboy star named Randolph Scott to become a Tarzan for a rival film company in 1933. He was not Weissmuller's equal, either, though he did make 21 mediocre movies. Glenn Morris, a hurdler from Colorado, set a world record in winning the Olympic decathlon title in Berlin in 1936 and two years later starred in a Tarzan movie opposite 1932 Olympic swimming gold-medalist Eleanor Holm, but his screen career ended after one more film failure. He was the fourth and final Olympian to play Tarzan. Ironically, the man who wanted most of all Olympians to play the part, Don "Tarzan" Bragg, never got to do it. From boyhood on, Bragg swung from trees in his backyard to practice for future performances as the jungle idol. As he rose in sports, he spoke of his ambition often. He was the top pole-vaulter of his time and when he won the gold medal in the Olympics in 1960 at Rome, celebrating with a Tarzan yell, he was sure he was a cinch.

He was perfect for the part, too—dark, handsome, long-haired, powerful, and agile, as well as well known. And he was hired for the role in a movie, but he lost it when he hurt his foot practicing swinging from some ropes at home, sidelining himself for six weeks.

The dream did not die. Four years later he auditioned and was chosen over Weissmuller's son for the lead in another Tarzan movie, but the company collapsed. A year or so later, he was offered another opportunity in a TV version of Tarzan. At the time he was going into a hospital for a back operation. Finally, the dream had died.

He went to work and today operates "Kamp Olympik" in New Jersey.

It is Weissmuller's Tarzan that is remembered—his swift swimming with his body well out of the water, his swinging from tree to tree on vines, his breast-beating call, which really was a recorded mix of several such yells he attempted. Many of these movies are still shown on television. After the once skinny Weissmuller got too fat to play Tarzan, he portrayed Jungle Jim in movies and on TV and similar roles for awhile until he was not in demand any more, just as Buster Crabbe became Flash Gordon in films after Tarzan, and then Captain Gallant on TV before bowing out of acting.

Both Crabbe and Weissmuller have sold swimming pools for a living. Crabbe has run boys' camps and been a sports supervisor at a resort in the Catskills. Remarkably fit in his sixties, he set swimming records for men his age in a seniors' meet in Los Angeles in 1971. Weissmuller meanwhile had run through many marriages and many millions of dollars and was living in Florida fronting for an amusement park at last sighting.

Weissmuller was big when "B" movies were big, before television stole the show, but if he has drifted into the shadows, he remains a memorable athlete and actor. In the 1950 Associated Press poll, he was selected the greatest swimmer of the first half-century, primarily on his Olympic exploits.

"I've had my ups and downs, good times and bad times, but the heights I hit when I was an Olympic king were the best times of my life," he observed not too long ago.

6
LOS ANGELES AND LAKE PLACID, 1932
The Babe Leads the Ladies

IN LOS ANGELES, late on the last day of July, 1932, a Sunday afternoon, a slender, agile Mildred "Babe" Didrickson began a spectacular series of Olympic performances. At the starting mark for the javelin throw she sighted in the distance a tiny German flag stuck in the turf. It signified the world record throw of just under 133 feet achieved two years earlier by Ellen Braumuller, who was the favorite in this competition. The Babe did not know much about the art of hurling the spear, but she could see what she had to beat. Instead of arching it, she threw it flat, as a catcher would peg to second base. The javelin flew low, 14 feet past the flag for a new world record. And the Babe tore a tendon in her shoulder with her throw. She had won, anyway, with her first throw. Neither the German girl nor any of the others could top that throw.

Four days later, the Babe lined up for the start of the 80-meter hurdles. She had vowed to set another new world record. She was so anxious to do so that she jumped the gun at the start and the field was recalled. One more false start and she would be disqualified. Cautiously, she held back as the gun sounded a second time. She got off last, then started to catch up. At the halfway mark, Evelyn Hall of Chicago led her by four feet, and the Babe was fourth. One hurdle later, the Babe was within two feet. Another hurdle and she had drawn even. Over the sixth and last hurdle Didrickson and Hall, side by side, elbowed each other as they came too close to one another. In the short sprint to the wire of the rough race, the Babe got there first, by maybe an inch. The time was a world record of 11.7 seconds.

The crowd stood and cheered the Texas gal who had gained her second gold medal.

On Sunday, the final day for the women's track and field, she went in the high jump against Jean Shiley of Philadelphia. After the others were eliminated, the Babe and Jean both cleared a world record, 5 feet 5 inches. Each failed three times at just under 5 feet 6 inches. The bar was returned to near 5 feet 5 inches for the tie breaker to settle first and second places. Up first, the Philadelphia girl made it. Now, the Texas gal had to make it or settle for second. She went for it and made it. They were tied again.

But then a judge stepped forward and waved the Babe away, ruling she had made an illegal leap. He ruled her head had gone over the bar before her legs. That was made legal later, but it was not at that time. You could not "dive" over. The Babe protested that her legs had gone over first. Anyway, she added, she had been jumping the same way all day without anything having been said about it by any of the officials earlier. Movies later proved her right on both counts. But her protests were ignored, and she received the silver medal to go with her two golds.

An interviewer asked her how she felt about it.

"I jumped as high as she did," the Babe said flatly.

"Have you ever been warned not to jump that way?"

"Nope."

"Do you feel bad, Babe?"

"Nope."

"Are you glad Jean won?"

"Yep."

"Have you got any complaints?"

"Nope."

That was it. She did not have much to say. She did not complain. She had made her protest, it had been ignored, and that was that. She was tough. She was the toughest and best athlete, man or woman, in the Los Angeles Olympiad of 1932, and the noted sports authority Grantland Rice later wrote that she was the greatest all-around athlete of all time. She was special.

Mildred Ela Didrickson was born in June, 1914, the sixth of seven children of Norwegian immigrants who had settled in Port Arthur, Texas, at the turn of the century. Her father, Ole, was a furniture refinisher and a sports fan. She had four brothers who kept busy in all sorts of sports. The father set up bars in the backyard for jumping and hurdling. He hung a basket from the side of the house. He fashioned a barbell from an old broomhandle and flatirons for weight lifting in the garage. He pitched to his kids and threw footballs to them.

The Babe grew up to be a tomboy who could beat her brothers and other boys at many games. With her sister, she got into games of baseball, basketball, and football with the boys. But her sister was not as outstanding an athlete as she was. Babe once said, "Before I was in my teens, I knew exactly what I wanted to be. I wanted to be the best athlete who ever lived."

Opportunities for girls in sports were limited. At fourteen, her father read her newspaper stories of the Olympics in Amsterdam and of great female athletes who did well there. She announced to him, "Next year, I'm going to be in the Olympics." When she was told the Olympics were held only every four years, she set her sights on the 1932 Games. The fact that they would be in Los Angeles made them seem more within her reach.

Batting against the boys, she hit a baseball so hard and so far she was nicknamed "Babe," after Babe Ruth, who was in his prime at the time. She became the star of her high school girls' basketball team. Until she made the team, she practiced barefoot on the gym floor because she had no sneakers. In her spare time, she worked out at the football field, which was encircled by a running track. She ran as fast and as far as she could. All by herself, she learned how to hurdle, high-jump, long-jump, and throw the javelin and discus. She had no coach. She copied the boys who worked out afternoons. She often worked out until after dark.

This was during the depression, and her family had fallen on hard times. They had moved to Beaumont in hopes of finding more opportunity. Her father went to sea to make some money he could send home. Her mother had to go to work as a laundress. The children had to help her. Mildred had to iron her brothers' shirts and pants. After school, she sewed up burlap potato sacks in a factory. She grew skilled on a sewing machine and won a prize with a pleated dress she entered in the Texas State Fair. But she was shy and sensitive about what she called "sissy things." She preferred playing ball with the boys. "I'm gonna' whup you," she would challenge foes.

Some of her basketball exploits were written up in the newspapers of her hometown and came to the attention of Colonel M. J. McCombs, a man who believed in liberated women and ran a women's sports program at his Employers Casualty Insurance Company in Dallas. Babe had learned to type and do secretarial work in school, and he offered her a job with his firm so that she could play for his basketball team. After graduation, she accepted and went to work for $75 a month. She was a good worker who could type 85 words a minute. And she was a brilliant basketball player, who scored 100 points in one game, won Women's All-American Honors three straight seasons, and led her Cyclones to the National AAU team title.

All along, she still had her sights on the Olympics. When the women's national championships came to Dallas in 1930, she was ready. She convinced the colonel to sponsor her track and field career and entered the meet. It was the first meet she had seen, much less entered. She won the javelin throw and the baseball throw, and she set a world record of better than 18 feet 8 inches in the long jump but finished second when Stella Walsh bettered it. The Babe broke the world record five times in that event that day, but Stella broke it six times. It was incredible competition.

The next summer the Babe went to Jersey City for the championships and won the long jump, as well as the 80-meter hurdles and the baseball throw, which was a woman's event at the time. She set a women's world record that still stands in this event with a toss of 296 feet.

The 1932 meet was at Northwestern University, near Chicago, and was also the qualifying meet for the Olympic team. There were nearly 200 girls there competing. Some track teams had more than 20 girls. The Employers Casualty Company Team of Texas had one girl. Each team was introduced to the crowd in a group. When this one-girl team was introduced, the intrigued crowd responded with a standing ovation. Years later she admitted, "It still sends shivers down my back just thinking about it."

It inspired her. Not that she needed extra inspiration. She had worked hard at almost every event and entered eight of the ten events, passing up only two of the sprints. Although not big, a little over 5 foot 6 in height and weighing slightly more than 105 pounds, she was strong and quick, but not really a fast runner.

Officials tried to talk her out of it. They felt she was being foolish. They figured it had to hurt her chances of making the Olympic team in any one event and feared she might get hurt. But she was sure of herself. And she did not overestimate herself.

For three hours she rushed here and there to stay alive in the various events. She'd take one of her leaps in the long jump, rush to the track and run a heat in the hurdles, shift over to take a toss in the javelin throw, and so forth, in an incredible display of strength and stamina. She finished first in five events—the 80-meter hurdles, baseball throw, javelin throw, shot put, long jump, and high jump. She had never even tried the shot put before. She set world records in the hurdles, javelin, and high jump. She finished close to the top in two other events and lost out only in the 100-meter dash.

The United Press story reported it was "the most amazing series of performances ever accomplished by any individual, male or female, in the history of track and field." All by herself, she had scored 30 points. The one-woman team had won the meet. The next team had 22 points.

The Babe was bitterly disappointed when she learned she would be allowed to enter only three events in the Olympics because of the rules of the Games. She picked her three, and she won two of them, and she might have won the third. She and many others felt she could have won four or five gold medals if she'd been given the opportunity.

As it was, Grantland Rice sought to console her by offering to take her golfing the next day. She took him up on it although she'd never been on a golf course or swung a golf club in her life. She hit 250-feet tee shots and scored 102, which was astonishing. It was her introduction to her future career.

She had just turned nineteen, and suddenly she was well known as the greatest woman athlete in the world.

More than 3,000 fans welcomed her at the airport on her return to Texas. She was honored with a parade of motor cars through main streets lined with cheering spectators.

Promoters dreamed up get-rich-quick schemes and pursued her to turn professional. She did, needing money to support herself and to send home, though she continued to work at her secretarial post for awhile. She pitched an inning for the St. Louis Cardinals in an exhibition game and shut out the Philadelphia Athletics. She played an exhibition tennis match against the men's champion, Vinnie Richards, and did well, though defeated. She toured as the only female and only beardless member of the House of David baseball team. She toured with her own mixed basketball team of men and women players, "The Babe Didrickson All-Americans."

For awhile, she played in vaudeville, singing poorly, telling a few bad jokes and donning a brief uniform to demonstrate her athletic skills within the limits of the stage. However, she missed competitive sports. About the only way a woman could make money in sports at the time was in golf, though there was not much money there for them. She practiced her golf game until her hands bled, literally. She entered her first tournament—the Fort Worth Women's Invitational—in 1934, and led all qualifiers, but once competitive play commmenced her game came apart. She still needed practice. She worked at it 12 to 16 hours a day. Her first triumph came in the Texas State Championships in 1935. It was an amateur event, but she still was regarded in golf as an amateur at that time.

She got better and better and became by far the best player on the women's pro tour in her time, some say the best the tour ever had.

At the Los Angeles Open in 1938 she was paired with professional wrestler George Zaharias in the preliminary pro-amateur event. The promoters figured it would be funny to put the 130-pound Babe alongside the 250-pound bruiser. Asked to embrace for photographers, they did so shyly. And they liked it, kidding one another. "You're my kind of girl," the burly Zaharias whispered to her. "And you're my kind of man," the Babe whispered back. They began to date one another whenever possible. Before the year was out, they were married, with Leo Durocher as best man, and honeymooned in Honolulu.

The marriage surprised cynics, who could not conceive that her marriage to a burly wrestler would last. But it did. They bought a home and the Babe kept going at golf. She won the British and American Amateur titles before she was declared a professional, then won the women's National Open and World Championships. At one point in the late 1940s she won an astonishing 19 consecutive tournaments.

At the age of thirty-nine, in 1953, she was not feeling well, had some medical tests made, and was found to have cancer. She made no effort to conceal her condition. "I don't hide nothin'," she said. "It's nothin' to be ashamed of. I'm hard to beat. I'm not gonna let this beat me if I can help it."

She went in for surgery and was swamped with letters, telegrams, and gifts from admirers. Less than four months later, she finished third in the Tam O'Shanter Tournament in Chicago. She was voted a trophy for the Sports Comeback of the Year. The following year, she won the U.S. Open by 12 strokes and returned to win the Tam O'Shanter with a near-record score.

But she had little left. She rapidly was growing weaker, her condition growing worse. Soon she had to leave the tour and take to her bed. Her husband had quit wrestling to devote full time to her. He cooked her meals, waited on her. To see them together in those last days was deeply touching. Babe Didrickson Zaharias died in September, 1956. In the 20 years since, George Zaharias has seldom spoken of anything else. He has devoted himself to raising funds for the fight against the disease which beat the Babe and to a memorial for the amazing athlete who dominated the Los Angeles Olympics in 1932.

There were other great women Olympians that year. Stella Walsh was one. She won the 100 in the world record time of 11.9 seconds. She competed for Poland because she was not yet a U.S. citizen. Born Stanislawa Walasiewicz in Poland in 1911, she was brought to this country at the age of ten months when her family settled in Cleveland. "Growing up, all I wanted to do was run. I don't think I ever walked," she once recalled.

She went on to win 40 American national women's titles in the sprints and long jump. She became a bitter rival of the Babe's and beat her in most long jumps. She was not as versatile as the Babe, but more durable. She was one of the most durable athletes ever. She won her first national sprint title in 1930 at the age of nineteen and her last title 18 years later in 1948 at the age of thirty-seven. At forty-two, she won the western women's national pentathlon title with a record performance in the grueling five-event competition.

In swimming, Helen Madison of the United States swept both freestyle sprints for women. Eleanor Holm, an American of awesome beauty, who had competed in the 1928 Games at the age of fourteen without winning a medal, won the gold medal in the 100-meter backstroke event in 1932.

The daughter of a Brooklyn fire chief, she won 29 world titles, held 6 world records and was on her way to the 1936 Olympics in Berlin when she controversially was kicked off the team by Avery Brundage for "improper conduct." A free spirit, it turned out she had been guilty of no more serious crimes than sipping champagne and shooting dice with the newspapermen on board the boat and staying up past the 9 P.M. bedtime.

She was bitter at the time, but because of the publicity was offered opportunities to make movies and star in night club acts. "It turned out to be best thing that ever happened to me," she sighed years later. "It made me a star, a glamour girl, which another gold medal never would have done." She even made a Tarzan movie, opposite Berlin decathlon champion Glenn Morris. She married Billy Rose, the fabulous showman, and became the star of his Aquacade at the New York World's Fair and elsewhere. Eventually she settled down in Florida, where she lives.

In the Winter Olympics at Lake Placid, New York, early in 1932, Sonja Henie, the tiny Norwegian, won her second straight gold medal in figure skating. She was at her peak but returned to make it three straight in the Winter Games at Garmisch-Partenkirchen, Germany, in 1936. Between 1927 and 1936 she won 10 consecutive women's world titles in competition all around the world. She, too, was an amazing athlete.

The daughter of a former bicycle-racing champion, a wealthy furrier, Sonja was born in Oslo in April, 1913. As a child, she loved to dance. She began ballet school at four. She was given roller skates at six and soon could cut clever patterns in the street. At eight she was given her first ice skates, which she had wanted since she had seen a winter carnival and been entranced by the skaters.

She skated and skated. Coached by her father, she became incredibly skilled. Figure-skating competition is divided into two parts. A graceful and stylish skater of imagination can easily shine in freestyle routines, but that is only the last part, which the public sees. Meticulous tracing of patterns on the ice, "the school figures," form the first and for many years the most important part of the judging. Most placings are all but settled by the time these first-day efforts are completed. Yet Sonja was able to master these dull details sufficiently to win the Oslo women's title at age nine and the Norwegian title at ten.

A doll-like blond, less than 5 feet tall and less than 90 pounds in weight, she debuted in the first Winter Olympics in Chamonix, France, in 1924 at the age of ten. She was placed last by the judges but captivated the fans. Three years later, at thirteen, she won her first world title, and the next year she won her first Olympic gold medal.

She revolutionized the sport. "Even freestyle figure skating had been stiff and formal until I came along, but I loved to dance and brought ballet to my routines," she once explained. "I suppose I was so young I didn't know you shouldn't do it. I didn't know how daring it was, but what I did won acceptance. After all, ours is not simply a sport, but also an art. It combines beauty with athletics."

By the time she had won her third Olympic crown, she was the most prominent woman athlete in the world. She drew capacity crowds to exhibitions in major arenas around the world. An American promoter, Jeff Dixon, dreamed up the idea of starring her in ice shows that would tour the world. She was signed and on her way to her first million at twenty-six.

She wound up with her own ice show, the first of many Olympic figure-skating stars to turn professional in these touring shows. She blazed the trail they followed. She made ice shows big business. She attracted capacity crowds wherever her show played, and became a Hollywood movie star, although she spoke broken English. She skated through 10 films and at her peak ranked with Shirley Temple and Clark Gable as the biggest box-office attractions of the early 1940s.

She lived like a queen, too. She married a wealthy man. She wore expensive furs and jewels. Once when her skates needed sharpening in Chicago, she sent for the fellow who did this for her in New York. He flew in, did the job in two minutes, and flew back. It is estimated that she earned almost $50 million, more than any other athlete, man or woman, of all time.

The only one ever to win the women's figure-skating title three times, she soared toward the heights in the Olympics.

The men had their moments during the Olympic year of 1932, too.

At Lake Placid, U.S. competitors ended the domination of Norwegians in the Winter Games by winning six gold medals, two each by speed-skaters Irving Jaffee and Jack Shea. Falling in the face of a 40-mile-an-hour gale, Jaffee skidded across first in the dramatic finish of the grueling 10,000 meters.

Austrian Karl Schafer narrowly upset three-time Olympic men's figure-skating champion Gillis Grafstrom of Sweden. Pierre Brunet teamed with Andrée Joly to win the pairs skating for the second time. The U.S. nearly upset Canada in hockey but settled for second place after losing to and tying the Canadians in overtime struggles.

That summer, the Games were a smashing success, although the distance Europeans had to travel to Los Angeles cut the entry rolls in half. More than 1 million persons paid more than $2 million to see the international competition, primarily in the new 105,000-seat Coliseum. A notable absentee, however, was U.S. President Herbert Hoover. It was the depths of the depression, and the president was unpopular and reluctant to make personal appearances.

He sent his vice-president, Charles Curtis, instead. It was the first time the head of state had not attended an Olympics in his country, at least the ceremonial openings welcoming representatives of most of the world's great nations. And the second and last time to date this has happened came when another American president, Dwight David Eisenhower, did not appear at the Winter Olympics in Squaw Valley, California, in 1960. He, too, sent his vice-president instead, who happened to be Richard M. Nixon.

Aside from Babe Didrickson, the only double winner in track and field competition in 1932 was Eddie Tolan, who swept the sprints in controversially close contests with Ralph Metcalfe. They remain revered as among the fastest humans of all time.

U.S. athletes won 11 of the 23 track and field events. Among them, William Carr set a new world record at 400 meters and Bill Miller one in the pole vault. Eight months later, Carr broke both legs in an auto accident and never ran again. Kansas fullback Jim Bausch captured the decathlon, defeating Akilles Jaervinen, whose brother won the javelin and whose father had won Finland's first Olympic gold medal.

But the Americans suffered some disappointing defeats. The glamorous Kansan, Glenn Cunningham, faded to fourth at the finish of the 1,500 meters, which was won by unheralded Luigi Beccali of Italy. Badly burned on both legs as a boy, Cunningham overcame his handicap, running to build himself back up at first, then for records, setting a new world mark in the mile of 4:06.7 in 1934.

His mile runs against several serious and skilled rivals perhaps did more than anything else to popularize indoor track in the U.S. in the 1930s. But when he tried again in the Olympics of 1936 in Berlin, he was outsprinted down the stretch by Jack Lovelock of New Zealand, and his dream of a gold medal ended. He retired and in recent years ran a boys' camp in Kansas.

Ralph Hill of the U.S. tried to catch Lauri Lehtinen of Finland down the stretch of the 5,000-meter run, but the Finn moved back and forth in front of him, preventing the American from passing him, then lunged to win by inches at the tape as bedlam broke loose in the cement bowl. The fans booed, but there was no disqualification. Hill refused to protest, which won him praise as a sportsman.

Japanese swimmers won five of the six gold medals in their sport. Clarence "Buster" Crabbe, 400-meter freestyle champion, was

Los Angeles and Lake Placid, 1932

the only American gold medalist. Ivar Johansson of Sweden scored a remarkable wrestling double. He won the freestyle middleweight title, then went into the sauna, worked out, sweated off 11 pounds, went without eating for four days, went back to the sauna to sweat some more several times, then won the Greco-Roman welterweight title. "I thought I would die," he noted later. Another Swede, John Richtoff, won his second straight heavyweight wrestling crown.

Maybe the most interesting gold medalist in 1932 was Eddie Eagen, who was a member of the winning four-man bobsled team at Lake Placid. Twelve years earlier, the Yale student from Denver had won the Olympic light-heavyweight boxing crown at Antwerp. Maybe he was no Weissmuller or as big a sports star as the Babe, but Eagen, who later became chairman of the New York State Athletic Commission, was one of the few performers ever to win in two totally different sports in the Olympics and remains the only person ever to win in both the Winter and Summer Games.

7
NAZI GERMANY, 1936
The American, Jesse Owens

THE NAZI DICTATOR Adolf Hitler had brought the world to the brink of war in 1936 when Germany hosted the Olympics, first in the Winter Games at Garmisch-Partenkirchen early in the year, then later in the Summer Games at Berlin. Under threat of having the international contests canceled or removed, he temporarily suspended his reign of terror against Jews and other minorities. He concealed his military might that normally marched across his country. But brown-shirted storm troopers posing as police added an ominous air to the festivities.

The Winter Games went well enough. German athletes had been trained to points of perfection, and while they won only 2 of the 17 events, these were not their specialties. Fair-skinned, fair-haired Nordic types from Scandinavian countries won 12 of the other contests. Ivar Ballangrud of Norway won three gold medals in speed skating. Birger Rudd of Norway won his second straight gold medal in ski jumping. Blonde-haired, blue-eyed, pink-complexioned Sonja Henie of Norway fulfilled Hitler's image of Aryan racial perfection, and when she won her third straight women's figure-skating title, he welcomed her warmly. An Austrian, Karl Schafer, won the men's title, and Adolf was Austrian.

The U.S. won the two-man bobsled event for the second and last time to date and Canada's domination of hockey was ended by Great Britain, but that was bearable to the dictator.

The Summer Games represented the true test of his theories of Aryan supremacy. He had constructed the cavernous cement

Nazi Germany, 1936

saucer, the Third Reich Sports Field, to showcase his marvelous men and women performers in track and field. When the German shot-putter, Hans Woellke, won the first event, the 110,000-seat stadium exploded in a din of cheering.

When, next, three Finns swept the first three places in the 10,000-meter run, their appearance confirmed the dictator's racial beliefs, and they received Hitler's handshakes at his box. When two German girls, Tilly Fleischer and Luise Kruger, finished one-two in the women's javelin throw, Hitler beamed as he greeted them, and his aide, Herman Göring, hugged them. Then, however, the black American Cornelius Johnson captured the high jump, and Hitler left his box and the arena before the victory ceremonies.

Reminded by Count Baillet Latour, the IOC chairman, that if he honored some winners he should honor all, Hitler replied that he could not continue to take the time to greet further winners. Nor did he again, despite other victories by other Germans. But he did continue to attend during most days. He was there when the black American Jesse Owens, after setting a world record of 10.2 seconds in the semifinal of the 100-meter dash, won the final in 10.3 seconds, and as another black, the marvelous Ralph Metcalfe, settled for a silver medal for the second straight Olympiad. Again Hitler departed before the presentation ceremonies.

Hitler was there, too, two days later, when, after setting another world record of 21.1 seconds for 200 meters around a curve in a trial run, Owens went for his second gold medal in the long jump and almost lost at the outset.

Each competitor had three jumps in the morning to pare the field to the afternoon's finalists. The qualifying standard was set at 23 feet 5½ inches, which was well within Owen's range, since he had set a world record with a leap of more than three feet further two years earlier.

However, as Owens warmed up in his sweat suit and jogged down the runway to check his "steps," an official waved a red flag at him. To his surprise, Owens realized he had stepped past the takeoff bar and had been charged with an official attempt and a foul. He protested but was denied.

Well, he still had two jumps left. He stripped off his suit and took his second jump. Shaken by his first "foul," his concentration shattered, he moved indecisively down the runway, landed past the takeoff bar as he leaped, and, while he went far enough, was charged with his second foul. Suddenly he had only one chance left, and he was shaken.

All eyes were on him as he went back to his starting mark and nervously sought to steady himself. He felt a hand on his shoulder. He turned and to his surprise saw that it was his major rival, the blond Luz Long of Germany, who was smiling at him.

Long could not speak English and Owens could not speak German. But Long made himself understood. He pointed to suggest Owens should start further back and take off further back to play it safe, for he did not need a great jump to make it to the finals. Grateful Owens agreed, nodding, realizing it took tremendous courage for the German to comfort and counsel the American black at this time in full view of Hitler.

As the German moved away, the American moved back. He began his run a full foot behind his normal starting point. He ran so cautiously, he took off two feet behind the takeoff bar. He leaped, landed, came out of the pit, and waited warily as officials measured his jump. It was measured at nine-sixteenths of an inch beyond 23 feet 5 inches. It was barely enough, but it was enough. One-eighth of an inch less would have eliminated him from the competition he was to win.

Almost all who follow sports know he won four gold medals in these Olympic Games to embarrass the Nazis, but few remember how close he came to losing the long jump, indeed even of failing to reach the final, or how the German who was his strong rival risked stature to assist him. "I will never forget it as long as I live," Owens has said, "not the sportsmanship of that marvelous man nor how hard it was to beat that great athlete."

That afternoon, with a wind at their back, Owens and Long had a dramatic duel. His composure recovered, Owens leaped almost 25 feet 5 inches to take the lead. Then he leaped 25 feet 9¾ inches to increase his lead. On Long's third leap, he landed an inch short. But on his fifth, he landed exactly where Owens had, tying for first.

They were left with one leap each, and the tension was tremendous.

Owens went all out. He sprinted down the runway, took off in flight—scissoring his legs to sustain himself in the air—landed, and lunged forward to keep from falling backwards. His effort was measured at one-half inch past 26 feet, and he was in front again.

Now it was left to Luz Long, and the pressure pounded at him. He may have tried too hard. He ran so hard down the runway he went past the takeoff bar as he flew out, and fouled.

Finally, it was finished. Owens was the winner, and Long rushed to embrace him in congratulations. Hitler hurriedly left. And Owens never made another long jump in his life.

The following day, another American, Mack Robinson, ran faster than Owens in the semifinals of the 200. The older brother of Jackie Robinson, the great all-around athlete who later would break baseball's barrier against blacks, Mack was a marvel, and he got off in front in the final as a drizzle dropped from the dark clouds overhead. But Owens caught him coming around the curve and pulled away as they sped down the stretch to win by three yards in 20.7 seconds.

As Hitler left, the German fans for the first time rose to render an ovation to this brilliant black man who could not be denied his due.

Three days later, Owens led off for Foy Draper, Frank Wykoff, and Ralph Metcalfe as they set a world record of 40 seconds flat in the semifinals of the 400-meter relay. The following day, in the final, the U.S. team lowered the mark to 39.8 seconds as Owens won his fourth gold medal. No other man or woman ever has won as many in track and field events that still are contested.

Hitler was gone as Owens joined his teammates atop the victory stand and had a laurel wreath as well as a fourth gold medal draped around his neck. He admits tears came to his eyes as the U.S. flag was raised and his country's national anthem was played. "I felt great patriotism and a great sense of accomplishment," he recalled almost forty years later. "It was the most marvelous moment of my life."

It scarcely is remembered how controversial the racial and religious issues were at that time in America and other countries as well as in Nazi Germany. The Games are awarded to the different cities that apply by vote of the Olympic Committee years in advance, and the 1936 Games were awarded to German cities before Hitler came to power. The world was not yet truly aware how oppressive were the policies of the new regime in Germany and how determined the Nazis were to make war on the world. It was generally felt political differences should not be brought into a sporting festival.

There was some sentiment for American withdrawal, but Avery Brundage said, "Jews must realize they cannot use these Games as a weapon against the Nazis." Both Brundage and American coach Dean Cromwell, as well as many others at the time, were supporters of the "America First" movement, which argued against American interference in the affairs of foreign countries, including Germany.

Even within Germany there was sentiment against the Games being based there. Nazi youth campaigned against non-Aryans being entertained and brought into competition with Germans for honors.

Hitler felt to give in to either side would be an embarrassment to the great new nation he was building. His propaganda minister, Josef Goebbels, pleaded that they should put on a spectacular show to impress the world. The dictator convinced his countrymen they could offer a show of strength. And he courted Olympic officials of the world with impressive preparations.

He spent $25 million to provide the finest facilities possible. Nine new arenas were built. A lavish village was constructed to house the athletes, which later would be used as military officers quarters. He insisted talk of awful acts within his country and aims of conquest beyond were wrong. He conspired to conceal signs of oppression.

A Jew even was included on the German team. She was Helene Mayer, who had won a gold medal in women's fencing in 1928. She was living in Los Angeles but still was a citizen of Germany and was invited to return to represent her country in the contests in 1936. She accepted, and when she won a silver medal and gave the Nazi salute to Hitler, she was cheered by her countrymen. She then returned to America, but after World War II returned to Germany.

A record total of more than 4,000 athletes from 49 countries gathered in Germany for the Games. In a close vote, the American Olympic Committee decided to send a full team. However, therewere only 10 blacks, all track and field athletes, on the entire team. And the two Jews in the track and field group were the only members of the entire unit who were not chosen to compete in any events.

The United States was not without its racial and religious prejudices and problems, then as now, though much more so at that time.

Marty Glickman, now a New York sports broadcaster, and Sam Stoller, a Virginia television executive, were the two Jews on the team. Lawson Robertson of the University of Pennsylvania at the time, and Cromwell of the University of Southern California, both now dead, were the coaches.

Nazi Germany, 1936

Originally, the first three finishers in the Olympic trials, Owens, Metcalfe, and Wykoff, were assigned to the individual 100, while Stoller and Glickman were selected to run with Owens and Metcalfe on the sprint relay team and practiced with it. However, during the week before the relay the coaches added Wykoff to it and requested a trial run among Stoller, Glickman, and Draper to determine the final spot. Stoller won, with Glickman second and Draper third. Then, on the morning of the event, the coaches called a meeting and announced Draper would run in the final position because he was more experienced.

It might be noted that Draper had not practiced with the unit. And also that he as well as Wykoff were from Cromwell's school, the University of Southern California. However, it might also be noted, as Avery Brundage did later, that the four who did run were the first four finishers in the sprint in the Olympic trial. Still, Stoller, Glickman, and some of their sympathetic teammates, such as Metcalfe, now a congressman from Chicago, protested, to no avail. Glickman warned it might be regarded as an anti-Semitic move, which it was and still is by many. Owens, who already had three gold medals, offered to relinquish his spot to one of the others, but was refused.

As it was, Owens, Wykoff, Draper, and Metcalfe won their relay and their gold medals. Americans won a dozen gold medals in men's track and field, half a dozen in men's and women's swimming and a few in other sports, including basketball, which was brought into the program that year.

A thirteen-year-old American girl, Marjorie Gestring, won the springboard diving event. Dorothy Poynton-Hill won her second straight in platform diving. But the leading lady in the 1936 Olympics was Hendrika Mastenbroek of Holland, who won three gold medals and one silver medal in swimming. She was first in two freestyle sprints, second in a backstroke sprint, and a member of the first-place sprint-relay team.

As usual, the host nation did well, and the intensive practice routines put in by the Germans paid off in 33 gold medals, though only 6 in track and field. The Germans virtually swept the gymnastics, equestrian, rowing, and canoeing events.

A number of Americans other than Owens shone in track and field. Helen Stephens helped the U.S. to its only two gold medals in women's events when she won the 100 in a world record 11.5 seconds from Stella Walsh and anchored the 400-meter relay team to triumph. American blacks Archie Williams and John Woodruff won the 400 and 800, respectively. The first famous football player among blacks, Fritz Pollard of Rutgers, who became a U.S. State Department official, won the bronze medal in the 110-meter high hurdles. Americans Forrest Towns and Glen Hardin swept the hurdles.

Earle Meadows captured the pole vault after George Varoff, who had just set a new world record, failed to qualify for the team a week later in the trials. Ken Carpenter took the discus, and Glenn Morris the decathlon. Finns finished first in most of the distance events, but a standout was Lovelock of England, who sprinted through the stretch to outrun Americans Glenn Cunningham and Archie San Romani in a world record time in the 1,500.

However, the outstanding athlete of the Olympics in 1936 and maybe of any single Olympiad was Owens, who was born in September, 1913, in Danville, Alabama, one of seven children of a poor tenant farmer's family. Jesse picked cotton in the fields as a child. He was christened James Cleveland. Asked his name by a teacher, he gave his initials, "J.C." The teacher wrote down "Jesse," and that was the way it was to stay.

Like many southern rural blacks, the Owens family went north in search of greater opportunities and settled in Cleveland, where work in factories could be found. A shy, skinny lad, Jesse did not go out for sports until he was fifteen, when Charlie Paddock, then the "World's Fastest Human," stood on the stage at Jesse's junior high school and spoke of the Olympics. Jesse figured that would be fine for him, too, especially after he found he could outrun his friends.

When he got to high school, he went out for the track team and astonished the coach who clocked him in a sprint by running near world record time. The coach, Charlie Riley, later recalled, "He ran so fast I thought my stopwatch wasn't working right.

"Unlike distance runners and field event men, who can be built up, you can teach technique to dash men, which will help them, but, basically, sprinters are born, not made, and Owens was a natural. He had natural speed and a naturally smooth style and he learned form fast. He may have been the most amazing natural athlete ever."

Because of the strength and spring in his legs, he was a natural leaper and hurdler, too.

As a junior at Cleveland East Tech, he swept both sprints and the long jump in the Ohio high school championships. As a senior,

Nazi Germany, 1936

he swept them again and set national scholastic records which endured for many years. He even tied the world record for 100 yards at 9.4 seconds and won the national long jump title against the best amateur athletes in the country. He is considered the outstanding high school track performer of all time.

Offered countless scholarships to college, he selected Ohio State and became the greatest college track man ever. His coach, Larry Snyder, refined his form and he progressed rapidly. As a freshman, he set a world indoor record in the long jump and he improved it as a sophomore, but he was beaten by the better sprinters until he filled out to 160 pounds and seemed to mature during his second college campaign.

He hit his peak at twenty-one at the end of his sophomore season, when he had what may be the best day any athlete ever had. This was in the Big Ten Track Championships at Ann Arbor, Michigan, in May, 1935. The 10,000 or so fans in the wooden stands at Ferry Field that hot spring afternoon saw a spectacular performance by Owens, although he was suffering from a bad back.

At 3:15, he won the 100-yard dash in 9.4 seconds to tie Frank Wykoff's world record. Ten minutes later, he went for the world record in the long jump. Awed observers watched him place a piece of paper at a point depicting the existing mark, then leap past it, setting a new standard of 26 feet 8¼ inches that would last for 25 years. At the announcement, those in attendance went wild. He took only the one jump that day.

At 3:45 he whipped to the tape in 20.3 seconds to set new world records for both 200 meters and 220 yards, and a roar arose from the fans again. Fifteen minutes later, he swept over the low hurdles in 22.4 seconds to set world records at both 200 meters and 220 yards which were to endure a dozen years. The crowd stood and hollered itself hoarse. In less than one hour, Owens had equaled one world record and surpassed five others in winning four championships.

"It's funny, I'd hurt my back fooling around, wrestling with some friends. It hurt so much I could barely bend down to start the first event. But once I started to compete, I forgot about it. Then, as soon as I was finished, it started to hurt again," Owens later recalled with a grin. "At both ends of that meet others had to help me get dressed and undressed."

He went on to become the only man ever to win four events in the National Collegiate Championships, which were contested at

Berkeley, California. But then he was upset by a brilliant rival, Eulace Peacock of Yonkers, in the 100 and long jump of the National AAU title meet. He lost twice more to Peacock and quit for the season, fearing he had gone stale. He returned to school, and was married during his junior year.

In 1936, he defended his four titles in the Big Ten Meet, winning the hurdles despite falling down at the halfway point and having to get up and catch up. He won all four events in the NCAA Championships, running 100 meters in a world record 10.2 seconds, which lasted 20 years. He won the long jump and the 100 in the National AAU title-taking at Princeton, New Jersey, finally overcoming Ralph Metcalfe, who had been beating him at this distance.

Owens passed up the hurdles, but won the 100, 200, and long jump in humid heat in the Olympic trials at Randalls Island, New York, a week later and he was on his way to Berlin. Clearly, he was an established star by the time he reached Germany, but the brilliance of his accomplishments there still were dazzling.

Offers poured in requesting Jesse's appearances following the Games. The AAU, anxious to pay its Olympic expenses, accepted many without his consent and assigned him to run all over Europe and Scandinavia. He extended himself into exhaustion, started to lose, and left to return home instead of accepting an assignment to a meet in Sweden. The AAU suspended him.

Angry, Owens announced he was turning professional. "I'm burned out, I'm busted, and I'm tired of being treated like cattle. I know how hard it is for a member of my race to make money and earn financial security and I have to reach for it while it's being offered me." So he passed up his remaining college eligibility and retired from amateur track.

Owens, who'd pumped gas at a filling station to support himself at Ohio State, toured the stage circuit for awhile in a tap-dancing act with Bill "Bojangles" Robinson, led a band, made a movie, and opened a dry-cleaning establishment. He made a lot of money in a little while and invested in other businesses. He lost his money in the stock market, however, his business failed, and within three years after his Olympic heroism he went bankrupt.

A fighter, he battled back. He went into physical education and youth work for major national concerns, started to tour the world on behalf of the United States government, and got himself on his feet financially and spiritually. Today he heads a public relations, marketing, and merchandising firm in Phoenix.

Acclaimed the greatest track athlete of the half-century in a 1950 Associated Press poll, approximately a quarter-century later and almost 40 years after his triumphs in the Olympics, he is, if anything, more famous now than he was then. A dignified and extravagantly articulate man, he remains in great demand for public appearances and travels the world preaching sports, patriotism, and brotherhood.

8
ST. MORITZ AND LONDON, 1948
A Young Man Named Mathias

WITH WAR BEING waged around the world, the Olympiads were canceled in 1940 and 1944. In 1948, the Games were resumed, though without the losers, Germany, Italy, and Japan. Twenty-eight nations sent more than 700 athletes to the Winter Games at St. Moritz in the neutral country of Switzerland early that year, while 59 nations sent more than 4,000 athletes to the Summer Games later, which were staged amid the rubble and rebuilding of London and the rain of an English July and August.

Curiously, the International Olympic Committee lists the 1916, 1940, and 1944 Summer Olympic Games as the 6th, 12th, and 13th, although they were canceled. The canceled Winter Games are ignored, as would appear more logical, with the 4th renewal at Garmisch-Partenkirchen, Germany, followed by the 5th at St. Moritz, Switzerland, in its official records.

In any event, there were 12 years between Olympiads, and many marvelous athletes lost opportunities for glory in the Games at their prime.

For the first time in the history of the Winter Olympics, Americans gained gold medals in figure skating and skiing at St. Moritz in 1948.

Dick Button may have been the best men's figure skater of all time. Born in Englewood, New Jersey, in July, 1929, he began as a boy with borrowed or rented skates at local indoor rinks. At twelve, he asked for his own skates, and his father bought him hockey skates. "I was disappointed," Dick has recalled. "I had been practicing figure skating and I wanted figure skates, which are different

St. Moritz and London, 1948

from hockey skates. It was hard to admit that to my father, who thought I wanted to play hockey. It was as if figure skating wasn't manly. But I told him and he accepted it. He was great about it. He said if that was what I wanted, it was fine with him. He not only traded the hockey skates in for figure skates, but took me to a teacher so I could learn right. Unfortunately, the teacher shortly decided I couldn't learn at all. He said I'd be a figure skater when hell froze over. Fortunately, it didn't take that long."

Dick learned. It was hard work. Some may not regard figure skating as athletic, but no athlete works harder than a figure skater. To master the dull details of the school figures, which must be traced meticulously, and to perfect the leaps and spins, the ease of motion of his freestyle routines, Dick worked out for 8 to 10 hours a day and often 7 days a week for his entire career, which is typical of others who've done this. He started later than most great skaters and without the natural ice available outdoors many months of the year as in the cold-weather countries.

He had to get up before dawn and return late at night many times to get the use of facilities when they were available to him. It was expensive paying for ice time, and teachers, and travel to competitions, and his parents had to support his sport. Dick's parents didn't push him into the spotlight but simply supported and encouraged his passion. A studious sort, he worked hard at school but otherwise sacrificed most of his private life growing up on the ice. He fell again and again and kept getting up.

"My parents took me to Lake Placid in upstate New York for lessons and I flunked my first tests. I don't know why I went on with it because all the signs were I didn't have the skill for it, but I was very determined and didn't let defeat discourage me. I made myself into a figure skater with work. I wasn't born to it, but I became what I wanted to be," he has recalled.

In 1943, at fourteen, he entered his first contest, the Eastern States Tournament, and finished third in the judging. He was on his way. A year later he won the Eastern Junior title and a year after that he won the American novice crown. The following year, in 1946, at 16, he became the youngest U.S. champion in history. And another year later, he became the world champion, winning the first of his five consecutive world crowns.

He was sensational. He had grown graceful and sure of himself. The slender, swift, agile athlete not only was good at the details of the first-day figures, but imaginative, inventive, and often inspired in the balletlike soaring and spinning of the second-day freestyle routines.

A Harvard freshman at eighteen, he won the gold medal in the Olympic Games at St. Moritz in 1948 by a wide margin over his nearest rival. He had the highest point total ever recorded in this competition. Figure skating is not an exact science. A panel of judges from various nations scores each competitor on his work each day and nationalistic pride sometimes prevails over impartiality. Also, judges are establishment figures, resistant to innovations in their sport and reluctant to reward new young performers. A sort of seniority system prevails in which skaters advance year by year up the ladder to the top. When it is the next person's turn, he is recognized as the current standout and is scored accordingly. Among the skating family it is tacitly acknowledged that the best man or woman does not always win. Accordingly, it is a cruel sport in which pure performance is not always recognized. Of course, most competitors never come close to the top. But Button hit the heights early. He was clearly the class of the competition. In 1949, he became the first skater ever to hold the five major championships at one time—the United States, North American, European, world, and Olympic crowns. In the world competition at Paris, he averaged 5.9 points out of a possible 6.0, and the crowd stood and cheered him for five minutes.

In an exhibition for fund-raising for the Olympic team at Madison Square Garden in New York, he did a Charleston routine that sent the crowd, conditioned to the rough physical sports such as boxing, basketball, and hockey, into a frenzy, demanding encore after encore. It was one of the most exciting moments the writer has had watching athletes in action—a never-to-be-forgotten moment when a performer puts the fans in the palm of his hand.

However, Button chose not to become an ice-show performer, as have most other champions of his sport. He was studying law. He kept up his skating practice and successfully defended his Olympic crown in 1952 in Oslo, Norway, but then retired from the sport. After receiving his law degree in 1955, he went into private practice.

He had also learned to play the piano, loved music, studied dramatics, and appeared in musicals such as *Pal Joey* and *South Pacific* in summer stock and in the children's skating classic *Hans Brinker* on television in the late 1950s. Still trim today, he appears

St. Moritz and London, 1948

regularly on television as an expert commentator on figure skating, which has spurred the popularity of the beautiful and spectacular sport in recent years. And he manages some skaters.

That year of 1948, Barbara Ann Scott of Canada, a lovely young lady of nineteen, ended European domination of women's figure skating. Norwegians won three of the four men's speed-skating titles. Swedes won three of the four men's Nordic skiing events. Women's skiing was added to the Alpine events and Gretchen Fraser, a pretty pigtailed young woman from the state of Washington won the first skiing medal America had ever captured. She streaked to triumph in the new slalom competition, which is a test against time with the speedsters wending their way downhill through a series of flagpoles, called *gates*. The skiers depend on rapid reflexes as they cut this way and that down a slippery course. Gretchen Fraser was phenomenal.

Her mother was born in Norway and was an enthusiastic skier. After marrying William Kunigk of Tacoma, she worked in developing Mt. Rainier as a resort and at popularizing skiing. Her daughter, Gretchen, started skiing at sixteen and, in 1939, married Don Fraser, a member of America's 1936 Olympic ski team. Both husband and wife were chosen for the 1940 Games, but the events were canceled. While Don served in the Navy during the war, Gretchen taught skiing, swimming, and riding to amputees in Army hospitals and became an accomplished flier.

After the war, the Frasers went into business with a small fuel distribution company at which they both worked. As another Olympiad neared, Don encouraged Gretchen to try out again. Although almost thirty, she resumed competition. She had not won a major American crown in six years when she was elected for the 1948 Games, and she was an unknown and definitely an underdog when she arrived in Europe.

She startled the experts when she finished second to an Austrian, Trude Jochum-Beiser, in the combined Alpine event, winning the silver medal in a test of speed and endurance that was never held again. Still, she was not well regarded when she led off as first of 31 entrants in the slalom the next afternoon. The first skier charts the course for those who follow, so she was at a handicap.

Substituting daring for perfection, she did well, weaving her way down the tricky course in less than a minute; but others behind her did better. The test is settled on total time for two runs, however, and by the time she went back for her second run she was ready. The countdown commenced, she was sent off, and wheeling this way and that with the aid of poles, spraying snow as she shot through the gates, speeding daringly at better than 60 miles per hour, she set fast time for the entire field and left the rest far behind her.

When the bundled crowd lining the course and waiting at the bottom bellowed their surprise, her frosted face broke into a big grin. She got her gold as a Swiss contender settled for silver, half a second short, and an Austrian accepted the bronze, another three-tenths of a second behind.

Gretchen Fraser gave American skiing a boost when it was badly needed and inspired others. Americans have been becoming increasingly competitive with the Europeans, who have superior natural conditions for training and vastly superior public support in their sport.

Gretchen Fraser managed the women's team at Oslo, Norway, four years later. While she retired from active competition, she continued to enjoy the outdoors, frequently camping with her husband in the Canadian wilds. One year she became the first woman ever to live on an ice cap when she and her husband spent two weeks in Juneau, Alaska, filming a television special with the famed broadcaster Lowell Thomas.

Another American triumph of note at St. Moritz in 1948 was by a four-man bobsled team. It was the last time the U.S. has won this swift, dangerous race.

Lord David Burghley, gold medalist in the 400-meter hurdles in the 1928 Olympics at Amsterdam, was chairman of the British Olympic Committee in charge of conducting the 1948 Games in London. He did a splendid job despite the debris of war that remained. No new facilities were constructed, but old Wembley Stadium still was serviceable as the main arena and there were adequate accommodations for the 19 sports contested.

American gold medalists ranged from 4-foot-6-inch-tall Joe DePietro, who won the bantamweight weightlifting title, to 7-foot Bob Kurland, who centered the winning U.S. basketball team. Americans won four of the six weight lifting titles. Massive John Davis beat out big Norbert Schemansky as the United States swept the one-two spots in the heavyweight class. Turks took four of the eight wrestling titles, but an American, Henry Wittenberg, won in the light-heavyweight class.

The Olympiad had its disappointments, too. Jack Kelly, Jr.,

St. Moritz and London, 1948

world champion in the single sculls and son of the 1920 gold medalist, was eliminated in the semifinal of this rowing event, won by an Australian.

A Mexican, Humberto Mariles, became a great hero by winning his country's first gold medal. He won the individual grand prix jumping event and helped his team to the title in this equestrian sport. Ironically, when Mexico City hosted the 1968 Games 20 years later, the wealthy Mariles had been imprisoned for shooting another man after an argument.

Americans swept all seven gold medals in the men's competition and captured half of the six women's contests in swimming and diving. Wally Ris, Bill Smith, Jimmy McLane, and Joe Verdeur won individual men's races, while Sammy Lee, later a doctor in California, beat out Bruce Harlan in the platform diving and was third to Harlan in springboard diving. Vicki Draves became the first ever to sweep the diving events in the women's competition. Silver medalist in the springboard diving was Zoe Ann Olsen, who later married football and baseball star Jackie Jensen.

Another American gold medalist was Ann Curtis. Taught to swim by the sisters at Ursuline Convent in northern California, she won her first national championship at the age of eleven. She had won 25 national championships and in 1944 had become the first swimmer and the first woman of any sport to be voted the Sullivan Award as America's greatest amateur athlete. She finally got a chance at an Olympics in 1948. She made the most of it at London, capturing two gold medals and a silver medal. Runner-up at 100 meters in the freestyle, she won at 400 meters and helped the 400-meter relay team win.

Drizzle dampened the track and field events, but could not dull the brilliance of the thirty-year-old mother of two who dominated these contests as has no other woman. Fanny Blankers-Koen, the wife of the Netherlands track coach, was the oldest competitor at the Games but also the best. The sturdy blond swept the two sprints and set a world record in winning the 80-meter hurdles. She was considered capable of winning the high jump, too, but was limited to three individual events. She did run in the 400-meter relay and after taking the baton came from far behind to win on the anchor leg. She is the only woman ever to win four gold medals in one Olympics. Only three men have managed this feat in track and field—Ralph Kraenzlein, Paavo Nurmi, and Jesse Owens.

Another wonderful competitor was Micheline Ostermeyer of

France, a most unusual woman who was a concert pianist, yet powerful enough to win gold medals in the shot put and discus throw and a bronze in the high jump.

Many of the greatest trackmen of all time found fame in the 1940s but had no Olympics to contest until after they were retired or past their prime. They can be added to a long list of world record holders who failed to gain a gold medal in the Games. When you get right down to it, each event in the Olympics finally is contested in one day, perhaps in a few minutes, and the enormous pressure produces some stunning upsets.

Cornelius "Dutch" Warmerdam of California was the greatest pole-vaulter ever. Competing with the bamboo pole long before metal and then fiberglass poles sent vaulters soaring skyward, Warmerdam burst over the 15-foot barrier in 1940 and set indoor and outdoor records at around 15 feet 8 inches that lasted 17 years. It was more than a decade before another vaulter even reached 15 feet. At one time, Warmerdam had the 43 finest vaults ever. By the time the Olympics arrived in 1948, he was thirty-three and retired. In London, it took only a little more than 14 feet for Guinn Smith to win this event.

In 1948, Charles Fonville of Michigan sent the world record for the shot put past 56 feet 10 inches, but he failed even to qualify for the American team in the one-meet test which has deprived so many standouts of their shot at the Games over the years. Wilbur Thompson, who had never even won a U.S. title, got the gold with a lesser effort.

Harrison Dillard was one of the greatest hurdlers of all time. He was the world record holder and had lost only once in 100 races when he hit the first hurdle in the final trials, lost stride, and lost out on an Olympic berth in his event. However, he squeezed onto the team by finishing third behind Barney Ewell and Mel Patton in the 100-meter dash, then upset them to win the gold at London. He got his gold in hurdling four years later in Helsinki, Finland.

Dillard was a poor black youngster of thirteen when he watched from a curb as Jesse Owens was welcomed back to Cleveland as a hero after his Olympic success in 1936. So scrawny he was named "Bones," Harrison had found an idol to emulate. "I was struck by a spark that afternoon," he later recalled. He went to Owens's old high school and wore Owens's old track shoes. He set out to be a sprinter, too, but was converted by his coach into a hurdler, also. He kept sprinting, but found he liked hurdling better. "I've always felt that sprinters are a dime a dozen, but when you combine running with the gymnastics required to hurdle you get a high art," he explained.

He swept the hurdles in the state track meet, went to Baldwin-Wallace and became collegiate champion. By 1948, the 5 foot 10 150-pounder had set a world record of 13.6 seconds for the hurdles at both 110 meters and 120 yards and had an incredible streak of 82 consecutive victories before he was beaten. When he was beaten, it was because he insisted on running both the sprints and hurdles and was wearing out with heat races as well as finals in the big meets. Doubling in sprints as well as hurdles saved him, however, when he tripped in the trials of the hurdles, but made the American Olympic team as a dashman.

Though deeply disappointed, he was a determined athlete. He was an outsider among the world's speediest sprinters in the Olympic final at London, but he got off to a great start and held off the fast-finishing, brilliant Barney Ewell at the tape. Ewell thought he had won and clasped his hands over his head in triumph—until the official finish was announced, which reduced him to tears. Dillard's coach, Eddie Finnigan, sprinted from the stands to embrace his runner, weeping.

Dillard said, "I would have settled for the silver medal. I never have gone through anything in my life like that long wait to hear the result." His coach confessed, "We weren't in his best event and I never thought we had a chance. Fate is strange, but wonderful. We'd waited for this a long time. I went to find a church to give thanks to God."

It is considered by some the most dramatic upset triumph in Olympic history.

Patton beat Barney Ewell in the 200-meter final and all ran on the 400-meter relay winner as Dillard got his second gold medal. Actually, this team was disqualified for not passing the baton at the right point, but after a review its triumph later was restored.

Dillard toured the world waiting for another Olympics. The tension in the trials at Los Angeles in 1952 was tremendous. There were six false starts before the runners got away. Never beaten to the first hurdle, Dillard led from the start but hit the seventh hurdle and stumbled. Faced with failure again, he steadied himself somehow and held on to win at the wire.

In Finland, he could not help being cautious and was being caught by Jack Davis at the tape but again had just enough to win.

"It was one I wanted, in my event," he sighed. After he ran on the victorious sprint relay team again, he received his fourth gold medal. Second twice in the voting, he finally finished first to win the Sullivan Award in 1955 and retired before the Olympics the following year.

Mal Whitfield, a Texan who went on to set the world record for the half mile at 1:48.6, won the 800 in the 1948 Olympics and again in the 1952 Games. He was a silver medalist at 400 meters, a gold medalist member of the 1,600-meter relay team in 1948, and a silver medalist member of the 1,600-meter relayists who finished second in 1952. America's Gil Dodds and Greg Rice were a great miler and two-miler, respectively, who had slowed with injuries by 1948. The world's best miler and two-miler was Gunder Hagg of Sweden, who set world records in both and at 4:00.2 came within a fraction of a second of becoming the man to break the four-minute mile barrier. The second best was countryman Arne Andersson. But both had been declared professionals for having accepted excessive expense money by 1948.

At London, a lesser Swede, Henri Eriksson topped his countryman, Lennart Strand, at 1,500 meters, while a Belgian, Gaston Reiff, beat Czech Emil Zatopek at 5,000 meters. However, Zatopek came back to win at 10,000 meters to get the first gold medal of an outstanding Olympic career which would peak four years later in Finland.

The most amazing athletic performance in London was by Bob Mathias, a seventeen-year-old Tulare, California, high school boy, who won the toughest test of them all, the decathlon. It was only the third one he ever had attempted in his life.

Bob's father, a former football player at the University of Oklahoma, had moved to Tulare to take over a general medical practice the year Bob was born, in November, 1930. As a boy, Bob was athletic, but he gained height before weight. He was so skinny at the age of eight that his doctor dad decided he was suffering from anemia. For five years Bob had to take afternoon naps and was restricted from sports. He was playing trumpet for the high school band before he even was allowed to try out for sports.

However, in his teens he filled out fast. By the time he was seventeen and a senior, he stood 6 foot 2 and weighed 190 pounds. And he had matured into a marvelous all-around athlete who averaged almost 10 yards a carry for the football team, averaged 18 points a game for the basketball team, and regularly won any one of four or five track and field events he entered in meets. He was not great at any of these events, but he was good at all.

His coach, Virgil Jackson, was thinking about this one day when he heard there was going to be decathlon competition in a meet at Pasadena to prepare competitors for the Olympic trials later in the summer. Mathias recalls, "He came to me and suggested I try the decathlon. I asked him what a decathlon was. He said it was 10 events, but he didn't know which ones. I said if he could find out, I could try 'em. We found out some of them were events I had never tried, including the long jump, the pole vault, the javelin and the metric mile. He said he'd try to teach me so I said I'd try to learn. We had three weeks."

At first it seemed likely that if Bob didn't spear himself to death in trying to learn to handle the javelin, he probably would impale himself on the pole while vaulting. But he was a natural athlete and picked up technique fast. Within three weeks he pulled off one of the most remarkable upset achievements of all time in sports by beating a field that included the national champion Moon Mondschenin to win the first decathlon he ever entered.

Startled experts suggested Mathias shaped up as a contender for world decathlon honors by the 1952 Olympics. Bob and his coach didn't want to wait. The Olympic trials to select the 1948 team were only six weeks away in Bloomfield, New Jersey, and Bob and his coach decided they had nothing to lose by trying out. Bob worked hard, went, and won. Some said it was ridiculous to send a boy into a man's event against the best in the world, but he was on his way to London, the youngest member of the American men's track and field team in history.

He was still learning half the events when he went up against such veteran stars as the towering Ignace Heinrich of France and the Argentine Enrique Kistenmacher on the first day. No one gave him any chance at all except a small group of fans who gathered around the youngster's proud parents at one corner of the stadium.

The first event was the 100-meter dash. Bob didn't win his heat, but he ran a respectable 11.2 seconds. Next came the long jump. Bob leaped 22 feet. After two events, he had fallen behind Kistenmacher and Heinrich. Then came the shot put. Bob put the 16-pound iron ball 45 feet, the best throw of his life. He hopped out of the ring happily and found a red flag being waved in his face. It turned out he had left from the front of the ring. The rules require competitors to depart from the rear. He couldn't believe his best-ever effort was lost. He had other throws, but the best he could do was 42 feet, and he fell further behind the leaders.

Then came the high jump. His opening height was set at 5 feet 9 inches. It was one of his best events, and he had jumped half a foot higher. Confidently, he didn't bother to take off his warm-up suit for his first attempt. He went up but knocked off the bar. He was surprised. Suddenly he was worried. He figured he'd better do it on his next attempt. He took off his suit, tensed, went into his approach, got a bit mixed up, took off too soon and brushed off the bar. Shades of Bill Toomey 20 years later, Mathias was left with one jump to clear an opening height or lose any hope of winning a medal.

"Suddenly, I started to panic," he recalls. "I didn't know much about the decathlon, but I knew with a zero score in this event I'd finish far back. I didn't know I could win the whole meet or I'd really have lost control. I tried to get a grip on myself but I was scared. I was only a kid, after all, and now my confidence, my cockiness was gone. It was a height I should make, but with only one chance left I felt I was going to blow it. Then I heard a cheer, 'C'mon, Tulare!' I looked and saw the group around my folks. I didn't want to let them down. It gave me the little bit extra I needed. I grit my teeth, went right at that bar, and went over it."

After that dramatic reprieve, he went to 6 feet 1 inch before failing. It was darkening and drizzling, and he wrapped himself in a blanket while waiting for the day's final event. This was the 400 meters and he ran it in 41.7 seconds. Finally, the first long day was done. And he was within 32 points of Heinrich and 51 of Kistenmacher. He suffered through the long night waiting for the next day. It dawned miserably, the worst day of the Olympics, a steady rain falling, the stadium surface turning to mud.

The first event that morning was the 110-meter hurdles. Another American, Floyd Simmons, sped over them so swiftly he shot into the lead in the meet. Bob lost points with a 15.7-second effort. Then came the discus, maybe Bob's best event, and he spun the saucer 144 feet 4 inches, by far the best in the field. Now the kid from California was in front, with the Frenchman second, the Argentine third, and the other contending American fourth.

It was getting late in the day and darkening. The rain continued to fall and the crowd in the stands through the afternoon had begun to thin out. The decathletes were at the pole vault. Heinrich and Kistenmacher failed to get above 10 feet 6 inches. Bob did not yet know how to do it, he just did it. He gripped the slippery pole, ran, planted, and went over at 11 feet 2 inches. Only one man went higher, and he was not in the running.

This left two events, the javelin and the 1,500. Mathias knew he was mediocre in the metric mile and would go so slow he'd give up points to the others. He led the meet, but knew he needed an exceptional toss of the spear to put himself safely in front. His best ever had been 157 feet, but now Bob was bone-tired. He had not eaten. He huddled under his blanket in the chill gloom waiting for the call. It came and he hurled the spear more than 165 feet, more than 30 feet past Heinrich's mark. Suddenly, Heinrich was beaten. Mathias had only to finish the 1,500 to win.

At 10 that night, wearily, aching from every muscle in his body, constricted by cramps, the youngster struggled around the black oval in the cold drizzle four times in 5 minutes 11 seconds. As he crossed the finish line his father came out of the stands. The boy fell into his father's arms while the remaining fans stood and cheered Bob's startling triumph.

He had led only one event, but he had done well enough in the others to total 7,139 points, winning decisively. He was the youngest person ever to win the decathlon, in fact the youngest ever to win in men's track and field. He was still just a schoolboy, but he remembers, "I felt like a man as I stood on that victory platform and got that gold medal and heard our national anthem."

He was an instant celebrity, who came home to parades and banquets and proposals of marriage from female fans. An astonishingly handsome, husky, and clean-cut lad, he seemed the perfect sports superstar. But his life was only beginning. And he still was learning the decathlon. Two years later, he broke the world record for the event, which had been established by Glenn Morris. Mathias at nineteen became the first man to top 8,000 points. He went to Stanford and became a football star as well as a track star. His 96-yard scoring run defeated Southern Cal and put his team in the Rose Bowl.

In 1952 in Finland he returned to the Olympics and became the only man ever to win a second decathlon gold medal. He entered only ten decathlons in his life, won them all, and retired at the peak of his athletic career. Taking his examination before he entered the marines during the Korean conflict, he was declared by a doctor "the only physically perfect specimen I've tested out of thousands of men over the years."

But there were other things Bob wanted to do besides sports. After completing military service, he accepted an acting contract and made movies and television dramas for awhile, but he was not a great success at it and swiftly tired of it. He entered politics, ran for Congress, won, and remains now a member of the House of Representatives. Married and with a growing family, he remains active at tennis, swimming, and other sports, but strictly for pleasure.

"The Olympics gave me the opportunity to do other things," he says today. "The Games made me a star, a celebrity when my life was really only beginning, but I don't think I was spoiled by it, and it opened a lot of doors to me. The thing is to take advantage of your openings in life. I treasure my gold medals. The Olympic experience is incomparable and remains the most memorable moment of my life, but I would hope I have used it as a base on which to build a better life."

Records are broken, but Olympic triumphs remain in the records forever. The Games put competitors on sharp points of pressure in the prime of their lives. "The athlete dies young, but the man goes on to grow old," Mathias smiles.

9
OSLO AND HELSINKI, 1952
Boxers Strike Gold

QUICK-HANDED AND explosive, a youngster from Brooklyn, Floyd Patterson, battled his way through the field, outmaneuvered Vasile Tita of Romania in the final, and won the middleweight boxing championship in the 1952 Summer Olympics at Helsinki, Finland. Filling out and progressing rapidly, he became the first of four professional heavyweight boxing champions to emerge from five Olympiads.

Patterson was an awesome amateur. He was astonishingly quick and hit hard with either hand. His performance at Helsinki in 1952 was impressive. However, he won there as a middleweight and was at his best at 160 pounds. Probably he should never have risen beyond the 175-pound light-heavyweight class professionally. Although beefed up, he was a small heavyweight and did not have the strength to take a big heavyweight fighter's best punches. He adopted a defensive style and never became the boxer he might have been. Still, he held the heavyweight title on and off for almost six years.

Born in Waco, North Carolina, in January, 1935, brought to Brooklyn as a boy, he was reared in poor circumstances but battled his way out of the ghetto. He became a Golden Gloves king and won his Olympic laurels by defeating a Frenchman, a Dutchman, and a Swede before flattening the Romanian for the gold medal. He turned professional later that year and won 13 consecutive fights before his first defeat.

Patterson won the professional heavyweight crown in November, 1956, with a fifth-round knockout of Archie Moore in a fight to fill the throne vacated by the retired Rocky Marciano. In August, 1957, Patterson defended his title a second time with a sixth round knockout over Pete Rademacher, who had brought the United States the Olympic heavyweight title in Melbourne in 1956, but was built up beyond his ability for his first professional fight.

In June, 1959, Patterson lost his title to Ingemar Johansson of Sweden, a finalist in the 1952 Olympic heavyweight class, who stopped the champ in three rounds.

Curiously, Johansson had been disqualified for not fighting enough in the heavyweight final against America's Ed Sanders at Helsinki in 1952, the year Patterson captured the middleweight gold medal. As a result, the silver medalist's slot in the Olympic record books is blank. However, as professionals the American Sanders was killed in a bout while the handsome Swede, a playboy who was not a skilled or rugged fighter but had a good and powerful punch, went on to win the title. But Patterson regained his crown the following June by a knockout and retained it the next March with another knockout of Ingo.

When Patterson won the heavyweight title at twenty, he was the youngest man ever to capture it. And after losing it, he became the first man ever to recapture the heavyweight honors. Although he has had his ups and downs, Patterson has fought professionally for more than 20 years and earned more than $8 million in the ring. Even today he refuses to retire, though he seldom has fought in recent years and appears to be drifting from the ranks of the active performers.

Patterson lost his title the last time in September of 1962 when KO'd in one round by big Sonny Liston. Liston in turn lost the title when stopped in seven rounds in February, 1964, by Muhammad Ali, who as Cassius Clay of Louisville had won the Olympic light-heavyweight boxing title in Rome in 1960. Ali later stopped Patterson in Floyd's effort to reclaim his title.

After Ali was stripped of his title on his conviction for draft dodging, Joe Frazier, the 1964 Olympic champion at Tokyo, stopped Jimmy Ellis in February, 1970, to take over the vacated throne. He proved his right to it by decisioning the reinstated Ali in March, 1971. However, Frazier, in turn, was dethroned in one round in January, 1973, by George Foreman, who had won the Olympic heavyweight title at Mexico City in 1968.

The trend is not likely to continue, since Theofilio Stevenson, the skilled Cuban who won the heavyweight crown at the Games in

Munich in 1972, has not turned professional in accordance with the wishes of the Cuban government. Duane Bobick, the highly touted American eliminated by Stevenson in an earlier round, is attempting to rise to the top professionally, however.

For many years now, boxers have struck gold professionally after gaining gold medals in the Olympics, although capitalizing on their amateur attainments in the Games goes against the standards of Olympic officials. Still, figure skaters do it, as do others, so why not boxers? Their gold medals give the Olympic champions drawing power as they turn professional, and Olympic success often is a sign of prospective professional success. Even some losers in the Games have gone on to scale the heights.

Rademacher, who topped the Soviet Lev Mukhin in the Olympic heavyweight final at Melbourne in 1956, might have become a fair fighter but had no business trying for the title in his first professional fight. It ruined his future; but, of course, the paycheck was fat and he might never have made it to the title bout if he had tried to fight his way up.

Grandson of a slave, Cassius Clay came out of Louisville, tall, slender, and astonishingly fast for a big lad. He won the National AAU and Golden Gloves titles before outboxing Anton Pietrzykowski of Poland for the Olympic light-heavyweight gold medal in Rome in 1960. He did not take off his gold medal for 48 hours. He even wore it to bed. He added weight and went on to win world heavyweight honors as a professional, becoming a Muslim, changing his name to Muhammad Ali, and becoming the most boastful and colorful champion the ring has had, and maybe one of the best. He has continued to be the strongest gate attraction of his day, an effective fighter, and a man who has made millions.

Frazier should not even have been boxing for Olympic laurels in 1964. The Philadelphia butcher's apprentice out of South Carolina lost in the trials to 290-pound Buster Mathis, a fat fellow with surprising agility. However, Mathis was injured and Frazier substituted at the Games in Tokyo. Not a stylish fighter, but a busy one and a tough one who wore his foes down, Frazier won the final by a close decision from the German, Hans Huber. Joe turned pro, won the title, and successfully defended it against the challenges of Mathis as well as Ali before losing it to Foreman.

The huge Foreman, an awesome puncher, spent a troubled youth in Texas, landed in Oakland, and won his way to the 1968 Games in Mexico City, where he knocked out the Soviet Iones

Chepulis for the gold medal. On the heels of a controversial demonstration against U.S. racial policies by black trackmen Tommie Smith and John Carlos, Foreman's waving of a small American flag in the ring after his triumph endeared the black lad to some of his countrymen and earned him considerable patriotic publicity. He went on to wrest the professional laurels from Frazier with a stunning, swift KO.

Boxing is the most basic of sports. Man has fought man as long as life has been known. Formal fistfighting dates back to the 1700s, at a time when James Figg won some recognition as the world heavyweight champion. Modern historians prefer to recognize John L. Sullivan of the late 1800s as the first heavyweight king and the last of the bareknuckle champs. The development of boxing as an acceptable sport commenced with his successor, Jim Corbett, and the introduction of gloved fighting.

Despite its elemental brutality, boxing has been a sport in the Olympics since the third Games in St. Louis in 1904. The American O. L. Kirk won both the bantamweight and featherweight titles to become the only man ever to win two boxing crowns in a single Olympiad. The Hungarian Laszlo Papp, who won the middleweight title in 1948 and the light-middleweight titles in 1952 and 1956, remains the only man ever to win three gold medals in boxing.

Several Olympic medalists went on to win world titles in classes other than heavyweight over the years. Frank DeGenaro, who won the flyweight title from the Dane Anders Petersen at Antwerp in 1920, later won the professional flyweight crown as Frankie Genaro. That year of 1920, Eddie Eagen won the light-heavyweight title. Two others on the U.S. team were Jack and Pete Zivic, whose brother Fritzie won the world welterweight title as a pro.

Four years later at Paris, Fidel LaBarba won the flyweight laurels, Jackie Fields won the featherweight honors and both went on to be world champs as pros. Joe Salas actually had won the amateur featherweight title of America in the trials as Fields was eliminated. However, Olympic rules at the time permitted two entrants from each country in each class and both went for the gold and wound up meeting in the final. Fields won a close decision after toe-to-toe battling over the three two-minute rounds.

At Los Angeles in 1932, Argentine Alberto Lovell won the heavy-

Oslo and Helsinki, 1952

weight honors. His son, Pedro, recently has been boxing successfully as a pro heavyweight in the Los Angeles area. An interesting finalist four years later in Berlin was the bantamweight Jackie Wilson of Cleveland, who stood 6 foot 2 but weighed only 117 pounds and surely was one of the skinniest competitors the Games have had.

Runner-up to Papp in 1956 in Australia was Puerto Rican Jose Torres, who later became world light-heavyweight champion as a pro. Four years later in Italy, Nino Benvenuti won welterweight honors to thrill his countrymen in Rome, and he later became professional middleweight king.

Heavyweights are the glamour guys of boxing, and Floyd Patterson started the most spectacular series of emerging professional champs Olympic ring action has produced when he won in Finland in 1952.

In wrestling in 1952, Axel Gronberg of Sweden won his second straight Greco-Roman middleweight gold medal. Lightweight Tommy Kono, middleweight Pete George, middle-heavyweight Norbert Schemansky, and heavyweight John Davis gave the United States four of the seven weight-lifting titles, while Russia, making its debut as an entrant in the Olympics, captured the other three crowns. Russians won 9 of the 16 gymnastics titles.

A Czech, Josef Holecek, won his second straight in canoe singles at 1,000 meters, while Frank Havens brought the United States a rare triumph in this sport in the canoe singles at 10,000 meters. The American team twice trimmed Russia to triumph in basketball, as usual.

In swimming and diving, world records were surpassed in all 14 events. Winning one individual race, the American Ford Konno gained two gold medals and one silver. Sammy Lee won his second straight in the platform diving, and David "Skippy" Browning won the springboard competition to complete the fifth straight sweep of the diving events for American men. Pat McCormick swept both of the women's diving events, but these were the only water triumphs for American women.

Growing up practically in the water at Santa Monica, California, Pat McCormick grew brave surfing the big waves and turned to the dangerous, exciting diving events. Over the years, she cracked her scalp, spine, ribs, fingers, and jaw and she cut and bruised most of her body banging into boards and the sides of pools as she mastered her aerial acrobatics. But she was tough and determined. "A doctor once told me he'd seen worse survivors—from building cave-ins," she laughed.

She did as many as 100 dives a day, six days a week for many years. She was the first woman to sweep the American national outdoor and indoor diving titles in 1950 and 1951, and in 1952 in Helsinki she swept the Olympic crowns. Later, she was one of the rare women to be voted the Sullivan Award as America's top amateur athlete.

The main thrust of the Russian Olympic bid was in track and field, but the U.S.S.R. won only two women's events and failed to win a man's event. The Americans did not win an individual event in the women's competition, which was dominated by Marjorie Jackson, an Australian who swept the sprints. However, Americans won 13 of the 23 men's events. Among them were dramatic triumphs by Charlie Moore and Horace Ashenfelter over Russians in the 400-meter hurdles and 3,000-meter steeplechase, respectively.

Ashenfelter, a twenty-nine-year-old FBI agent, was a mediocre middle-distance runner who turned to the steeplechase in desperation. It is a difficult event that does not draw a lot of outstanding athletes. He had run only half a dozen of these in his life, had not done well in any of them, and was not well regarded in world circles. He was not supposed to have a finishing kick and seemed doomed when he trailed far behind the Russian Vladmir Kazantsev, the world record holder, on the last lap.

However, the American put on an amazing sprint, caught the favorite at the last water jump, cleared the barrier, exploded out of the pond, and hit the tape in front in the fastest time ever recorded for the event. It was one of the most memorable upsets in Olympic history and Ashenfelter later noted, "Olympic competition is so inspiring and representing your country produces so much unexpected patriotism that some men are moved to do more than they had thought possible."

Another amazing upset was scored by diminutive American Lindy Remigino in the 100-meter dash as he surprised Jamaica's Herb McKenley. The magnificent McKenley was a luckless Olympian who also lost at 400 meters to countryman George Rhoden. Another Jamaican, long-striding Arthur Wint, was second at 800 meters to American Mal Whitfield, who won his second straight gold medal in this event. American Andy Stanfield won the 200-meter sprint and Harrison Dillard finally got his gold in the 110-meter hurdles. Bob Mathias repeated his decathlon triumph.

Americans Walt Davis, Jerry Biffle, and Bob Richards won the high jump, long jump, and pole vault, respectively. As a boy, Davis suffered from polio, but he recovered, built himself up with heavy exercises, shot up, and cleared his own height of 6 feet 8 inches to win his Olympic gold medal.

Short, stocky Richards escaped a crime-ridden neighborhood in Illinois through sports and the influence of a local church. He was ordained to the ministry in 1946 but continued to compete in sports. At the University of Illinois he was a good all-around athlete, and he later won the American decathlon championship but specialized in pole-vaulting.

He became the second man in history to top 15 feet and won the Olympic crown in 1952 and again in 1956 at Melbourne before retiring. The Reverend Richards became most famous as a television spokesman for Wheaties breakfast food in commercials, before becoming a full-time evangelist who preaches around the world. His son became a good pole-vaulter.

Among winners in the throwing events were Americans Parry O'Brien in the shot put, Sim Iness in the discus throw, and Cy Young in the javelin throw. Young was the first American to win the javelin.

From Santa Monica, the son of a former football star, O'Brien became a football player but turned to the shot put as he grew into an enormous young man. He went to the University of Southern California on a football scholarship but gave up football when his shot-putting skills showed themselves. He was a hard-working, dedicated fellow, who carried the 16-pound iron ball with him wherever he went and would stop to practice whenever he passed an open field.

"I used to climb into the Coliseum over the fence and work out by moonlight," he once recalled. He revolutionized his event by introducing a new form in which he turned completely around before starting and whirled into his throw. He won gold medals at Helsinki in 1952 and again at Melbourne in 1956, and in between he became the first shot-putter to break through the 60-foot barrier. He continued to compete and won the silver medal in Rome in 1960 but finished fourth at Tokyo in 1964. He was national titleholder eight times and held the world record seven years, eventually putting the shot past 63 feet before retiring to become a banker in California.

In 1952 an American came close to a stunning upset at 1,500 meters, the glamorous "metric mile," which the United States has not won since 1908, but Bob McMillen was edged out by inches at the tape by Josey Barthel of little Luxembourg, although timers clocked them in the identical time. Finishing fourth was Britain's Roger Bannister, who two years later became the man who finally burst through the four-minute-mile barrier but retired to become a doctor without ever having won an Olympic gold medal.

However, the hero of the distance races was the Czech Emil Zatopek, who was one of the outstanding Olympians of all time. Second in the 5,000 meters and first in the 10,000 meters in 1948, Zatopek finished first in both and also in the marathon in 1952, setting Olympic records in each. For the barrel-chested but frail little twenty-nine-year-old, it was an astonishing feat of endurance that never has been matched.

He had the world's worst form. He ran with short, choppy strides, his fists clenched, and an expression of agony on his face from the first. He made you feel he could not run another step, much less finish, yet he went on and on, faster and farther than the freshest and greatest distance runners to win his four gold medals, three in a single Olympiad.

At sixteen he had gone to work for a shoe factory that sponsored a race in the streets and required its young employees to run. Emil asked to be excused from it, saying he was no good at running, but was refused. He finished second. Surprised, he started to run often. He did well and was selected for coaching and training by the government ministry of sports. He was not especially fast, but he seemed to have natural endurance. The sort of fellow who gives himself completely to anything he enters, Zatopek built himself up with dedication, running every spare moment until he could run no more.

After he won his first gold medal in London in 1948, he married a track star. His wife Dana also was a gold medalist in Helsinki in 1952, winning the women's javelin throw. By then, Emil had become the best in the world, and he ran over his smoother rivals like a runaway locomotive, in agony all the way, but astonishing the track world with the pace he could keep up apparently on sheer determination. His three winning races at Helsinki covered about 35 miles.

He was an army lieutenant by then, but he continued to run into 1956, when he was ailing from a hernia operation and aging but still finished sixth in the Olympic marathon in Melbourne. He retired the next year. By then he had set 18 world records from 5,000 to 30,000 meters and another in the marathon. He even set one for the one-hour run, covering more than 12 miles.

A spirited man, he once said, "after all the bombing, starvation, and death I have seen in Europe, the Olympics were like a ray of sunshine in the darkness. They were the warmest of terrible times."

Zatopek had become a member of the Czechoslovakian Communist party and a colonel in the army. Then he openly sided with his countrymen's bid for freedom in 1968. When Russian troops put down the revolt, Zatopek was expelled from the party and the service and reduced to collecting garbage. When sympathizers were seen helping him in the streets of Prague, he was fired and assigned to work out of sight as a laborer at construction sites, where he still toils.

A man's star seldom shines forever, but those Olympics in 1952 in Helsinki were brightened when the famous Finn, Nurmi, opened the ceremonies by striding into the stadium carrying the Olympic torch, which had been relayed from Greece. The ovation he received remains one of the most memorable in the history of sports.

Earlier that year, at Oslo, the Winter Games had been a brilliant show. In figure skating, Dick Button won his second straight men's title, while Britain's Jeanette Altwegg beat out Tenley Albright in the women's division. In speed skating, Ken Henry of the United States won at 500 meters, and Hjalmar Andersen of Norway won the other three races, the first man ever to win three golds on three consecutive days. Germany, having returned with Japan and Italy to Olympic competition, swept both bobsled events.

Norwegians, Finns, and Austrians dominated much of the skiing. Trude Jochum-Beiser of Austria won her second straight gold medal in downhill skiing. However, the United States had a heroine, too.

Nineteen-year-old Andrea Mead Lawrence defeated Austrian movie actress Dagmar Rom to score a striking upset in the giant slalom with a daring run, collapsing in the arms of her husband,

David, at the finish. Then, despite a fall on the first run, she recovered and went on to a spectacular run in the second heat to win the special slalom, becoming the first skier to win both Olympic alpine events.

Born in Rutland, Vermont, in 1932, the year the Winter Olympics were held in nearby Lake Placid, New York, Andy was put on skis by her inspired parents before she was four. They skied each year on vacations in Switzerland, established a ski resort in Vermont, and in 1938 brought back a pro, Carl Acker, to teach their daughter and others.

Before Andrea was twelve, she was doing well against adults in major eastern meets. At thirteen she broke her leg but recovered and never suffered another major accident in this bone-breaking sport. At fifteen, she won her way to St. Moritz as the youngest member of the U.S. skiing team and finished eighth. And she met her husband, who was a teammate.

Four years later, she was primed for a super performance. She won from an Austrian and a German by a wide margin in the giant slalom over a rough course after soldiers shoveled snow to cover the bare spots. Three days later, she nosed out two German girls in the special slalom. She lost precious seconds with her spill in the first run but bounced up to finish fast, then made by far the best time of all in the second run. She flashed through almost 50 gates over the 500-yard course to capture her second gold medal.

"I think maybe my advantage lay in my nature," she later observed. "The pressure on Olympic competitors is just awful, which is why there are so many upsets. Someone who doesn't think he will win is a bit more relaxed than the favorite, just goes all out to take a shot at it, and sometimes surprises even himself. I always want to win, but mainly I just want to do well. Which is why when I fell I didn't give up. I didn't want to look bad. I didn't think I would win, but I thought I could. I just threw caution to the winds. Instead of breaking my neck, I got gold medals to hang around it. You work a long time and dream a lot of such a moment. Winning once in the Olympics is staggering, but winning more is just about unbelievable."

Jim Thorpe played football at Carlisle, and went out for baseball and track as well. *Culver Pictures, Inc.*

Babe Didrickson (far right) got off last at the start of the 80-meter hurdles, but went on to win, setting a world record in the Olympiad of 1932. *Wide World Photos*

Jesse Owens won four gold medals in track and field events in the Olympic games of 1936. *Track and Field News*

Bob Mathias was the only athlete to win the Decathlon in two successive Olympiads, first in 1948 and again in 1952, when this picture was taken.

Harold Connolly won a gold medal in the hammer throw in the 1956 Olympics. *E. D. Lacey*

Weldon Olson (left) of the United States and Miroslav Vlach of Czechoslovakia battled for the puck in a fierce hockey game during the 1960 Olympics at Squaw Valley. *Wide World Photos*

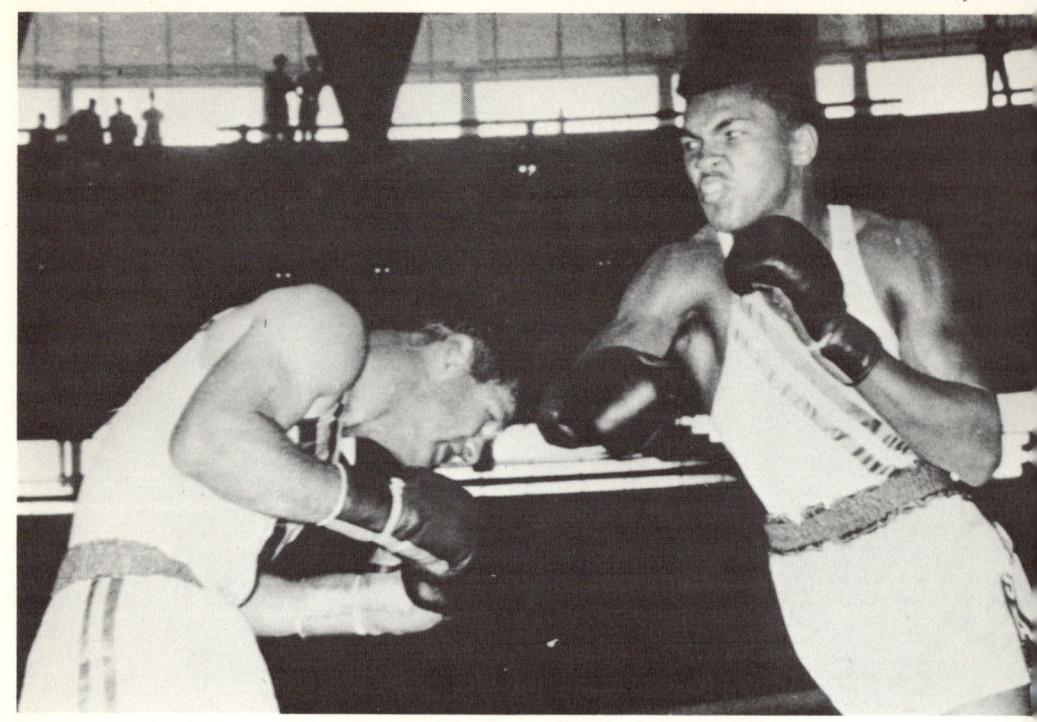

Cassius Clay (now Muhammad Ali) was only eighteen when he won the light-heavyweight boxing title in the 1960 Olympiad in Rome. *Wide World Photos*

Wilma Rudolph, who won the 100-meter dash on September 2, 1960, was winner of the 200-meter dash three days later, making her the first American woman to win both Olympic sprints. *Wide World Photos*

Billy Mills (left) of the United States had overtaken Ron Clarke of Australia and was about to pass Mohamed Gammoudi of Tunisia when this photo was taken at the 1964 Olympics in Tokyo. Moments later he won the 10,000-meter run. *E. D. Lacey*

Another victor in the 1964 Olympics was Peter Snell of New Zealand, here winning the 1,500-meter run. *E. D. Lacey*

Mary Rand of Great Britain won the long jump in the women's events of the 1964 Olympics. *E. D. Lacey*

In 1967 Mark Spitz won this 200-meter butterfly in a meet between the United States and Great Britain, then went on to win three gold medals in the 1968 Olympics and an unprecedented seven gold medals in the 1972 Olympics. *E. D. Lacey*

Nineteen-year-old Peggy Fleming won a gold medal in the Olympic Games of 1968 for her excellence in the freestyle skating event. *Wide World Photos*

In 1968, for the fourth Olympiad in a row, Al Oerter won the gold medal for the discus throw. *E. D. Lacey*

Debbie Meyer (foreground) led Jane Barkman in the 200-meter freestyle finals of the 1968 Olympics. *E. D. Lacey*

Bob Seagren won the pole vault contest in the Olympics of 1968. *E. D. Lacey*

Bob Beamon's jump of 29' 2½" won him the gold medal at the Olympics in Mexico City in 1968. *E. D. Lacey*

Kip Keino of Kenya outran Jim Ryun of the United States in the 1,500-meter run at the 1968 games. *E. D. Lacey*

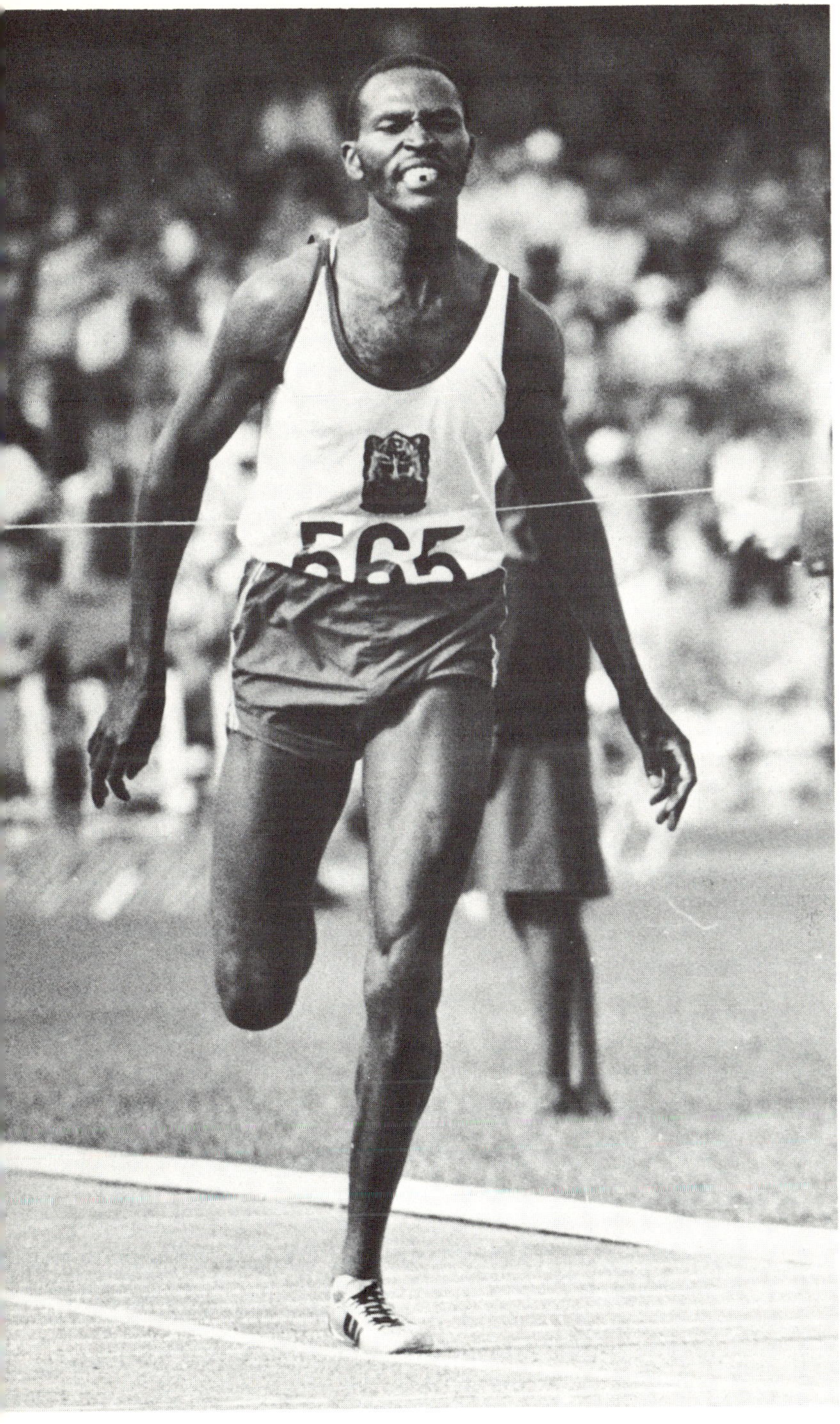

Pole vaulting was only one of the many events in which Bill Toomey excelled to win the decathlon gold medal in 1968. *E. D. Lacey*

Barbara Cochran was the first American woman in twenty years to win an Olympic skiing event when she earned her gold medal at Sapporo in 1972. *Wide World Photos*

Anne Henning won a gold medal for her speed skating in the 500-meter sprint, and a bronze medal in the 1,000-meter event. *Wide World Photos*

Air Force officer Micki King won her Olympic gold medal for springboard diving in the 1972 games. *Wide World Photos*

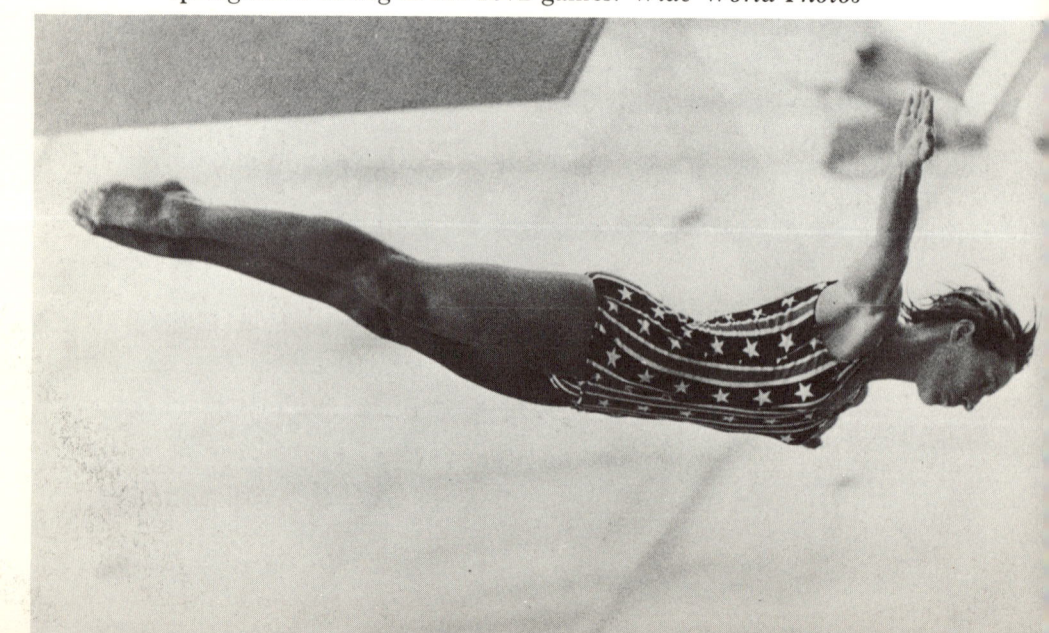

In the 1972 Olympic lightweight wrestling tournament Dan Gable of the United States won over Kikuo Wada of Japan. *Wide World Photos*

Olga Korbut of the USSR won two gold medals and enormous popularity for her gymnastic skills in the 1972 Olympiad. *E. D. Lacey*

Dave Wottle of the United States won the 800-meter run in the 1972 Olympics as second place Yevgeniy Arzhanov of the USSR fell and Mike Boit of Kenya came in third. *E. D. Lacey*

10
CORTINA AND MELBOURNE, 1956
One from the Shadows

THERE ARE EVENTS in the Olympics, even in track and field, which are not noticed much. They are not exciting events. They do not attract the eyes of the world, but men and women drift into these specialties, dedicate themselves to them, and spend the best part of their lives practicing and perfecting them. They are amateurs in the truest sense in that not many people would pay them to perform or pay to watch them. They receive little publicity. Though overshadowed by the more prominent performers in the more publicized events, they strive for perfection in the true spirit of sport.

One such event is the discus throw, though it is one of the oldest events and was contested in Greece before the Games themselves. It probably is as basic an Olympic event as any. And it is only every four years at an Olympiad that the best discus throwers in the world attract any attention at all, which also is true of those in the marathon and some other events.

Many track and field fans cannot tell you who holds the world record for the discus throw today. But they can tell you that Al Oerter is the greatest discus thrower of modern times, if not of all time. He may be the greatest Olympian. It is not that others did not often throw farther from meet to meet and from year to year, but no one threw farther for four consecutive Olympiads. He often was beaten, but not in the Olympics. His record of four consecutive gold medals in one event is unmatched.

"It is one thing to set records, but another to win Olympic gold medals," he says. "There are several men in any event who are capable of breaking the world record in their event. There are discus throwers who, when they are feeling just right and the conditions are just right, will catch a throw just right and break the record, but they will only hold it so long, their record will be broken. Setting records is just one part of sports or of track and field. Competition is the other part and for many of us the most important part. Winning, beating the best, is what matters the most. You can set a record any time, but you can win an Olympic gold medal only one time every four years. You come down to one day when you are against the best in the world and if you win the gold on that day no one can ever take it away."

His unrivalled string of successes started at the Melbourne Cricket Grounds in Australia in 1956, in front of the triple-tiered stadium packed with more than 100,000 fans. Oerter, who was born in August, 1936, had just turned twenty. He was one of the youngest contestants in an event traditionally led by older, more mature musclemen, and he was far from the most accomplished thrower in the competition.

The favorite was another American, Fortune Gordien, the world record holder at 194½ feet, who was third in the Olympics in 1948 and fourth in 1952 and regarded as ready at the age of thirty-four. The chief threat was Adolfo Consolini of Italy, the gold medalist in 1948 and the silver medalist in 1952, who still was among the best at the age of thirty-nine. Oerter, a husky young man from Astoria, New York, had never come within 10 feet of the world record, nor come close to even a national title, but the 6 foot 3, 220-pounder said later, "I thought I had a shot at it because I felt inspired."

No one ever had thrown the discus 200 feet, but Gordien came close in practice to put fear into his foes. However, on the first round, Oerter moved into the concrete circle, grabbed the metal saucer, set himself, spun and sailed in 184 feet 10½ inches, breaking the Olympic record, and by far the best he had done. The crowd roared when the distance was announced. Oerter tensed. "I don't know how I did it. I just did it. Everything just went right. I couldn't come close to it again. And I almost went out of my mind wondering if one of the others could." They couldn't. Gordien came closest, but fell 5 feet short. When the last throw was made, Oerter mounted the victory stand and had the gold medal draped around his neck. "I was as surprised as everyone else," he admits.

That was just one time. It can happen even in the Olympics, an upset of major proportions by an unknown who "catches one just right." The pressure produces upset of that sort. But when it happens more than once, it cannot be considered a freak. Oerter proved himself when he won the National AAU title for the first time in 1957 and was acclaimed the number one discus thrower in the world with a throw of more than 190 feet and a Pan-American Games triumph in Chicago in 1959. By then he was married, raising a family, and working in data processing for an aircraft company, but budgeting his time so he could work out every evening and continue to compete.

At Rome's Olympics in 1960, the touted contender was another American, the enormous Rink Babka, a 267-pounder who had thrown past 200 feet unofficially. And after Rink spun the caucer more than 190 feet on his first throw, the pressure on Oerter and the rest was tremendous. Each entrant has six throws in this event. Through the first four rounds, Babka's best held up. Falling short throw after throw, Oerter admits, "I was getting so tense I could barely lift my arms." He stood there long seconds calming himself, stepped into the circle, took a deep breath, unwound, and whipped the disk the furthest he ever had thrown it, 194 feet 2 inches, on his fifth throw. This beat Babka and the Olympic record. "It was unbelievable," he admitted, after he got his second gold medal.

Beefed up to 250 pounds, Oerter became the first man to break through the 200-foot barrier officially in 1962. He lost the record to the Russian Vladimir Trusenyov, reclaimed it, lost it again to the Czech Ludvik Danek. In Japan in 1964, Danek was favored. The whiplike action of throwing the discus had been pinching a nerve in his neck, provoking pain in his arm, compelling Oerter to wear a cushioned collar. And then in practice in Tokyo, Oerter tore rib muscles and was hospitalized. he was told to rest six weeks, but he would not. Even with his side frozen by ice, taped up like a mummy, Oerter was in awful pain as he limped onto the field.

He was fourth after four throws. Each one had hurt worse than the one before. He figured a fifth throw was all he could stand. The lead wad Danek's at close to 200 feet. Oerter treid to relax. The harder you try, the harder you throw, the shorter the throw in this event. It is the relaxed perfection of form that produces the best results. Almost effortlessly it seemed, his form perfect, Oerter threw the discus 200 feet 1½ inches and collapsed in pain as the applause and cheers washed over him. Danek could not match it. Oerter had gotten the gold again.

By 1968, at 260 pounds, thirty-one years of age, long a working man with a growing family, Al Oerter was an outsider in the Olympics at Mexico City. No one really figured he could win another title. Others such as Silvester and Danek were throwing farther. But Oerter was the consummate competitor. He started serious training more than a year before the Games, lifting weights, running to get his legs in shape, throwing to recapture perfect form. On the day of the finals, there was a deluge of rain. Oerter removed his collar and continued to throw despite the rain. On his third throw he spun the saucer 212 feet 6½ inches. For the fourth straight Olympiad he had thrown a personal best and broken the Olympic record in his event. Silvester and the rest cracked. Silvester fouled on his final three efforts, spinning out of the ring each time. For the fourth straight Olympiad, Al Oerter was the gold medalist. Finally, he was finished.

"I long ago had to start working for a living," he said. "I continued to throw for recreation. I competed because I loved competition. It was easy because I won the big ones, but I like to think I would have wanted to continue just for the joy of competition even without winning. There is nothing comparable to the Olympics. You work and sacrifice for years trying to bring out the best in yourself and have to come up to the test of the best in one day when you're so scared you're sick and shaking.

"It doesn't matter that my event is not a popular one. I don't suppose people would pay to see us perform ordinarily, unless Silvester and I threw the thing at each other until one hit the other. But that gold medal is sufficient recognition of all the pain you've put up with.

"I couldn't have done it without my family letting me do it; but I didn't do it for them, I did it for myself and for sport. Of course I am proud of my four straight Olympic victories. After all, no one else ever did that. But I think I'll remember best the Olympic experience itself, all those athletes from all over the world coming together not only to compete but to make friends, meet one another, and learn to love."

There were other noteworthy winners that year of 1956 when Oerter started his fantastic string of success at Melbourne. Parry O'Brien won the shot put for the second straight Olympiad. The Reverend Robert Richards became the only man ever to win the pole vault two times. Lee Calhoun won the high hurdles and Glenn Davis the low hurdles, and those were the first of two straight

Olympic championships for these men in these events. Bobby Joe Morrow, a tall, slender Texan, swept the sprints and added a third gold medal in the sprint relay. Americans Charley Jenkins and Tom Courtney captured the 400- and 800-meter runs, respectively.

Finishing fourth and narrowly missing making the U.S. Olympic team as a hurdler, Milt Campbell more than made up for it by making it in the decathlon and narrowly winning a classic competition from American Rafer Johnson and Russian Vasily Kuznetsov. Campbell, a twenty-two-year-old Indiana University graduate, from Plainfield, New Jersey, was a marvelous all-around athlete who went on to play professional football.

The silver medalist in the decathlon in 1952, Campbell went on to win the gold in 1956. At one time coholder of the world record in the high hurdles, Campbell finished first in the hurdles, sprint, and shot put and second in the long jump, high jump, 400-meter run, and discus throw in the decathlon, but a poor performance in the pole vault cost him the world record.

The 6 foot 3, 215-pounder never attempted another decathlon and eventually became director of an athletic program for underprivileged children in his home state.

Like Campbell, Johnson would advance from the silver to the gold in four years. However, Kuznetsov, the greatest Russian and European decathlete of all time, and two-time world record holder, wound up with the bronze medal and bitter disappointment in both his Olympiads.

The most exciting race in Melbourne was the metric half-mile. The Americans Tom Courtney and Arnie Sowell were challenged by Britain's Derek Johnson and Norway's Auden Boysen. Courtney leaped into the lead at the gun with the other three right behind him and the rest of the field falling back. The slender Sowell, however, sped swiftly past the bullish Courtney and held the lead through a fast first 400.

Bounding into the bell lap, Courtney began to come on. In the backstretch Courtney caught his smaller rival and they raced shoulder to shoulder round the final corner. Coming into the homestretch, Johnson suddenly surged between them from behind, with Boysen right behind. Sowell wearied and fell back. He was beaten, but Courtney still had to beat back Johnson.

Johnson forced himself in front, but Courtney refused to cave in and stayed with him as they raced down the stretch. His face contorted with the agony of his effort, Courtney, stride by stride, with the fans standing in the stands and screaming, inched even with Johnson. With an enormous exertion of will, Courtney pushed ahead at the tape. Right behind the two leaders, Boysen nipped Sowell for the final medal.

Courtney collapsed and could not walk or talk for an hour while doctors tended to him. It was that long before he could regain his senses and realize he had won, much less get to the victory stand to get his gold medal. "It took absolutely all I had in me for years right to the final second to get this medal," he sighed.

As usual, the distance events in 1956 were dominated by Europeans. Ron Delany from Ireland, who had developed in the United States as a collegian at Villanova, and who ran to win, not set records, flashed from far back to win the prestigious 1,500 meters in an upset. The glamorous former world record holder John Landy of Australia settled for third place. And Vladimir Kuts, a twenty-nine-year-old blond sailor wearing the blood-red uniform of the U.S.S.R., executed his competition with methodical, murderous record-setting triumphs at 5,000 and 10,000 meters.

An interesting triumph was scored by the little Algerian Alain Mimoun, who had been silver medalist behind the great Czech Zatopek in three distance races over two Olympics. He finally got his gold medal by coming from behind to win the marathon in the Melbourne Olympics, with the aging, ailing Zatopek sixth.

Mimoun had been stricken with sciatica only two years earlier. Unable to find a doctor who could cure him, unable to run, he made a pilgrimage to the Basilica of St. Theresa of Lisieux, prayed for recovery, and recovered within weeks. He claimed a miracle—and then at thirty-six, he made one, himself, covering the more than 26 miles of the marathon in less than 2½ hours. Zatopek saluted and embraced him while Mimoun wept. "From him, that meant even more than the medal," he says. He went home to name his home Olympia and a new daughter Olympe. He calls the room where he keeps his gold and silver medals a chapel. He says, "The Olympics are religion, the Games sacred."

Two other interesting winners were Harold Connolly, who gained a gold medal in the hammer throw, and Olga Fikotova, who won one in the discus throw. The American man and Czech woman met, fell in love, and, after fighting through the politics and red tape of their democratic and Communist countries, won the right to wed. Their glamorous marriage lasted more than 15 years before it ended in divorce in 1973.

The leading lady in track and field in Melbourne was an Australian, Betty Cuthbert, a blond of eighteen, who won three gold medals by sweeping the sprints and running on the winning sprint relay team. Another Australian, Shirley Strickland, aging at thirty-one, won her second straight Olympic gold medal in the hurdles and added a third gold in the sprint relay. An American, Mildred McDaniel, set a world record for the woman's high jump by topping 5 feet 9 inches.

Australians won seven of the dozen swimming events with nineteen-year-old Dawn Fraser gaining two golds and one silver. The powerful 150-pound Melbourne mermaid went on to win two more golds and two more silvers in the next two Olympiads, winning the 100-meter freestyle three straight times before being barred by her country's Olympic committee, presumably for "breaking training and consorting with a bookmaker."

Bookmaking is legal in Australia, and the bookmaker she consorted with was her husband. She did drink beer, stay up late, and play pranks, such as leading an expedition in quest of souvenir flags, speeding through the grounds of Emperor Hirohito's Imperial Palace at Tokyo in 1964 on a borrowed bicycle, with the police in pursuit. The authorities decided she did not give a good image for her nation's athletics, and her amazing amateur career concluded.

The American Pat McCormick became the first woman to repeat a sweep of both diving events. Juan Capilla of Mexico, bronze medalist in 1948 and silver medalist in 1952, finally won the gold medal in 1956 in platform diving. Impressively persistent, he frustrated American Gary Tobian by a fraction of a point in the cumulative voting of the judges. Australian Murray Rose was the dominant man swimmer, sweeping the 400- and 1,500-meter freestyle races.

Hungary won its second straight and fourth title in five years in water polo. Gert Fredriksson of Sweden won his third straight gold medal in the kayak singles event at 1,000 meters and his second in three Olympiads at 10,000 meters. Trying for the third straight Olympiad to match the triumph of his father in single sculls in 1920, Jack Kelly, Jr., failed, fading to third at the finish of the event in 1956.

Americans did score the most exciting of water victories, rowing to triumph in the featured eight-oared shell event. It was the eighth consecutive triumph by a U.S. team in this event, but by far the most dramatic. This is one event in which a loser can win. Teams row in heats, four teams in each heat, until finally, four are left for the final heat. However, a system called "repechage" permits losers in the first round a second chance to win a heat and rejoin the race for the finals. No crew in 36 years ever had returned from a first-round loss to gain the gold, but the Yale crew representing the United States did so in 1956.

Third behind Australia and Canada in the first round, the Americans defeated Italy, England, and France in the repechage, overcame Russia, Japan, and, in the last few feet, Australia, their earlier conqueror, in the semifinals, and, finally, Australia again, Canada, and Sweden in the finals. These faceless fellows who sweat their way through the back-breaking ordeal of oaring a slender shell swiftly over smooth waters are among the most shadowed of sportsmen.

In an unusual situation, American Paul Anderson at 304 pounds won the heavyweight weight-lifting title because he was lighter than his foe, Humberto Selvetti, a 316-pound Argentinian. Anderson and Selvetti each raised a total of 1,102 pounds in the three lifts, and by rules the title in such a tie goes to the lighter man. A wrestling star was the Turk, Mustafa Dagistanli, a freestyle bantamweight who won in 1960, too. Italian fencer Christian D'Oriola, who had won in foils in 1952, won again in 1956.

In gymnastics, the gold medalist for the second straight Olympiad in the individual combined exercises was the great Russian Viktor Tchoukarine. In the women's competition, Larisa Latyinina won three of the five gold medals she was to win in two consecutive Olympiads and her first of two straight individual combined titles.

Because of quarantine restrictions in Australia, the equestrian events had to be staged in Stockholm, and Swedish riders captured three of the six gold medals with their sharp horsemanship.

Because Melbourne was such a great distance from most countries, the Australian Summer Olympics drew only 3,300 entrants, more than 1,500 less than had contested the previous Summer Olympiad at Helsinki. However, a typical turnout of more than 700 athletes from 32 countries, including, for the first time, the Soviet Union, competed earlier in the year in the Winter Games in Italy at Cortina d'Ampezzo.

The Russians scored an enormous success in these cold-weather contests. They won 6 of the 24 gold medals and 3 of 4 in speed skating. Yevgeniu Grischin won 2 of 3 golds for Russia in speed skating. He had been a cyclist in the 1952 Games. The Soviet team scored an especially impressive upset triumph in ice hockey, conquering Canada, which had won six of the seven previous Olympiads. Even the American team overcame Canada to collect the silver medal.

Childhood chums from Colorado Springs, Hayes Alan Jenkins and Carol Heiss contended for figure-skating titles. However, the fifteen-year-old Miss Heiss was defeated by Tenley Albright. Jenkins did win, with his brother, David, third, and Ronnie Robertson second, as Americans swept the three medals. Hayes Alan Jenkins had just won his fourth consecutive world crown.

Tenley Albright was the daughter of a Boston surgeon and was to become a surgeon herself. At eleven she suffered from polio, but she fought it off. Later, she used to arise at 4 A.M. so she could practice skating before pursuing her studies. She finished second in the Oslo Olympics in 1952 before becoming the first American woman to win the world title, then the Olympic title. Persistence and sacrifice had paid off for her. She retired from skating and today is a practicing surgeon as well as a wife and mother.

The great ones do not always win. Bad luck beats many. Jill Kinmont was American women's slalom champion when she suffered a severe spill at Alta, Utah, in a tryout for the 1956 U.S. Olympic skiing team. She crushed a vertebra in her back and became permanently paralyzed.

Before her accident, she was romantically involved with Olympic skier Buddy Werner. He later was killed in an avalanche in Europe. After her accident, she became engaged to another Olympic skier Dick Buek, who was killed in a plane crash at Donner Lake. She is stoical and as active as she can be today. From her wheelchair she has taught remedial reading to troubled children in Beverly Hills and Paiute Indians in Bishop, Utah.

In Italy, the host country captured only the two-man bobsled event. A Finn, Antii Hyvarinen, ended Norway's string of six straight ski-jumping gold medals. However, a lumberjack from Norway, Hallgeir Brenden, successfully defended his gold medal in the 15-kilometer cross-country ski race and gained the silver medal in the 30-kilometer event won by Veikko Hakulinen of Finland. Hakulinen, winner of the 50-kilometer race in 1952, finished second to Sixten Jernberg of Sweden at 50 kilometers in 1956. Jernberg was second at 15 kilometers.

The star of the Winter Olympics at Cortina was a handsome, daring twenty-one-year-old Austrian plumber, Anton "Toni" Sailer, whose flawless form made him the first ever to win all three Alpine skiing events. The agile, swift Sailer won the giant slalom by almost six seconds, the special slalom by four seconds, and the downhill run by two seconds.

Born in mountainous country in November, 1935, Toni's fascination with skis started as soon as he could walk and talk. Begging for skis, he was promised a pair for his second birthday and talked his father into giving them to him two weeks early. Because he could not afford to buy as many rides up the ski lift as he wanted, he'd sneak into the resort office, pocket tickets, and use them up practicing.

Good, too, at tennis, soccer, and swimming, skiing remained his true love. Inspired when his older sister started to date an Austrian champion, young Toni took his first title when he was ten and won his country's national title at twenty. He broke his leg in a spill practicing for the Olympics in 1952 but was ready four years later. He explained, "The secret is to go not so fast that you fall, but faster than the rest."

The 6-foot, 175-pounder came close to perfection at Cortina. After his triple triumph, he refused to remove his number from his back so he would be recognized wherever he went the remainder of the Games. He gave his autograph to everyone who walked near him. He returned home to become a movie star and a recording artist, bought a hotel, made profitable investments, and became wealthy as well as famous.

He said later, "I had great hazards and I overcame them, so why should I not be proud? What can compare to sweeping all of your events in a single Olympics, to winning three gold medals, to knowing you do your thing better than anyone else in the world?"

But if the single star of the Olympic year of 1956 was an Austrian skier, it was the American discus thrower who went on to what some say are the greatest heights ever attained in the Games.

11
SQUAW VALLEY AND ROME, 1960
Rafer and Wilma

WILMA RUDOLPH WAS born in July, 1940, in St. Bethlehem, Tennessee, the 17th of 19 children of a poor porter, who was so sick he often could not work, and a mother, who worked as a domestic, cleaning other people's houses so her family had food to eat. They did not have much and moved to Clarksville, near Nashville, while Wilma was still an infant, because here there were more people and more homes for the mother to clean.

At four, Wilma was stricken with severe pneumonia and scarlet fever, and one leg was left useless so that she was unable to walk. For more than two years, Wilma was confined to a chair or to her bed, except when twice weekly her mother bundled her in a blanket and carried her by bus to a Nashville clinic for medical care. On doctor's orders her legs were soaked and heated, and the other children took turns massaging them.

Her mother says Wilma did not complain but simply made the best of things and kept trying to walk. At six, with the help of special shoes, she started to walk again a little, though mostly hopping or limping on one leg. Gradually, for the next five years, the bad leg built back up again and she began to walk better and even started to run. Soon she could run as fast as her friends and began to play basketball with the other girls and boys on outdoor playgrounds.

Clarksville High School had a girls' basketball team, and at thirteen Wilma went out for it and made it. She had already reached her full height of 5 foot 11, and while she was skinny, she was quick and energetic. Her coach, Clinton Gray, nicknamed her

"Skeeter" because he thought she "buzzed around like a mosquito." At fifteen, she averaged 30 points a game and earned all-star honors. Ed Temple, the track coach at nearby Tennessee A&I, a black college, saw her, was impressed by her speed, and suggested to Gray that he start a girls' track team for her. The coach did, entering his few interested girls in whatever meets were available. Wilma developed rapidly as a sprinter.

Within one year, at the age of sixteen, she had made the 1956 U.S. Olympic team as a spare. She earned a bronze medal by running with the American relay team, which finished third in the 400-meter event. She enrolled at Tennessee A&I, where Temple rounded up the four fastest female sprinters in the country, who went on to win six gold medals in the 1960 Olympics at Rome. Wilma won half of them.

Filled out to 132 pounds, long-legged, with grace and good form, she won the 100 and 200 to become the fourth straight woman and first American woman to sweep the sprints. Then she anchored her teammates to triumph in the relay to become the only American woman ever to take three gold medals in track and field in a single Olympiad.

A relaxed young woman who slept late, dined on hot dogs, hamburgers, and soda pop, and never showed any nervousness in her races, she was hailed around the world as a heroine. In Italy she was called *La Gazelle Nera* (the Black Gazelle) and in France *La Perle Noire* (the Black Pearl), but at home she stayed simply "Skeeter." Temple took her and her teammates on a tour of the world, where she was mobbed wherever she went, before she returned home to become the third woman ever selected for the Sullivan Award as the outstanding amateur athlete in the United States.

At one time she held the world records at 100 and 200 meters and shared in the one for the 400-meter relay, but she never entered another Olympics.

"It was the greatest experience of my life, and especially satisfying after my childhood problems, but I couldn't top what I did," she said. "I could match my three gold medals, but I've already done that now, and if I got two, instead of it being a thrill it would be a disappointment. Jesse Owens quit after one Olympics while he was on top, so I sort of figure that's what I should do, too, and I'll be remembered for when I was at my best."

Which she was.

She was a popular performer in Rome. She inspired her teammates. After she won her third medal, she was embraced by Earlene Brown, who weighed almost twice what Wilma did. Wilma encouraged Earlene to go out and show the world what American women could do. Earlene did, promptly putting the shot almost 54 feet, which was farther than she ever had thrown it in her life. It was good for a bronze medal, though not good enough to win. **The Russian Tamara Press won the shot and was second to** teammate Nina Ponomaryeva in the discus. Tamara's sister, Irina, won the hurdles. Other Russian women won the 800 meters, long jump, and javelin throw. Russian women were the best female athletes in the world.

Among many disappointments for Americans were the seventh and eighth place finishes in the women's discus throw and men's hammer throw, respectively, by the defending champions Olga and Harold Connolly. Olga Fikotova had represented Czechoslovakia in 1956, but in 1960 she was Olga Connolly and an American citizen representing the United States.

Another American who disappointed was nineteen-year-old John Thomas, who had put the world record at close to 7 feet 4 inches in the high jump. He jumped 7 feet at Rome but failed at 7 feet 1 inch and was beaten there by two unknowns from the U.S.S.R., Robert Shavlakadze and Valery Brumel. They tied, but Shavlakadze was awarded the gold medal on the basis of having had fewer misses along the way. However, it was Brumel who became the best, boosting the world record to 7 feet 5½ inches and beating out Thomas in the 1964 Olympics in Tokyo before breaking his leg badly in a motorcycle crash that curtailed his career prematurely.

Another American disappointment came when Ray Norton, the slender record-holding dashman who went around Rome with Wilma Rudolph, not only failed to win either the 100 or 200 but failed even to gain a medal. He then topped it off by running out of his zone before the baton was passed to him, causing the winning U.S. team to be disqualified in the sprint relay. Twisted by the pressure which produces so many upsets in the Olympics, Norton was sick during the Games, resulting in the end of U.S. domination of the sprints.

Armin Hary of Germany barely defeated Dave Sime at 100 meters, ending a string of five straight successes by Americans. Livio Berrutti of Italy took the 200 as the United States was blanked in the dashes for the first time since 1908. Then Hary anchored Germany to the gold in the 400-meter relay when the Americans were disqualified. U.S. runners did win other short races, as Otis Davis won the 400 and Lee Calhoun and Glenn Davis repeated as gold medalists in the hurdles.

Wilma Rudolph's Tennessee A&I teammate Ralph Boston broke the oldest world record on the track books when he leaped almost 27 feet to win the long jump while shattering the standard set by Jesse Owens more than 20 years earlier. The brilliant Boston, who became the first man to leap past 27 feet, settled for the silver medal at Tokyo in 1964 and the bronze in Mexico City in 1968, though he otherwise dominated his event for a decade. His closest competitor most of the time, the Soviet Igor Ter-Ovanesyan, who twice took the world record from Boston, never won a single gold medal in five Olympic attempts, nor even a silver. He bagged the bronze in both 1964 and 1968.

"Tarzan" Bragg took the pole vault and Al Oerter won his second of four straight discus throws, but Bill Nieder beat back Parry O'Brien's bid for a third straight success in the shot put. Poland's Josef Schmidt won his first of two straight triple jumps.

Runners from New Zealand and Australia dominated the middle and distance runs. Virtually unknown, powerful Peter Snell pulled off a stunning upset when he shocked Roger Moens of Belgium at 800 meters. Leading not far from the finish line, Moens looked over his right shoulder to see if anyone was close to him, saw no one, and relaxed, even as Snell shot past on his left, blind side at the tape.

Moens was the world record holder at 800 meters and one of the best at 400 and 1,500 meters, but he never got a gold in three Olympiads during his injury-flawed, frustrated time at the top. Bitterly disappointed after losing to Snell, he said, "Don't tell me the silver medal is something, after all. Finishing second is like finishing last. I should have won. I will not even try again." But Snell became better known, to say the least, gaining two golds four years later.

Herb Elliott of Australia won the 1,500 in the world record time of 3:35.6 in the only Olympiad he ever entered. He also held the world record for the mile at 3:54.5. He ran 17 four-minute miles from 1957 through 1960. He never was beaten in international competition during that time and continues to be regarded by many as the greatest his glamorous event ever has produced. The smooth, swift, and strong Aussie retired while still in his prime in his early twenties.

Snell's teammate Murray Halberg, who became a great distance runner despite a lame left arm suffered in a severe rugby injury, "stole" the 5,000 meters with a startling mid-race sprint, his bad arm hung, as usual, limply by his side. Halberg also finished fifth in the 10,000, won by Pyotr Bolotnikov of the U.S.S.R.

The most dramatic distance triumph was scored by barefoot Abebe Bikila from Ethiopia in the marathon. The weather in Rome was severe, but the scorching sun did not bother Bikila, nor did the hot pavement blister his calloused bare feet. He was small—only 5 foot 9 and 135 pounds—but he was wiry and tough. He was not young, but at twenty-eight he was mature and ready. He was unknown, but he had stretched himself with long, lonely runs over the African plains, and he knew what he could do.

It started with eight forging in front over the first few miles after the runners ran from the stadium and began to wend their way through the city streets that had been routed for this 26-mile marathon run. At 6 miles, the leaders were reduced to six. At 12 miles, as the afternoon faded, they were reduced to four—the Briton Ken Keily, the New Zealander Barry Magee, the Moroccan Mhadi Ben Abdesselem, and the unknown Ethiopian Abebe Bikila, who, it was reported with laughter, was running without shoes.

They trotted along at a steady pace faster than this race ever had been run before, sucking in air, spilling water over their sweating heads from cups passed to them along the way, feeling the aching building up in their bones and muscles, on and on and on. Mhadi made a move. It was madness, but designed to discourage the rest. He increased speed and pulled far in front. Only Bikila lengthened out to remain within reach of him. The others fell back, but Bikila remained pit-patting behind him. Mhadi could hear the footsteps, and he could not shake them.

And then Abebe Bikila picked up the pace and closed in on Mhadi, catching up to him as they turned in the dark night down the torchlit Appian Way, down the route Romans had driven Abebe's ancestors as slaves centuries before. With the throngs who lined the way back to the stadium cheering him, Bikila began to pull away, his bare feet beating on the hard pavement. He did not even seem tired. By the time he entered the stadium, he was well ahead, and the surprised fans hollered for him.

The lithe Ethiopian burst the tape 25 seconds before Mhadi got there. The barefoot Bikila had run the grueling event seven minutes faster than the immortal Zatopek, faster than any man ever had run it before. He refused the blankets that were offered him and the cool drinks, and, instead, trotted through a victory lap, which astonished everyone. Later, through interpreters, he said, "We are a poor people, and not used to mechanized transport. We run everywhere. Twenty-six miles is nothing to me. Of course I could have kept going for a long time." And he grinned. He had begun what was to become domination of distance events by untutored but tireless runners from African nations.

In Rome, Bikila was running only his third marathon, but he ran a record 2 hours and 15 minutes. Four years later at Tokyo, wearing track shoes, he ran even more strongly to beat his nearest rival by more than four minutes, setting a new world record of less than 2 hours 13 minutes.

He is the only man ever to win the murderous marathon in two Olympiads. He tried to win a third straight at Mexico City in 1968 but had to give up after 10 miles because of a broken bone in his foot.

Before he could try for a fourth time, a Volkswagen he was driving near his home in Addis Ababa overturned, crushing and crippling him. It is sad irony that he was then confined to a wheelchair, never to walk again, much less run; but the emperor of his country, Haile Selassie, visited him almost every week.

A private in the emperor's palace guard when he went to his first Olympics, Bikila became the greatest sporting hero his nation has known and received promotion rapidly. Eventually he became a captain, though confined to desk work. He lived with his wife and four children in a fenced-off, comfortable cottage, surrounded by the humbler homes of his poor countrymen, until his death in 1974.

Bikila had said, "I accept my tragedy as I accepted my triumphs. It was the will of God that I won the Olympics and its was the will of God that I met with an accident. God gives, God takes away."

The greatest athlete in the 1960 Olympics was the American Rafer Johnson. Born in August, 1935, one of five in a family so poor they lived awhile in an abandoned railroad boxcar, Rafer almost had his sports career cut short when he was a boy of twelve in Kingsburg, California.

He was fooling around with friends at a peach cannery, dropping from the limb of one tree onto an outdoor conveyor belt and grabbing the limb of another tree to get off farther down the line. Rafer dropped too close to the beginning of the belt and got his left foot caught between the rollers. His brothers heard his screams and ran to the workers, who stopped the belt and removed Rafer's foot from the rollers. It had been badly mangled and doctors had to operate to mend it. He spent eight weeks on crutches before he started to recover.

At this time, Tulare, 25 miles away, was celebrating the first Olympic decathlon victory of its native son Bob Mathias.

Rafer did recover, though even today his foot is sensitive and aches under stress. But he became a brilliant all-around athlete who starred in baseball, basketball, and football as well as track in high school. He won state scholastic honors in the hurdles and long jump in track. After his coach, Murl Dodson, took him to Tulare to see Mathias set a world record in the decathlon in 1952, Rafer, at sixteen, decided to devote a lot of time to the decathlon. He became one of the world's best hurdlers and long jumpers, and the very best decathlete.

In 1955 he beat Bob Richards to win the decathlon in the Pan-American Games and went on to set a new world record for the event at nineteen. For six years he traded the record back and forth between himself and such superlative foes as the Russian Vasily Kuznetsov and the Formosan C. K. Yang.

In 1956, he made the U.S. Olympic team as a long jumper as well as in the decathlon, but he suffered a knee injury that caused him to withdraw from the long jump and kept him from winning the decathlon. He says, "Under the circumstances I was satisfied to finish second to Milt Campbell, ahead of Vasily Kuznetsov. But for four years after that, I knew nothing would satisfy me in the next Olympics except first place."

By then he was at the University of California at Los Angeles, where he played basketball but also worked regularly on his decathlon events. Yang joined him there and the two trained together and competed against one another, good friends, but fierce rivals.

Their decathlon duel at Rome in the searing summer of 1960 was the all-time classic contest of this 10-event test. Kuznetsov fell out of it early as the other two battled bitterly. On the first day, Yang won four of the five events, but Johnson was so close in the four he lost, and so far in front of his foe in the other one, the shot put, that he finished the long day in the lead by 55 points.

The second day started with one of his best events, the high hurdles, but he hit a barrier and did so badly he fell 138 points behind

Yang. The Formosan's strength was in the running, while Rafer was superior in the weights. Johnson moved back in front after the discus throw. Yang's best event was the pole vault, but he not do as well as usual, while Johnson did better than usual and they finished with Rafer 24 points in front. Johnson figured to have to gain a lot in the javelin to offset what Yang would gain in the 1,500, but Rafer gained only a little and led by just 67 points.

That took them to the final event, the metric mile, and if Yang could beat Johnson by more than 10 seconds he could win the decathlon title. Many felt he would, but Rafer would not give in to him. The event started at 8:30 P.M. and try as he would, Yang could not pull away from the determined Rafer as the two weary athletes struggled through the last laps in the gloom.

"I just wanted to stay with him," Rafer explained later, which is what he did, within steps of him all the way. Yang came across at the finish and then, less than two seconds later, Johnson came home.

Johnson had won by only 58 points and both bettered the Olympic standard. The crowd stood to cheer the two gallant rivals.

In the dressing room later, Yang mourned, "I beat him in seven events, yet lost to him. I knew he would win. I have trained with him two years and I know him. I know he will do what he has to do to win. I had to get far in front of him in our last race to win and I tried but I couldn't do it and when I heard him behind me all the way I knew he would win." He hunched over and began to cry.

Johnson saw him and shook his head and said, "Well, that is the way it is. It is a tough event, and I will never do it again. I am sorry for him and happy for me and now I am just going to walk away from it."

A broad-shouldered, slim-hipped marvel of physical fitness, Rafer became a broadcaster but gave it up to work in politics. He was a supporter of the Kennedys and was with Robert Kennedy when the presidential candidate was shot to death at the Ambassador Hotel in Los Angeles during the 1968 primary campaign. Johnson later became director of the Kennedy Foundation.

Almost a quarter of a century after Jesse Owens had made a shambles of Adolf Hitler's theory of white supremacy, black athletes were becoming the best in the world and dominated American sports in general and track and field in particular. And two of them, children of poverty, overcame severe sickness and injury in their youth to become the stars of the 1960 Olympics in Italy—Wilma Rudolph and Rafer Johnson.

As Wilma Rudolph starred in track, winning three gold medals, another American woman Chris von Saltza starred in swimming, also winning three gold medals. She swam on two winning relay teams, won the 400-meter freestyle, and almost won a fourth gold medal, but settled for the silver as she was defeated by Dawn Fraser in the 100-meter freestyle. At twelve she had narrowly missed making the Melbourne Olympics and at sixteen she was a sensation in the Rome Olympics.

Daughter of a doctor in San Francisco who had been a college football and swimming star, Chris was a well-rounded young girl—a straight-A student, a cheerleader in football, and a super swimmer, who complained only that the chlorine in the pools turned her blonde hair green. She got to the top young, but that is typical of swimmers, who train hard, sacrificing almost all social life, and usually seem to be burned out by the time they are out of their teens.

Of all sports, swimming seems the least advanced. World records in the various events are broken so regularly that it is apparent swimmers have only scratched the surface of their potential. The relay teams anchored by young Chris von Saltza broke world records in the 400-meter medley by three seconds and in the 400-meter freestyle by nine seconds.

Lynn Burke missed matching Chris by only a silver medal, also gaining three golds by swimming on the two relays and winning the 100-meter backstroke. But the U.S. women failed in diving as the two titles were swept by Germany's Ingrid Kramer.

There were no double winners individually in men's swimming and diving, but American Jeff Farrell, who qualified for the U.S. team only six days after an emergency appendectomy, did anchor two relay teams to triumphs in world record times.

The big gold medal winner of the 1960 Games was Russian Boris Shakhlin, who won four gold medals in gymnastics. In weight lifting, American Charles Vinci won his second straight bantamweight title, while Russian Arkadi Vorobiev won his second straight middle-heavyweight title. In wrestling, Turki Mihat Bayrak won his second straight Greco-Roman light-middleweight crown. In fencing, Hungarian Rudolf Karpati won his second straight saber crown, the ninth in a row for his country. In yachting, Paul Elvstrom of Denmark captured his fourth consecutive gold medal in the finns class. In rowing, Germany ended the string of eight straight triumphs by the United States in the coxed eight crew competition.

The U.S. basketball team won for the fifth straight time with probably the best team it ever sent to an Olympics. Jerry West, Jerry Lucas, Oscar Robertson, Walt Bellamy, Bob Boozer, Terry Dischinger, and Darrall Imhoff were included on this incredible club, coached by Pete Newell, which won eight straight games, trimming Russia, 81-57, and, in the final, Brazil, 90-63.

Rome's Summer Olympics were the first to draw more than 5,000 athletes. They came from 84 nations. They put on a splendid show. The Winter Games earlier that year also were outstanding, the second to be contested in the United States. However, with Squaw Valley in northern California far from Europe, entrants were fewer than usual, only 665 athletes from 30 countries competing.

There were no dominant individuals, the only double winners in individual events being Russian speed skaters Lydia Skoblikova and Yuri Grischin, and Grischin actually tied for first in one race.

The United States retained its figure-skating titles with three-time world champion David Jenkins succeeding his brother Hayes as men's king, and five-time world champion Carol Heiss becoming women's queen.

In 1956 Carol, a beautiful girl, had finished second to Tenley Albright in the Olympics but later had beaten her in the world championship competition. She was sixteen at the time and the youngest skater ever to represent the U.S. team in the Olympics, the youngest ever to win the world crown for the United States. Her mother, devoted to her daughter's career, died of cancer shortly after seeing Carol win the world title. Carol kept a promise she had made to her mother not to turn professional until after she won an Olympic gold medal.

The most surprising success at Squaw Valley was scored by the U.S. ice hockey team, which won its first and to date only Olympic crown. Unlike Canada or Russia, this is not a cold-weather country that develops a lot of skilled hockey stars. There was not a player on the American club who could become a top pro, and the team was considered a rank outsider in the competition. But it went un-

Squaw Valley and Rome, 1960

defeated to score the biggest upset in the history of the Winter Games.

The Americans met the Czechs, one of the favorites, in the first game and came from behind to beat them 7-4 as Tom Williams iced it with his second goal of the game. The following night they trimmed Austria to move into the championship round.

With Roger Christian scoring the three-goal "hat-trick," and goaltender Jack McCartan making 36 saves, Sweden was stopped. Then Germany was put to rout.

Then came Canada, which had no stars but a strong team led by a smart player, Harry Sinden, who was to coach and manage Stanley Cup champions in Boston later. Don Head was beaten by Bob Cleary and Paul Johnson, while McCartan was beaten only by Jim Connelly. McCartan made 20 saves in the second period and 39 in the game to protect a 2-1 lead at the finish.

Russia remained to test the Americans. An overflow crowd of 10,000 fans filled the arena, while millions more watched the dramatic next-to-last contest of the tournament on television. Few felt the United States could sustain its success, but the team was inspired. Bill Cleary scored once and Bill Christian twice to put the Americans in front, 3-2. Christian's second score came with five minutes left.

Making 27 saves throughout the contest, McCartan was magnificent in the last minutes as the Soviets surged to the goal mouth again and again and were turned away each time. At one point he dove to knock a shot away, then while sprawling on the ice reached up with his gloved hand to catch a shot fired off the rebound. It was enormously exciting and when the final buzzer blew the Americans almost collapsed in exhaustion and joy.

Sometimes it seems you can still hear the cheers of hockey fans that sounded across the United States that night.

The Americans had only to conquer the Czechs a second time then to gain the gold. But they had been playing beyond themselves and were wearing down now. After the Russian game, the Czech game seemed a letdown. The Czechs were capable, and after two periods the Americans trailed 3-2. But they had come too far to quit now. They came out for the final period fired up, skating with determination.

The brothers Christian and Cleary carried them. In the sixth minute, Bill Christian passed to Roger Christian who scored to tie the game. Then Bob Cleary scored to put the United States in front. Four minutes later he scored again. Roger Christian scored. Then he scored again. Suddenly it was a rout, and Bill Cleary completed it at the buzzer.

A pickup team from the United States had won the final game 9-4, and the players seemed as surprised as anyone when they gathered their gold medals to the cheers of the capacity crowd in the arena that night. It was a team triumph by a team that was inspired to one of the more memorable of many Olympic upsets.

12
INNSBRUCK AND TOKYO, 1964
Schollander, the Superswimmer

AT TOKYO IN the Summer Olympics of 1964, Don Schollander became the first swimmer ever to win four gold medals in a single Olympiad and was disappointed because he was denied a fifth. A boyish blond with short, crew-cut hair, Schollander, whose name is pronounced Show-lander, was twenty and about to enter Yale University, when he became the dominant performer in the Games that year.

Most top swimmers master most strokes, and it is easier for one to win a variety of events and thus many medals than it is for a track and field man. Schollander was primarily a freestyle swimmer, but he won championships in events ranging from 100 to 1,500 meters, which would be like a runner winning titles in races from the 100-yard-dash to the mile, an unlikely occurrence.

In Japan, Schollander turned it on in the stretch to touch just ahead of Great Britain's Don McGregor at 100 meters, then pulled away from the field at the finish to come in far ahead at 400 meters. He set a world record of 4:12.2 in the latter event. He also spurred the American 400-meter and 800-meter relay teams to triumphs in world record times.

He was a relaxed young man who did not train as hard as many swimmers and had a number of interests other than just swimming, but he came as close as any swimmer ever has to having perfect synchronized stroking and kicking form. He was not as big or as strong as Johnny Weissmuller had been, but he was smoother. He also was far faster, but then all swimming techniques had been advanced enormously. He was a natural swimmer, a smart tactician, and almost tireless.

He could have done even more and should have, but was denied the freestyle spot on the 400-meter relay team so that another swimmer could get a gold medal, which he did when the team won. Schollander argued against it, which caused controversy and for which he was criticized.

He has said, "I just said what I felt. I was aware that I had done something no other swimmer had done, but by winning a fifth gold medal I could have done something no other athlete had done in any sport. However, it wasn't that and it wasn't that I was selfish, it was simply that I felt I had earned a place in the event purely on performance."

He came home a hero, anyway, his picture on the cover of many national magazines, sought after for television appearances, sent literally tons of fan mail, and welcomed at the White House, but says he didn't enjoy this part of it: "I'm a social animal, but prefer privacy to being a public figure. I won medals, I didn't want to be one myself." Still, he admits, "I was sorry if I'd done anything to spoil what I'd worked for and waited for a long time."

Possibly too much emphasis was placed on sporting success in Schollander's life. He came from a family of athletes. His uncle was outstanding at swimming, diving, wrestling, and football. His brother was a wrestler and football player. His father was a fine football player. His mother was a synchronized swimmer, who doubled for "Jane" (Mia Farrow's mother, Maureen O'Sullivan) in water scenes for Tarzan movies.

Don was reared in Lake Oswego, Oregon, where he spent every summer day swimming and began to race for fun before he was ten. He was small for his age, did not often win, and wanted to quit, but his parents would not let him quit a loser. As he got bigger, he began to win, but he also began to play football and found he preferred football to swimming. However, he was less successful and seemed to have less of a future at football than at swimming. His parents were proud of his success and wanted him to explore his potential in swimming.

When he was fifteen, it was suggested that he go to live in Santa Clara, California, where he could be coached at the famous swimming club there by George Haines, who turned out champions. Don didn't want to leave home, but his mother insisted, so he went. A family was found for him to live with, and he spent more time in the swimming pool than he did in high school. He trained twice a day, three hours a day.

Haines became a sort of father to Don, who developed rapidly under his guidance. He was a lonely lad whose life had become a series of tests. He says, "You are pushed until you push yourself past points of endurance in practice to prepare yourself for competition. You go in practice when it hurts like hell, so you are ready for races.

"When you reach the threshold of pain in a race you have two choices: You can back off, or you can force yourself to drive to the finish, knowing the pain will become agony. Most swimmers back off, but the champion pushes himself on into agony. It is the only way you can win. I don't know if it's worth it, but I do know it is oddly satisfying when you meet this sort of test."

He had few friends, but then there were few swimmers who could beat him. He found he could not only outswim them, but he could psych them out, too. He practiced a casual approach so his nervous rivals would think he was so sure of himself he had nothing to worry about. He'd say such things to them as, "Do you always start kicking before you hit the water?" so they'd start to think about every move they made, and it would throw them off. "Some races you can win before you even get into the water," he explains.

He was entered in his first major meet, the Spring Nationals, in 1962 and extended outstanding swimmers like Murray Rose of Australia and Roy Saari of El Segundo, California, before bowing. A month later, he took his first foreign trip—to Japan—and won races. That summer, he won his first national championship, in the 200-meter freestyle. A year later, he became the first man ever to swim it in less than two minutes, which was like Roger Bannister breaking the four-minute mile barrier.

He also won two national titles and narrowly missed a third. By the time of the Olympic trials the following year, he was on the verge of big things. He actually did not win any races, but qualified for the Olympic team with second-place finishes in two events. He was just turning into a top swimmer, but he was coming so swiftly that by the time of the events in Tokyo he would be a sensation.

His success was inspirational. Don's roommate, Dick Roth, suffered an attack of appendicitis three days before his event, the 400-meter individual medley. He was rushed to the hospital and the doctors wanted to operate, but he refused to permit it. He got out of the hospital so weak he barely qualified for the finals. But he said to himself, "If my roomie can win, I can win," and in the finals he not only won, he set a world record. Later, he had his operation. By then he had his gold medal.

Six-foot-six Jed Graef set a world record in the 200-meter backstroke. On the opening leg of the 400-meter medley relay, Steve Clark became the first man to swim the 100-meter backstroke in less than one minute. Australians won three races, but Americans swept the relays. And Americans Bob Webster and Ken Sitzberger took the diving events.

On the women's side, fifteen-year-old Sharon Stouder won gold medals in two individual races and one relay and a silver in one individual race, while Cathy Ferguson and Donna de Varona each won golds in one individual race and one relay. Another American, Lesley Bush, won one of the diving titles.

But the star of swimming and diving in 1964 at Tokyo and of the year's Olympic Games was Schollander, the 5 foot 11, 165-pound stylist.

After Tokyo, he entered college and started to expand in different directions. Most swimmers retire after such triumphs as he'd enjoyed, even at his age, but it had been so much of his life for so long that he didn't want to give it up yet. However, the pressures of living up to his image were so enormous that when he was stricken with mononucleosis in Switzerland during a competitive European tour, he was relieved that he could retire for awhile.

His studies improved and he still had time to get into campus politics, date girls, and go to parties. When he returned to swimming, he was inconsistently successful, but it no longer mattered as much to him as it had before.

As the 1968 Games in Mexico City neared, he began to bear down again, but found himself without his previous intensity. He qualified for only two events and won a gold medal in only one, the 800-meter freestyle relay. When he went into his only individual event, the 200-meter freestyle sprint, he realized, he said later, "This is my last race," and found himself so relieved that when he finished second he was strangely satisfied.

He says, "I would have liked to have gone out a winner, but I was glad to be going out. You have to put so much into becoming the best in the world in your sport that you take everything else out of your life and there comes a time when you have to start doing some of the other things there are to do in life. I'm proud of my performance in the Olympics at Tokyo in 1964 and I'll treasure the memory of it, but maybe I should not have waited so long to move on to other things."

Others offered super performances at Tokyo. In track, there was a stunning series of upsets scored by American runners, despite damp conditions as rains fell frequently on the 5,500 athletes who assembled from 94 nations. In the 400, Mike Larrabee, a twenty-seven-year-old veteran contending in his first Olympiad, came from behind to beat Wendell Mottley of Trinidad at the tape. In the 5,000 meters, Bob Schul came from far back with a sensational sprint to nip Harold Norpoth of Germany and become the first American to win the gold medal at this distance. In the 10,000, an unknown, Billy Mills, roared up on the outside from a pack of 38 runners in the stretch to speed past the favored Mohamed Gammoudi of Tunisia and Ron Clarke of Australia and become the only American ever to win the gold at this distance.

Mills's shocker was the most memorable. Half Sioux Indian, born in Pine Ridge, South Dakota, orphaned at twelve, he was sent to Haskill Institute, where he took up running to train for boxing. He became a better runner than a boxer and earned a track scholarship to the University of Kansas but had a mediocre career there. Entering the marines after college, he continued to train and race without winning anything of consequence. He did well enough to gain a berth on the Olympic team in 1964, but the United States had few distance runners of quality. It was said Americans were too soft to endure the ordeal of training for distance races.

The twenty-six-year-old, 5 foot 11, 155-pound marine lieutenant hung on through the torturous 25 laps at Tokyo and on the last lap startled the sporting world by racing past the strongest runners in the world. The nearly 80,000 fans huddled under umbrellas on this drizzly day in the enormous stadium and millions more watching on television shouted their surprise as Mills threw both arms high in the air, and a broad grin broke out on his face as he breasted the tape.

The day before the race he had gone to the store in the Olympic village where a major manufacturer provided free track shoes to the star runners. Told the shoes were free only for stars, Billy had to buy his. At no time before his race did a single reporter ask him a question. After the race, he was mobbed by the press. Nearby, the deeply discouraged Ron Clarke was asked if he had been worried about Billy before. "Worried about him?" Clarke responded. "I never heard of him."

Billy Mills wept openly when he got his gold medal and his nation's national anthem was played. He said later, "I suppose I was the only person in that place who thought I had a chance to win, and I didn't think so myself."

He proved himself a worthy winner the following summer, however, when he won a photofinish from luckless little Gerry Lindgren in the National AAU championship six-mile in 27 minutes 11.6 seconds to become the first American ever to hold the world record for the distance. Injuries curtailed his career after that, however, and he became assistant to the commissioner of the Bureau of Indian Affairs.

Americans swept the sprints, the hurdles, and the relays. Burly Bob Hayes, who became a professional football star, set a world record of 10 seconds flat in the 100. Henry Carr, who also went into pro football, captured the 200. Hayes Jones won the high hurdles and Rex Cawley the lows. One of the few non-Americans to win a running race was Peter Snell, the powerful lad in the all-black uniform of New Zealand, who repeated his success of the previous Olympiad at 800 meters and added success in the 1,500 meters, the first man in 44 years to double at these distances.

As a boy, Peter played everything from rugby to cricket, from hockey to golf. His favorite was tennis and he was one of the best of his age group at the game which is so popular in New Zealand and Australia. But he was so successful as a runner that he was picked up by a superior coach, Arthur Lydiard, and soon dropped other sports to concentrate on track. As he was beginning to run fast times, a broken bone in his foot set him back. He had just returned to top form when his upset of the Belgian Moens startled the track world in the 1960 Olympics.

In the next four years he established himself as one of the all-time standouts. Early in 1962 he lowered the world record for the mile to 3:54.4 and soon held the world records for the half-mile and 800 meters as well. He was favored in both the 800 and 1,500 at Tokyo, but doubling at these distances was so difficult some felt he would fail. However, he won going away with Canadian Bill Crothers second in the 800, then won all by himself with Czech Josef Odlozil second in the 1,500.

There are those who feel the 5 foot 11, 175-pound Snell, who trained with 20-mile mountain runs, was the outstanding middle-distance runner of all time. He came along after Roger Bannister retired, never met his Australian rival Herb Elliott when both were at their best, and was retiring when the great American Jim Ryun arrived at the top. However, neither Bannister nor Ryun ever won an Olympic contest, Elliott won only one, and Snell is the only one ever to win three gold medals in the middle distances.

Later that year of 1964, he lowered the mile mark to 3:54.1, but the following year his health was poor and he began to lose. Among other things, he seemed to have lost his incentive, and when he lost a swift mile in a bitter battle with eighteen-year-old Ryun and then a few races the following year, he retired at twenty-six.

In the field events at Tokyo, Lynn Davies of Wales upset Ralph Boston and Igor Ter-Ovanesyan in the long jump, and Valery Brumel beat back John Thomas in the high jump. The United States had won eight consecutive Olympic long jumps. Fred Hansen made it 15 straight for the United States in the pole vault. Al Oerter won his third of four straight in the discus throw. Dallas Long defeated fast-rising Randy Matson in the shot put. But Willi Holdorf of Germany ended a string of six straight championships for the United States in the decathlon. The favored Formosan C. K. Yang faded to fifth.

In women's events, Wyomia Tyus followed in the footsteps of Wilma Rudolph as American winner in the 100, and then four years later at Mexico City went on to become the only runner ever to repeat in this short sprint. An eighteen-year-old girl from Georgia, Wyomia held the women's world records at both 100 yards and 100 meters. At Tokyo, Edith McGuire at 200 meters was the only other American woman to win.

The only double winner was the enormous Russian Tamara Press, who won the shot put and discus throw. Her sister, Irina, captured the pentathlon. Mary Rand of Great Britain was second in the pentathlon and first with a world record beyond 22 feet 2 inches in the long jump. She later married the 1968 decathlon champion, Bill Toomey. Iolanda Balas of Romania won her second straight gold in the high jump. Betty Cuthbert of Australia, who had won the 100 and 200 in 1956 at Melbourne, won the 400 in 1964 at Tokyo.

A gorgeous Russian girl, Elvira Ozolina, who failed to win a medal in the javelin throw, went to a hairdresser and had her long hair shaved off in her shame.

The Czech Vera Caslavska won three gold medals in women's gymnastics. The following Olympiad she would win four, but since most of the entrants compete in all of the various contests in this sport it is not difficult for the dominant performer to take a lot of medals. The Russian women, however, won the team title both times to make it five in a row.

Equestrian sports are the only ones in which women compete against men in the Olympics. On the American team, which won a silver medal in one event, was Kathy Kysner, the first woman ever to make the team. She later became a jockey at thoroughbred racing tracks.

Perhaps the most impressive women at Tokyo were the Japanese athletes who won the volleyball crown from Russia. These Japanese girls were isolated from society and practiced six hours a day to points of exhaustion in preparation for the intense competition. They were driven by cruel coaching that would not permit a letup, but it paid off.

In rowing, Vyacheslav Ivanov of Russia became one of the rare ones to win three straight golds when he triumphed in the single sculls, as he had in 1956 and 1960.

Russia won the men's volleyball title. Hungary won in soccer. As usual, Hungary won in water polo. Predictably, India and Pakistan finished atop the field hockey standings, and the United States won in basketball. The United States also regained the eight-oar crew crown in rowing.

Bill Bradley, Joe Caldwell, Walt Hazzard, Luke Jackson, and Larry Brown were the stars of the basketball team that routed Russia in the final. Later Larry Brown stood admiring his gold medal. He said, "It's worth twelve dollars, that's all. And you couldn't buy it from me if you had a million."

As the athletes from 94 nations marched out of the stadium at the conclusion of the closing ceremonies and 75,000 people applauded, the word *sayonara* flashed large and bright on the scoreboard. A group of New Zealanders broke ranks and began to run around the arena and others joined them, holding hands, singing and dancing in celebration of friendship.

The earlier Winter Games in Innsbruck, Austria, had been a bitter battle. A fifty-year-old British tobogganist had been killed in a crash during a practice run, and a nineteen-year-old Austrian skier was killed when he tumbled into a tree. For the first time, more than 1,000 athletes participated.

The star of these was a twenty-four-year-old Siberian schoolteacher representing Russia, Lydia Skoblikova, who swept all four women's speed-skating gold medals. She became the only person ever to win four gold medals at one Winter Olympics, in fact the only person ever to win four golds in individual events at any Olympics, Winter or Summer. Terry McDermott flashed home first at 500 meters to become the first American winner in speed skating in 20 years.

Russian Klaudia Boyerskikh swept both women's cross-country ski races. A Finnish ski patrol border guard, Eero Maentyranta, won two men's cross-country races. Sixten Jernberg of Sweden won his third gold medal in three Olympics in another cross-country race. He also won three silvers in this time.

Marielle and Christine Goitschel of France traded one-two finishes in two women's Alpine skiing events to become the only sisters ever to take the top two spots in any Olympic event. Penny Pitou of the United States had finished second in two of these races in 1960, and now Jeannie Saubert of the United States finished third in two races in 1964. Billy Kidd and Jimmy Huega of the United States finished second and third in one of the men's Alpine skiing events. There were no dominant skiers this year. A 90-meter jump was added to the 70-meter leap, and Toralf Engan of Norway won it.

American domination of figure skating ended, probably because most of the American team had been killed in a tragic air crash in 1961. The newcomers had not yet developed sufficiently to come close to the winners, Manfred Schnelldorfer of Germany and Sjoukje Dijkstra of the Netherlands. A Russian husband and wife, Oleg Protopopov and Ludmila Belousova, won their first of two straight gold medals in the pairs competition.

The United States could not come close to repeating its ice hockey championship. The competition was close and savage. In one game, Karl Oberg of Sweden hit the Canadian coach, Father David Bauer, over the head with his hockey stick. The player was not even penalized at the time, but he was suspended for one game later and the referee who failed to penalize him was suspended for three games. Canada could have won the gold medal by winning the last game from Russia, but when it lost it, 3–2, it fell into fourth place and did not get a medal at all. And the Swedish team finished second to the Soviet team.

The ice melted and that summer an American youngster Schollander churned through the water to win stardom in the 1964 Olympiad.

13
GRENOBLE AND MEXICO CITY, 1968
Peggy and Debbie

WHEN THE BOEING 707 jet plane plummeted to earth near Brussels, Belgium, in February, 1961, all 73 persons on board died, including all 18 members of the United States figure-skating team. Gone with the tragic crash were sixteen-year-old Laurence Owen, the newly crowned North American women's champion and almost certainly a coming gold medalist in the Olympics, and her mother, Maribel Vinson Owen, who had won the American crown herself at sixteen and won a silver medal at Lake Placid in 1932 when Sonja Henie gained the gold. Gone also were all the other graceful women and agile men who carried the high hopes of United States figure skating.

Some said it would be at least a decade before this country could develop new skaters to replace those who had become dominant in the world. And the only American to win a medal in 1964 in Innsbruck was Scott Allen, who finished third in the men's competition. He was only fourteen then, the youngest figure skater ever to win a medal, and was rushed so fast that in following years he never was able to fulfill this first promise. But by 1968 in Grenoble, France, Peggy Fleming, who was just twelve when the air crash occurred and now was nineteen, was the winner of the gold medal in women's figure skating, and Tim Wood came close to completing an American sweep but in the judging was controversially placed second to Wolfgang Schwarz of the host country in the men's competition.

It was a dramatic comeback for the United States in figure skating, the most beautiful of all Olympic sports.

Just as the parents of Carol Heiss sacrificed for years to provide the costly instruction, equipment, and travel their daughter had needed to attain the heights in 1960, so did the parents of Peggy Fleming. Her father had been a pressman for the *San Francisco Chronicle*. When his daughter showed rare talent as a skater, he found work in Colorado Springs and moved his family there to spare his wife the long daily drive down the freeway to rinks where Peggy could practice only at odd times.

In Colorado, Peggy and her three sisters swam, water-skied, and learned to play tennis and golf, but it was skating that kept Peggy busy. She loved music and her parents tried to interest her in violin lessons, but she would not take the time or do anything that would distract from her skating. She began ballet lessons only because they were beneficial to her skating.

There is no rule that a homely lass cannot be a superior skater, but one has only to look at the women who have won world and Olympic titles to know that looks count considerably in this sport. A slender, beautiful brunette with delicate features, Peggy had a lot going for her on the surface. Inside, she was dedicated to perfection, practicing every spare second to make the intricate and difficult maneuvers of her routines seem effortless. She modernized her routines, though continuing to skate to a background of the most compelling classical music she could find to fit her style.

By 1964 she had won the first of five consecutive national titles, but in Innsbruck she finished sixth and realized she had to improve on the fine points of her performance. Still, this showing established the base from which a figure skater can hope to build championship prestige. "I was too bright-eyed in Innsbruck," she later observed. "I was deeply disappointed by my failure. But I was inspired by the experience. Maybe one doesn't think of figure skaters as tough, but I saw that I had to get tough. I had to work harder to build up to the best in the world, I had to believe I was the best before the judges would believe it, and I couldn't get carried away by the emotion of just being in with the best."

By 1966, she had become the best, winning the first of her world titles in Davos, Switzerland. She wanted to be a schoolteacher, but her studies at Colorado College were suffering and she just accepted the fact that she could concentrate only on her skating if she was going to get the gold medal in France in 1968. She won the world laurel again in 1967. And, finally, she won the Olympic laurel in 1968, piling up an impressive lead in the school figures the first day, then gracefully gliding, leaping, and spinning through an almost flawless freestyle routine that left Germany's Gabriele Seyfert and Czech Hana Maskova far behind.

Peggy went on to win a third world title before departing the amateur ranks to sign a half-million-dollar contract calling for her to appear professionally in ice shows and television spectaculars. Her annual television appearances have been beautiful and imaginative, revealing her as a charming and accomplished woman who has elevated her sport enormously.

At these tenth Winter Olympics in the Swiss Alps there were more television people—1,500—than athletes, who numbered 1,200, but there were other impressive performances besides Peggy's on display for an estimated 200 million viewers around the world.

Jean Claude Killy was as handsome as Peggy Fleming was pretty. If she was the heroine of the Winter Games, he was the hero. The flashy twenty-four-year-old Frenchman had won more major international skiing competitions than any other man ever. He had captured the World Cup, which was symbolic of supremacy in his sport, and he was expected to dominate the Grenoble Games. He bore a heavy burden and he came through, but it was close.

Killy, whose name is pronounced Kee-lee, won the downhill race with a combined total for his two runs of only one-tenth of a second less than the runner-up, the Austrian Guy Perrillat. Three days later, he won the giant slalom with two seconds to spare. Five days later he completed the first sweep of these contests since the Austrian Toni Sailer had pulled it off, but the Frenchman won only after it appeared he had lost.

Killy swerved through the 131 gates and sped down the 1,040-meter course twice in a total of less than 100 seconds. Haakon Mjoen of Norway beat this time but was ruled to have missed a gate and was disqualified. This left the Austrian veteran Karl Schranz as the best bet to beat the Frenchman.

By now, fog obscured the course. Schranz sped superbly through his first run, finishing close enough to Killy to catch him on the second run. But as he raced through the fog, an official who did not know he was coming stepped into his path and Schranz had to stop to avoid him.

Permitted another run, Schranz sidestepped back to the top, then tore through the run, finishing a split second ahead of Killy's time. Just when it seemed he had won, it was ruled that he, too, had missed a gate and had to be disqualified. Killy got the gold again.

In the best performance by a Canadian individual since 1928, Nancy Greene got a gold medal in the giant slalom and a silver in the special slalom in which she lost by less than a half second to France's marvelous Marielle Goitschel. In Nordic skiing, Italian Franco Nones was the first non-Scandinavian ever to win the 30-kilometer cross-country run. Czech Jiri Raska won the 70-meter jump, but was beaten in the 90-meter event by Vladimir Beloussov, who won Russia's first medal in ski jumping.

In speed skating, defending champion Terry McDermott of the United States lost his 500-meter title by one-fiftieth of a second to Erhard Keller of West Germany. Of such slender margins are victory and defeat, joy and despair often measured in Olympic competition. In the women's 500-meters there was an unprecedented triple tie for the silver medal by three Americans, Dianne Holum, Jenny Fish, and Mary Meyers, two tenths short the time of Ludmilla Titova of Russia.

Holum also was third at 1,000 meters. The seeds of success for American women in the following Olympiad had been planted.

Eugenio Monti of Italy had won nine world titles in bobsledding but he never had won an Olympic title, having taken the silver medals with his teams in two events in 1956 and a bronze medal in one event in 1964. Finally the daring club captain gained golds in 1968, piloting both the Italian two-man and four-man teams to triumph over the twisting, turning, breathtaking course. Monti was forty, but far from the oldest contestant in the Winter Games. The oldest was fifty-seven-year-old Matias Stinnes of Germany, who finished far back in the luge event, which is a sort of sledding test of speed and skill.

The youngest at Grenoble was eleven-year-old Beatrice Hustiu of East Germany, who, after skating for only two years, finished 31st out of 32 qualifiers in women's figure skating, and who received an ovation comparable to Peggy Fleming's simply for showing up, showing promise, and showing the courage to compete when other youngsters her age were at home playing games.

One of the stars of the Summer Games in Mexico was Debbie Meyer, a Californian who, at sixteen, became the first swimmer ever to win three individual gold medals.

The world had become a political powder keg when the Summer Games were held in the Americas for the first time in 36 years and in Latin America for the first time ever.

How much if any professionalism should be permitted amateurs eligible for the Olympics was a question that concerned Avery Brundage and other Olympic officials, but this was minor compared to other matters troubling the Games.

The demands of many countries to bar the participation of South Africans because of segregation in that country were accepted by the International Olympic Committee. Demands that Russia be barred because of its occupation of Czechoslovakia were denied, however, and Russians were booed and Czechs cheered.

In the United States, blacks urged a boycott by black athletes of participation in the Olympics in protest of racial oppression in this country. The boycott bogged down but not before such athletes as basketball's Kareem Abdul Jabbar had declined to participate in the games.

In the host country of Mexico there were student protests against the expense of staging the Games. Riots were put down violently with 40 or more students killed and hundreds more imprisoned. Yet by the time the Games began in mid-October, the majority of Mexicans seemed solidly behind this showcase celebration of the 19th Olympiad.

Magnificent Mexico City was at its most beautiful, its broad thoroughfares lined with trees and flower gardens, its spacious parks full of people picnicking on the grass, its modern business buildings reaching for the skies. Typical traffic congestions and periodic rain squalls did not dampen the spirits of the spectators and participants who filled the town. The sight of a million smiles and the sound of a thousand tongues was everywhere.

Housing developments designed to relieve the dreadful living conditions of the poor were rising. Dormitories constructed to house athletes and officials were designed for conversion into residential apartments afterwards. So many persons came from so many countries that they overflowed the hotels and were quartered in private residences. The marvelous restaurants of this cosmopolitan city were packed.

The sombrero-shaped soccer stadium, the Estadio, had become a track and field arena, and by the time more than 100,000 persons filled the cement saucer to greet the 7,200 athletes who marched in from 114 nations in the opening ceremonies, a spirit of peaceful friendship prevailed as the background for the intense sporting competition which was about to begin.

For the first time, the anchor runner on the torch-bearing relay team was a woman. Twenty-year-old Norma Enriqueta Basilio, a hurdler, skipped up the long, steep steps with her flaming baton to ignite the Olympic flame, which burned in a bowl atop the stadium. More than 6,000 doves were released symbolically against blue skies.

The flags of the contesting nations flew in the breeze encircling the saucer. The national anthem of the host nation was played and the chant *May-hee-co* produced a rhythm of pride. The controversial Olympic committee president, Avery Brundage, standing erect and proud, read a welcome in the best Spanish he could muster. The Mexican president, Pedro Ramirez Vasquez, declared the 19th Olympiad officially open. And the 16-day celebration started.

Mexico itself had won only a single bronze medal in the preceding Olympiad at Tokyo four years earlier. When word reached the stadium that a walker from Mexico, Jose Pedraza, was closing in on the lead in the last stages of the 20,000-meter event as it moved through the city streets approaching the windup within the stadium, a great roar rose from the nationals. As the contenders entered the arena, Pedraza was attempting to catch a Russian, Vladimir Golubnichy, both moving in the peculiar hip-swinging, feel-and-toe gait of the walkers, and for a moment an event few notice and most find laughable seemed the most important of all.

The Mexican could not catch the Russian. In an incredible din of noise, he fell just short of Golubnichy at the tape, buried his head in his hands, and began to cry. But then he realized the crowd was roaring *May-hee-co* and *Pay-drah-zah*. As he mounted the second step of the victory stand, saw his country's flag flying at the second level, and received his silver medal, he realized he was being acclaimed for what he had done, not for what he had not done. He held his head high as emotional Latins embraced him with their cheers.

It remained for Felipe Munoz to get the gold for Mexico. It was as though someone was bound to do it somehow, and the inspired swimmer churned past world record holder Vladimir Kosinsky of Russia midway on the last lap of the 200-meter breaststroke race to bring bedlam into the indoor arena.

Grenoble and Mexico City, 1968

As he touched the end triumphantly, he was hauled from the water, hoisted wet and dripping onto the shoulders of ecstatic countrymen and a sombrero placed on his head. He was paraded around the pool to the cheers of the crowd. The flag was hoisted high, the anthem played proudly. As word spread, a rumble of triumphant sound seemed to speed across the country.

Later, two Mexican boxers, flyweight Ricardo Delgado and featherweight Antonio Roldon gained golds unexpectedly.

The massive flag-waving heavyweight George Foreman was the best of the boxers. In freestyle wrestling, Japan's bantamweight Yojiro Uetake won his second straight gold medal, while in Greco-Roman wrestling, Hungarian heavyweight Istevan Kuzma won his second straight. Repeat winners in weight lifting were Japan's featherweight Yoshinobu Miyake, Poland's lightweight Waldemar Baszanowski, and Russia's heavyweight Leonid Zhabotinski.

Vera Caslavska, the incredibly controlled Czech, gained four gold medals and one silver medal in gymnastics to complete her heavy haul, but Russia won the woman's team title. Japan won the men's team title. In Mexico, Vera Caslavska married Josef Odlozil, the runner who was the silver medalist at 1,500 meters in Tokyo in 1964. But Czech team members were sent home as soon as each had completed his or her competition. After Odlozil ran eighth in the 1,500 in Mexico, he had to go home to await his wife, who went on to win and win and win and win in her events.

Marion Coakes of Great Britain became the first woman ever to win an Olympic medal in equestrian jumping, but she finished second to the veteran American Billy Steinkraus. West Germany won its second straight team dressage title, but its string of three straight golds in grand prix jumping was snapped by Canada. In cycling, France's Daniel Morelon and Pierre Trentin each gained two golds. In rifleshooting, Gary Anderson of the United States got his second straight gold medal.

In rowing, the West German eight won the featured crew event as the United States ran out of the money. Hungary won its second straight title in soccer. Pakistan captured its second title in three Olympiads in field hockey. Yugoslavia won in water polo. Russia swept the volleyball laurels. The United States team remained undefeated in the history of Olympic basketball as Spencer Haywood sparked its youngest-ever quintet to triumph despite the absence of the better-known black players.

Protests by black Americans marked the track and field competition. Jim Hines and Charlie Greene finished first and third in the 100-meter dash, announced they would not accept their medals from Avery Brundage, and were given them by Britain's Lord Burghley instead. Hines, Greene, Paul Pender, and Tommie Smith sprinted the U.S. team to the top in the 400-meter relay. But after Smith and John Carlos finished first and third at 200 meters, they lowered their heads while the American anthem was played and raised black-gloved fists to the skies in protest of their country's racial policies as they stood on the victory stand.

Their behavior was cheered by some and booed by most; they were expelled from the team and sent home. There were no further major demonstrations of this sort, although after Lee Evans won the 400, he waved a clenched fist heavenward, and he and other black Americans wore black socks instead of the customary uniform attire.

Many feel that political protests have no place in an Olympic celebration. However, Smith and Carlos insist that they were right to dramatize their sincere sentiments on a vast stage that was being watched by the world.

Smith says, "The fact is the fight for right among blacks is bigger than the winning of any one event in sports. Winning made my act more meaningful, but I used victory as a means to an end, which will be reached when blacks have reached equal status in society with all peoples."

Carlos says, "No one who was reared in the sort of oppressive poverty that I was in a New York ghetto would begrudge me the right to protest in a place where it would be seen."

In any event, they had performed superbly. Hines had tied the world record of 9.9 in winning the 100 meters, but Carlos became a superior sprinter. Some say he could have won the 200 but tried only to get into the top three so he could get to the victory stand. He says this. But possibly no one could have beaten Smith, who, despite a painful pulled muscle, added the world record of 19.8 seconds in winning the 200 to the world record he already held in the 400.

Evans set a world record of 43.8 in winning the 400, but he was condemned by the others for not joining their protest. Smith and Carlos paid a personal price for their act, for they were the focus of intense hostility when they returned to the United States, not from blacks but from whites. They soon left amateur track to try pro football unsuccessfully.

At an altitude of 7,350 feet above sea level, Mexico City's thin air posed unusual problems to those not used to it. It created a tremendous advantage for competitors, such as those from the emerging African nations, who were accustomed to high altitude conditions. It had an enormous effect on the middle-distance and distance races.

Wilson Kiprugut of Kenya was second to Ralph Doubell of Australia at 800 meters. Kipchoge Keino outlasted Jim Ryun of the United States at 1,500 meters and was second to Mohamed Gammoudi of Tunisia at 5,000 meters. Naftali Temu of Kenya was third at 5,000 meters and first over Mamo Wolde of Ethiopia at 10,000 meters. Wolde won the marathon, the third straight for Ethiopia. Amos Biwott of Kenya overcame Kenyan Ben Kogo in the 3,000-meter steeplechase.

Keino's conquest of Ryun was dramatic: Keino was born in Kapchemoiywo, Nandi, in 1940, of poor parents. He ran to and from school, but competed in sports without great enthusiasm or success, and at seventeen left school to become a policeman in 1957. Appointed a physical education instructor at a police training school five years later in 1962, he began to take his own running seriously. The enthusiastic sports officer there recognized his potential, but once Keino began to compete in meets he was uncoached.

The former American Olympic star Mal Whitfield visited Kenya on a U.S. State Department goodwill tour and at Keino's request laid out a training schedule for him on which the tall, slender African developed his own program. Running from dawn to dusk, up hills and down valleys, sometimes in army boots, Kip Keino, who often wore a cap he tossed aside in triumphant final laps, grew swift and strong. He began to win big races, set world records, and at the age of twenty-eight was peaking in Mexico.

Ryun was fron Wichita. Raised in middle-class circumstances in middle America by religious parents, he was a clean-cut kid who liked sports but was without special skills. He was frail and sickly and had a hearing problem that affected his balance. He ran some in junior high school, but it was not until he went out for cross-country in high school that he found he had the endurance to develop as a distance runner.

It is difficult to pinpoint the physical qualities that separate good runners from the rest, but Jim apparently had the heart, lungs, and other internal construction to succeed as a runner, and he was willing to put in the torturous practices necessary to improve. As a sophomore, he ran his first mile in a sad 5:38 but he swiftly started to cut the time down. He became the fastest high school miler ever, the first to run under four minutes.

Even before he finished high school he had made the U.S. Olympic team at seventeen, beating out veteran Jim Grelle at the tape for third place in the final trials in Los Angeles, but he was sick and eliminated in the semifinal at Tokyo. Two years later, however, as a young collegian at Kansas University, he set world records in the half mile and mile. The following year he lowered his mile record to 3:51.1, which still stands, and set a 1,500-meter world mark of 3:33.1.

Stricken with mononucleosis in June, 1968, he made a remarkable recovery and appeared ready for the metric mile in Mexico City, but the thin air and the contestant from Kenya conspired to foil him.

Ryun's finishing kick was considered superior to Keino's, and it was felt that Keino would have to start at a fast pace and maintain a large lead to trim Ryun. Keino's teammate Ben Jipcho obligingly provided the fast pace in the first lap, pulling the field along in 56 seconds.

Keino took over as Ryun restrained himself in the middle of the 12-man pack. At the midway mark, Keino was pulling away, 5 yards in front of West Germany's Bodo Tummler, 10 yards in front of another West German Harold Norpoth and 20 yards in front of Ryun.

On the third lap Keino was running easily, but Tummler and Ryun were increasing speed and beginning to gain ground. Keino was the only one of the three in other Olympic races, and he had run more than a dozen miles of trials and finals at this point and was supposed to weaken, but he would not; he was astonishing.

Early on the last lap Ryun launched his famed finishing kick. He sped past Norpoth and caught Tummler entering the final corner, but Tummler battled back and Ryun had to run wide coming around the curve before he could get free. He found himself 10 yards behind Keino, the crowd screaming. Ryun drove with determination down the stretch, but he could not cut into Keino's lead. Keino was maintaining his pace almost effortlessly.

Suddenly Ryun surrendered. He slowed, starved for air. Three times through the last strides Ryun turned around to make sure he was not being caught, even while Keino was pulling away. Spent, Ryun staggered across the finish line well back of the Kenyan Keino, who won in 3:34.9, second in history only to Ryun's record and a remarkable run at high altitude.

Ryun had been regarded as the greatest miler ever and almost certainly America's first gold medalist in the metric mile in the Olympics in 60 years. His defeat was deeply disappointing to his countrymen and to himself. By contrast to the extroverted, agreeable, grinning Keino, Ryun was introverted, sensitive, and serious. He mistrusted the press and disliked invasions of his privacy. He struggled to regain his interest, retired, married, and returned to track to expose his wife to the excitement of international competition.

Bespectacled, hard of hearing, asthmatic, he gypsied across the country seeking a comfortable place to train, supporting himself as a professional photographer. He performed erratically, ranging from 4:19 to 3:52.8 for miles in 1972, but made the Olympic team and appeared ready for a major run at immortality. Then he was tripped in a heat race and fell out of the Olympics for a final, frustrating time. Meanwhile, the carefree Keino finished second at 1,500 meters and first in the 3,000-meter steeplechase to climax an enormously successful career.

Mexico's thin air also destroyed another dominant runner's dream. Another Kenyan, Temu, triumphed at 10,000 meters as the world record holder; Ron Clarke of Australia, gasping for breath, faded to sixth at the finish, collapsed just past the finish line, and had to be administered oxygen. Gallantly, he returned four days later for the 5,000, in which he also held the world record, and led for nine laps, but again he faded at the finish as another African, Gammoudi of Tunisia, gained the gold.

Clarke was thirty-one and this was his last attempt to get a gold medal. He set 17 world records at from two to six miles, but the Australian never won a major championship race and retired in disappointment. The Olympic dream has been a nightmare for many.

The thin air produced one remarkable performance as the lanky American Bob Beamon flew through it on his first finals leap to win the long jump with a world record of 29 feet 2½ inches. It was so far past the previous standard—almost 2 feet—that it is regarded by experts as the single outstanding performance in track and field history. The twenty-five-year-old New Yorker had never come close to it before, nor has he or anyone else since. He bounced into the air in excitement and fell to his knees in prayer. He never has recaptured the magic of that moment, a once-in-a-lifetime thing. Dick Fosbury, who perfected the backwards bounce over the bar, which came to be called the "Fosbury Flop," won the high jump at an Olympic record above 7 feet 4 inches, and then also faded from the limelight.

Bob Seagren, a confident, movie-star-handsome Southern Californian from Pomona, who as a lad learned by vaulting his garage roof, increased his world record to 17 feet 8½ inches in the pole vault, but was tied by Claus Schiprowski of West Germany and Wolfgang Nordwig of East Germany. Seagren won only because he had made fewer misses to that height. He also had attempted fewer heights than most of his rivals along the way so won with a rule which seems unfair, but remains in the books. He increased the world record to 18 feet 5¾ inches in 1972, but after his new-styled pole was declared illegal and he had to use an unfamiliar one, he lost to Nordwig in the Munich Games.

Randy Matson, who almost died from double pnuemonia as an infant and was sickly as a lad, grew up to be a 6 foot 6, 270-pound powerhouse, who broke the 70-foot barrier in the shot put and advanced from the silver medal in the 1964 Games to the gold medal in the 1968 Games. He won with a toss of less than 67½ feet but at the time had pushed his world record to almost 71½ feet. The towering Texan went to work for a living and seemed to lose his edge after that, though he continued to compete as a pro, along with Seagren and others on the new play-for-pay tour.

Al Oerter won his fourth consecutive gold medal in the discus, but honors in other field events went to Communist countries. Russia's Viktor Saneyev won his first of two straight in the triple jump. Russia's Janis Lusis, longtime world best, finally won the javelin throw. Hungary's Gyula Zsivotzky won the hammer throw.

The American Bill Toomey dramatically outperformed the West Germans Hans Walde and Kurt Bendlin to become at twenty-nine the oldest winner ever of the grueling decathlon.

His wife Mary's world women's record in the long jump was surpassed at 22 feet 4½ inches by the Romanian Viorica Viscopoleanu. The only woman to win two gold medals was Wyomia Tyus, who repeated at 100 meters and helped the U.S. 400-meter relay team win. The only other American woman to win was Madeline Manning, who flashed in first at 800 meters.

However, it was an American woman, or maybe she should be called a girl, who starred in swimming. Sixteen-year-old Debbie Meyer, a plump speedster from Sacramento, California, won the three longest freestyle races for women—the 200-, 400- and 800-meter events, breaking an Olympic record in each—to become the first triple winner in individual races in the history of Olympic swimming and the fourth woman to win the Sullivan Award. Nothing expresses the improvement in swimmers better than the fact that this typical teen-age girl's time for 400 meters was 33 seconds faster than Johnny Weissmuller's when he won the men's event in record time in 1924.

Debbie was born in New Jersey in 1952 and began to swim in kids' meets at the age of eight without any wondrous results. Her father, an executive of the Campbell Soup Company, was transferred to Sacramento when Debbie was twelve. Once the family was settled there, she went to Arden Hills Swim Club and found out it had one of the best coaches in the country, Sherm Chavoor. Unlike track coaches, swim coaches believe athletes are at their best young and can be developed into world class competitors at an early age with rugged, demanding practice routines. Chavoor kids his young athletes, but he works them hard to bring out the best in them. Only the toughest and most successful stay with it.

Debbie responded to the challenge of Chavoor with determination. Being sturdy and strong and blessed with natural talent, she developed fast. Her parents encouraged her and were surprised by her success. They did not drive her—Chavoor drove her and she drove herself. She says, "With a coach like Sherm, you develop a love-hate relationship. But you only hate him from time to time when you get tired. You love him all the time when you see what he gets from you." She set her first world record at fourteen and soon held every women's record in the freestyle from 200 to 1,500 meters. Her spectacular success in Mexico City was not surprising. "I was well prepared and I wasn't about to tie up," she says.

So with Peggy Fleming she was one of the two young women who were the stars of the 1968 Olympiad. She became the fourth woman to win the Sullivan Award. Debbie was still just a teen-age high school girl, however, who had sacrificed enormously for early success in sports and was starting to wonder if it was worth it. "I've been a good student, but I didn't have time for much else besides studies and swimming," she said.

"I didn't have a lot of friends, because a lot of the kids were sort of in awe of me. I didn't date a lot, because the boys seemed afraid of me. I didn't go to a lot of parties. I just didn't feel like one of the kids, though I wanted to. I'm more mature than the average kid my age because I've been around the world a number of times and met a lot of different kinds of people on my travels, but I'm not sure I'm a well-rounded person.

"The Olympics were a fabulous experience and winning the three gold medals, doing something no one else has ever done, was a thrill. It made me proud. It made me feel like everything else had been worthwhile. But I wasn't sure I wanted to go through all I'd have to go through to repeat that performance. I wasn't even sure I could if I wanted to. There's a lot of tough thirteen-year-olds coming up," she sighed. The 5 foot 7, 130-pounder loved to eat and was weary of dieting. She did return to competition but seemed to lack the desire to succeed that had driven her before. She'd already succeeded. She'd been there before. Finally, she retired in 1972 at twenty on the eve of another Olympics. "I just don't want to do it any more. I don't want to give up everything else in life. I'm tired," she said. And began to eat. And date boys. And go to parties.

Similar sacrifices do not pay off in such success for most athletes who aspire to Olympic glory. But there were other swimmers who starred in Mexico City. Claudia Kolb won gold medals in two individual races. On the men's side, Germany's Rollie Matthes won two races, too.

The disappointment in swimming was the highly touted young American Mark Spitz, although he won three gold medals. He won all three in relay races. He had been expected to win three individual races and a total of six gold medals, surpassing any athlete in Olympic history. He had cockily predicted he would do so, which did not endear him to his teammates or opponents. No one wept when he settled for a silver medal in one race, a bronze in another, and got no medal at all in his other race. The pressure had pounded him emotionally to pieces, but he vowed he would be back in Munich in 1972.

To the sentimental strains of "Los Golandrinos," athletes, men and women, losers as well as winners, friends again now instead of foes, broke ranks from the parade in the closing ceremonies and hugged one another and held hands and danced, singing, around the great stadium. Around and around and around they went, hands locked, laughing and crying as the 20th Olympiad ended and the 21st, four years into the future, beckoned. The words *Munich '72* blazed on the enormous scoreboard.

14
SAPPORO AND MUNICH, 1972
Another Superswimmer, Spitz

THIS WAS SAPPORO, a city of one million persons, on the island of Hokkaido in Japan in the bitter cold of winter, 1972. It was the 11th of the winter Olympics and more than 1,100 athletes from 32 countries had convened for the competition.

On the night before her first race, an American teen-ager, Annie Henning, fretted nervously in her room in the Olympic village. At dinner, she could not eat. Through the evening she dipped into a jar of peanut butter, but she was not hungry.

When she awoke the next morning, she knew "this was it." The time she had worked and waited for had come. The sixteen-year-old, long-haired blond from America's midlands had come thousands of miles into the Orient, to speed skate against time and opponents.

Speed skaters compete in pairs, crossing over to exchange lanes in the middle of each lap encircling the icy rink. This provides them competition, but it is their time that matters most. It is time that determines the final placings.

Annie Henning had drawn as her foe in her heat a courageous Canadian, Sylvia Burka, who was blind in one eye, who skated with her head cocked to keep one eye on the other skater. Annie and her coach worried that the Canadian might crash into her on the crossover.

Their race was a sprint, 500 meters. At the start, Annie, in the outside lane, shot smoothly away. Skating as these speedsters do—bent forward, one arm resting behind her back, the other swinging free, her blades slashing across the ice in a relentless rhythm—Annie swept through the first corner and into the backstretch in the lead.

As they headed for the crossover, however, the Canadian, having skated the first half of the race in the shorter inside lane, was close. As she angled into the crossover she did not ease up to let the leader through. A collision seemed certain.

Suddenly, the American rose slightly and slowed to let the other through. By the time she was settled into the inside line, Annie had lost perhaps a full second and seemed beaten. But instead of surrendering, she dug in and drove harder. Her strong stride accelerated as she rounded the last turn. She sped down the stretch to the finish, far in front.

Her time was splendid, 43.7 seconds, which seemed sufficient to win. But the judges, ruling she had been fouled, allowed her a second run. She went back out and went even faster, 43.3 seconds.

She had to wait until the others had dashed to be sure she had won, but either time would have been enough to beat the two Russians who came closest.

Annie Henning got her gold medal—and she got a bronze medal, too, for finishing third to a West German at 1,000 meters. And afterwards, Annie said, "I'm so relieved I don't know if I ever want to skate again. I haven't had a normal life preparing for this. But then, now that I've got an Olympic gold medal, I don't suppose I'll ever have a normal life again, will I?"

Meanwhile, twenty-year-old Dianne Holum, who drew the Russian Nina Statkevich as her heat rival in the 1,500-meter race, shot into such a swift start that the other girl was left at the starting line. Holum melted the ice with murderous strokes of her skates. All the way, her father was hollering, "Come on, baby, come, baby," every time she flashed past. She came home having clocked in a new Olympic record of 2:20.8.

Smiling joyously, the brunette clasped her hands over her head and took a victory lap, skating triumphantly. Before it was finished, a couple of Dutch contestants came close to catching her. One, Stien Bass-Kaiser, a thirty-four-year-old housewife, came within two-tenths of a second of catching her. (You can't count that fast.) But she didn't catch her.

The Dutch veteran came back to beat the American at 3,000 meters, but Dianne Holum said she was satisfied with her gold and silver medals. "Speed skaters do not attract any attention in the United States," she sighed. "No one knew we were alive until this moment, and now we're being cheered all over the country. It's very strange, but it makes the sacrifices all very worthwhile."

Both Dianne Holum and Annie Henning came from Northbrook, Illinois, a Chicago suburb, which had installed a speed-skating facility. With similar support, others in what in America are minor sports might have done as well. By devoting its sporting interest to a single minor sport, other small towns might develop champions and contribute enormously to community pride and spirit. A great many of the citizens of Northbrook had saved up to go en masse to Sopporo. They were in the stands rooting hard when their girls came through.

The United States supports more major sports than any country in the world. Not considered a cold-weather country, it does not provide much financial support to its skiers and skaters and lags far behind many other countries in world competition.

Still, the United States made its best-ever Winter Olympics showing at Sapporo, winning eight medals, including three gold medals.

Gordon "Mickey" Cochran coached four of his children onto the Olympic team. He and his wife were ardent skiers who scouted around near their Richmond, Vermont, home for a place to fashion their own training course. The Cochran kids were on skis from the time they were five years of age.

He and his wife could not afford to attend the Games in Japan to see Bobby and daughters Marilyn, Lindy, and Barbara compete. They were watching on television when twenty-one-year-old Barbara, a tiny blond, dove and veered daringly twice through the fog to win the slalom event. And they wept when she called from Japan at 2 A.M., Vermont time, to tell them about it.

She was the last one of the leaders to go on the last run and when the time flashed on the electric scoreboard and everyone realized she had beaten the favored Austrian Annemarie Proell by a scant two one-hundreths of a second, a roar arose from the Americans at the base of Mount Teine. Her teammates vaulted a fence to hoist her onto their shoulders and parade her around in triumph.

She was the first American woman to win an Olympic skiing event since Andrea Mead Lawrence had turned the trick 20 years earlier, and hers was the third gold medal for the U.S. winter team this year. Susan Carrock won a silver medal in the downhill event to make it two medals for the U.S. women's skiing team.

Sapporo and Munich, 1972

The dominant woman skier was Marie-Therese Nadig of Switzerland, who gained two gold medals. The dominant man was Italy's Gustavo Thoeni, who won two, too. In Nordic skiing, the Soviet schoolteacher Galina Koulacova captured two cross-country golds. Norway's Magnar Solberg won the biathlon all-around event for the second straight Olympiad.

There literally was dancing in the streets as Japan's Yukio Kasaya, Akitsugo Konno, and Seiji Aochi, who had trained with almost fanatical daring and dedication, finished one, two, and three in small-hill ski jumping. The host country had captured only one medal in all the previous Winter Games.

Ondrej Nepela of Czechoslovakia and Trixi Schuba of Austria won the figure-skating golds in the individual events, while the team of Irina Rodnina and Alexei Ulanov gave Russia its third straight title in the pairs.

The stocky and methodical Trixi Schuba was not as attractive as the flashier Karen Magnusson of Canada and Janet Lynn of America, but was more efficient, especially in the dull compulsory school figures, which precede the freestyle part of the performance.

Despite a slip, Janet Lynn somehow was voted into third place, bringing the United States its seventh of the eight medals it won. The men won only one. This came from the young, spirited ice hockey team, which surprised everyone by finishing second, ahead of the Czechs and behind the Russians. The Soviets won for the third straight time and fourth time in the last five Olympiads.

Practically full-time hockey players although classed as amateurs, the Soviet team proved it could play with professionals by extending the National Hockey League All-Stars before bowing in a bitter eight-game exhibition series later in the year. Its path to the Olympic title had been paved by the withdrawal of Canada from world amateur competition. The Canadians decided that because its top players turn professional early it could not compete on equal terms with the veteran Russian and Czech teams.

The star of the eleventh Winter Olympiad was a speed skater, Ard Schenk, a husky, handsome physiotherapist from Amsterdam in the Netherlands. The twenty-seven-year-old, 6 foot 2, 190-pound powerhouse, a modern Hans Brinker, sped to victory in three events.

He fell in the 500, enabling Western Germany's Erhard Keller to win his second straight gold in that event. Otherwise, Schenk might have won a fourth to score an unprecedented sweep. As it was, he won at 1,500 meters, 5,000 meters and 10,000 meters. He was hailed as a hero almost everywhere in the world except the United States, where speed skaters are not recognized in the streets.

This was the first time the Winter Games had been staged in Asia and they were an enormous success, though not without their controversies.

Aged Avery Brundage, the retiring but still rigid president of the International Olympic Committee, presided over the disqualification from the Alpine skiing events of one of the favorites, the great veteran Karl Schranz of Austria, on charges of commercialism. Apparently, Schranz advertised and accepted sponsorship help from a commercial skiing concern. Most considered the ruling unrealistic and unfair. However, the fuss that was stirred up was small by comparison to the tumult in the 20th Summer Olympics in Munich.

Thirty-six years after the 1936 Games were staged in Berlin, the Germans spent an astonishing $650 million to mount the most magnificient Olympiad ever in Munich. They had dreams of erasing the dark shadows that lingered. The host nation's efforts for a show of international friendship would have been enormously successful except for a tragic interlude that blighted the athletic contests.

Arab terrorists invaded the quarters of the Israeli team and held athletes as hostages in hopes of securing the release of some imprisoned guerrillas. The Games stopped suddenly as television cameras sent pictures of the siege around the world through the long day and into the night.

The tragic final chapter was played out at the airport, where 16 died in an explosive conclusion. That Jews should be subjected to new horrors in this country where anti-Semitic tragedies took place through the 1930s and 1940s was the bitterest of ironies. The host nation protested theirs was a new Germany, which had no part in, nor any sympathy for, this latest outrage.

While the world mourned, the remainder of the Israeli team returned home. Many felt the Games should be ended, while others felt terrorist activities should not be permitted to destroy the spirit of this international sporting competition. The International Olympic Committee decided to continue.

Sapporo and Munich, 1972

There were the usual controversies stirred up during the twentieth Summer Olympiad, as more than 6,000 athletes from 115 nations competed.

American sprinters Eddie Hart and Rey Robinson were given old schedules and not informed of a new time plan for the sprint trials, with the result that they arrived at the track too late to compete. Their coach, Stan Wright, cried that it was simply an unfortunate mixup, but the runners were understandably bitter.

The powerful Russian Valery Borzov swept both dashes, but his Soviet team was beaten by the Americans in the 400-meter relay. Robinson was not, but Hart was given the chance to go for a gold medal here and made the most of it, anchoring Gerald Tinker and sprint silver medalists Larry Black and Bob Taylor to triumph.

Americans Vince Matthews and Wayne Collett ran one-two in the individual 400 meters, but their conduct on the victory stand—slouching, turned away from the U.S. flag as it was raised, and chatting while their country's national anthem was played—was deemed so disrespectful that they were barred from further Olympic competition.

With injuries to other American 400-meter runners, this resulted in the United States withdrawing from the 1,600-meter relay, which it usually won but which was won by the Kenyan team this time.

The actions of Matthews and Collett were reminiscent of the black-power protest staged by Americans Tommie Smith and John Carlos four years earlier in Mexico City.

Many now believe that the raising of the colors of the winner's country and the playing of the national anthems are out of place in what is intended to be nonpolitical competition among individuals. Even team scores are not kept officially, though reported by the press.

The 800 was the most exciting of the races in the track and field portion of the Munich Olympics. Wearing a golf cap, Dave Wottle, a slender, awkward, but determined American ran last for a full lap, then rushed around the entire field on the second and final lap for a dramatic triumph.

Wottle was born in Canton, Ohio, in August, 1950. No one in his much that he wore a baseball cap wherever he went. Unfortunately, he was not a good baseball player. Nor was he a good basketball player, though he tried out for his team in junior high school.

He almost turned away from track when he went to the tryout meeting and couldn't get the door open. Walking away, he realized he'd never return if he left. He decided to go back and knock. That was opportunity knocking.

"I was so shy, I used to be alone all the time until I started running track," he recalls. "Inside, I wanted to be something in sports, but it was awhile before I found something I was good at."

He tried the sprints and he tried the distances, but he wasn't successful until he tried races in between these extremes. He was so shy he used to wear his running clothes under his regular clothes so he wouldn't have to change in front of the other fellows in the dressing room. Once he began to win races, he became more confident personally and was not so withdrawn.

He wasn't great in high school, but he was good enough to get to Bowling Green University on a track scholarship. Here, he began to develop, mainly as a miler, until he fractured a bone in his ankle, which sidelined him for nine months. He came back as a junior in June, 1971, 14 months before the Olympics. He started to run 85 miles a week in practice. Soon he was approaching his peak.

Wottle was given little chance of making it in the metric mile in the U.S. Olympic trials, although America's premier miler, Marty Liquori, was sidelined with a severe and lingering foot injury. Jim Ryun was making a comeback and he won the trial. However, Wottle was second to make the team. Entering the metric half-mile, only to give himself an alternative, Wottle shocked the track world by setting a world record of 1:44.3 for the 800 meters. He was married just before the Games, which most figured would ruin his conditioning. Even if in shape, he had not mastered tactics. He was a long shot in classic competition.

A slow starter, Wottle usually had to come from behind with a finishing charge to win his races. He didn't always win. In the metric-mile trials at Munich, Wottle started so slow and fell so far back that his closing kick fell short and he didn't even make the final.

Neither did Ryun, who tripped in a tangle of runners, sprawled, stunned, for precious seconds, got up, and got going too late to catch the leaders and qualify. His 1964 Olympic conqueror, Kip Keino, the heat winner, put an arm around Ryun as the American walked off in despair, his dream of an Olympic gold medal gone.

"I'm just another good runner who for one reason or another didn't get the gold," said the disappointed Ryun, who gave up and turned pro.

Wottle, whose career cannot be compared to Ryun's, was one of the fortunate ones. He admits, "For three days before the 800 I was staring at walls, trying to psych myself up, trying to make myself believe I could win. Although I'd run the event in record time, no one believed I would win. I don't think I believed I would. The tension built and built and built.

"The morning of the race, I told myself, 'The heck with it. If you win, great. If not, you'll live. Making yourself sick won't help.' But just before the race I was so nervous my knees were shaking and I thought my legs would collapse under me. I felt weak.

"When the race started, I couldn't get going. I was off so slowly and fell so far back I thought I had no chance. Maybe that relaxed me. I said to myself, 'Well, what the heck, you might as well give it your best.' I reached down and found something I didn't think was there. As I started to pass runners, I began to realize I had a shot at it."

Wearing that peaked cap of his, he came bounding up, picking off other runners one by one around the last turn and into the stretch as the surprised fans stood up and started to holler for him. On the outside, he drove past Mike Boit of Kenya, caught the leader, the Russian Yevgeniy Arzhanov, and applied pressure to him as they approached the tape, straining with desperation.

As they reached the tape, Wottle drove ahead into it as the straining Soviet, leaning for it, fell forward and across the line second. "I couldn't believe it," Wottle recalls. Neither could many others, who cheered him as he hopped around in happiness.

On the victory stand, Wottle did not remove his cap. It was no gesture of protest. He was so excited, he simply forgot, and apologized later.

"I had the cap bronzed," he says now, laughing guiltily. It goes well with his gold medal.

Most of the gold in the distance events went to a new generation of Flying Finns, who interrupted the Africans' domination of endurance races.

Pekka Vasla upset Keino at 1,500 meters, while Lasse Viren won both the 5,000- and 10,000-meter races. The Finns, both bearded, were graceful, slender stylists of impressive speed and stamina, who had not dominated world runners previously, but were ready at the right time.

However, the Africans still took many medals. The incredible Keino of Kenya beat his countryman Ben Jipcho in the 3,000-meter steeplechase to give him two gold medals to go with two silver medals for his two Olympiads.

Keino had run this event only four times previously, but as so often in the past it was an event that could be won by someone who had come up short in more glamorous races.

John Akii-Bua of Uganda set a world record in winning the 400-meter low hurdles with American Ralph Mann second and the defending champion Dave Hemery of Great Britain third.

Rod Milburn, the world's greatest high hurdler for years, won the 110-meter highs in Munich. The world record holder from Opelousas, Louisiana, Milburn had lost only one of 31 prior races over two years, but, ironically, it was the final U.S. Olympic trial. Stumbling over a barrier, he barely made the team by finishing third, but went on to gain the gold medal.

It was reminiscent of the incident almost 30 years earlier when another American who was the world's best hurdler, Harrison Dillard, lost out in another of these cruel one-race trials, which so often cost classic competitors their best shot at immortality.

The only American to win in a field event was the youngest American winner on the Olympic track, nineteen-year-old Randy Williams, who got off a 27-foot leap to win the long jump in an upset.

Most thought massive shot-putter George Woods had won when his best effort hit the marker of the leader, the Pole Wladyslaw Komar, but officials ruled the American's iron ball had struck the ground a fraction of an inch short. "This can be a heartbreaking experience," Woods sighed.

Bob Seagren was so angry when his new pole was declared illegal that when he finished three inches short of the East German Wolfgang Nordwig in the vault, the American handed his substitute stick to officials and stalked off. The pole was made of a material that had not been approved by the IOC, although it had been permitted in previous meets.

Another American, Dwight Stones, fell an inch short of high jump winner Yuri Tarmak of Russia, who went seven feet. But by gaining the bronze, Stones became at eighteen the youngest man to win a track and field medal.

Viktor Saneyev, winning his second straight in the long jump, burly Aatoliy Bondarchuk in the hammer throw, and an amazing all-around athlete, Nikolay Avilov, who had personal bests in 7 of the 10 events and set a world record of 8,454 points in the decathlon, were other Russian winners. The great javelin thrower Janis Lusis was second to a bearded, balding West German, Klaus Wolferman.

The oldest winner in track and field was thirty-five-year-old Ludvik Danek, the great Czech discus thrower, who finally got his gold medal after settling for silver and bronze medals in the two previous Olympiads. Jay Silvester, the fine American thrower, however, failed for the third time to win in the Olympics, though he got a medal at last, a silver for second place.

At thirty-four the world record holder reluctantly retired to coaching. Danek's triumph was the first for a Czech since Zatopek.

The oldest medalist in track and field was the forty-year-old Mamo Wolde of Ethiopia, the defending champion, who finished third in the marathon. The Belgian Karel Lismont finished second. Finishing first by more than two minutes was Frank Shorter, the first American in more than 60 years to win this most classic of Olympic events. Born in Munich in October, 1947, he returned at twenty-six to triumph in this traditional test.

His father was a serviceman who was stationed in Germany when his son was born. Frank was reared in New York and New England. He admits his running career can be considered an accident. "I was in school and they were offering pies for running four miles in a certain time. I tried it and won a pie. So I tried out for cross-country but it was awhile before I won much else," he laughs.

Shorter graduated from New Mexico University, went to medical school at Yale, but transferred to law school at the University of Florida in 1972. At home on vacation from Yale earlier, he'd been training by running through an Indian reservation and over the desert around his hometown of Taos, New Mexico, but, after he interfered with a bunch of toughs who were roughing up a girl alongside a road during one run, they made life so miserable for him he moved to Florida and shifted his schooling to this state. Here, his wife, a skier, often ran alongside him.

He had become a good, but not great, distance runner, who won some big races, but lost others in college and postgraduate competition. His running did take him on travels to Africa, Russia, Japan, and other countries. In 1971, he won both the 10,000 meters and the marathon in the Pan-American Games in Colombia, so by 1972 he was rated a threat, if far from the favorite, in Olympic races. In fact, he finished only fifth in the 10,000 meters at Munich.

"I'd rather have been better at 5,000 meters or 10,000 meters, because the marathon hurts more," Shorter mourns with a wistful grin, "but it turned out to be the marathon or nothing, so I took it.

"The marathon is fashioned after the 26-mile run the Athenian messenger Philippides took from Marathon to Athens, but it is noteworthy he dropped dead at the finish. The first time I ran it, I began to wonder at about 20 miles why he didn't think to stop at 20 miles. I thought of it, but the farther I ran, the farther I got in front of other runners."

He upsets the purists by drinking beer during his training programs. In fact, he sat around with his wife drinking beer the night before the marathon in Munich, trying to relax. "I was trying to forget how much I'd suffer once I started to run," he laughs. The mustachioed German-born law student, who stands under 6 feet in height and weighs less than 135 pounds but is blessed with natural stamina, ran so hard in the Olympic marathon that he blistered his feet. He refused to stop and concentrated so hard on running that he forgot the pain after awhile. "Blisters just aren't important," he said later. "Winning this race was."

He ran relaxed at first, lingering back in the pack. At 5 miles, when he had fallen 10 seconds back, he started to pick up his pace. At 10 miles, he had caught and passed the leaders and he was starting to pull away from them.

There is a time in the middle of a marathon when it becomes murderously monotonous and all but the most determined begin to drop back. Shorter sped up, moving on five-minute miles through the streets of the ancient city.

At 15 miles, he was almost a minute in front of Wolde, Lismont, and teammate Ken Moore. At 20 miles, he was almost a minute and a half ahead. The others were wilting in the hot humidity, but the slender Shorter refused to slacken. At 25 miles he was more than two minutes in front. "What you do at that point," he explained, "is you try not to die."

He did not know it, but just before he got into the stadium, a young German in a track uniform trotted in and went for the tape. The crowd, which had been waiting to catch sight of the leader, started to cheer, until officials announed it was a hoax. The crowd was booing the boy when Shorter entered. Hearing the boos, Shorter wondered what he'd done wrong. "I'd suffered a lot to get there and didn't think much of the greeting," he laughed later.

Cheated of his cheers and the spotlight, Shorter burst the tape after 2 hours 12 minutes and 19 seconds of an astonishing American upset. "Well, they gave me the gold, anyway," he recalls. "I'd have really been upset if they'd given it to the other guy." He came home a hero.

The heroine of women's track and field in Munich was Renate Stecher of East Germany, who swept the sprints. East Germans won three other events, while the host West Germans won four. Clearly German women had become the class of the competition. Russian women won three golds. American women did not win a single event. Mary Peters of England did beat out two German contenders to win the pentathlon and recognition as the world's finest female all-round athlete.

Americans did better in other events. A dedicated Iowan, Dan Gable, won lightweight laurels to lead Americans to a surprising three gold medals in freestyle wrestling. Wayne Wells won the welterweight title. Ben Peterson won the light-heavyweight title, and his brother was second in the middleweight class. Rich Sanders was second in the bantamweight class but, sadly, was killed in a car wreck while touring Europe later.

The most publicized American wrestler, good-natured 400-pound Chris Taylor, was beaten by the Russian Alexander Medved in the first round of the super-heavyweight class and finished third in the final standings as Medved won his second straight gold medal.

Flyweight Petar Kirov of Bulgaria won his second straight gold in Greco-Roman wrestling. Super-heavyweight Vasily Alekseyeve of Russia won his second straight gold in weight lifting, hoisting 1,411 pounds in his three lifts.

Ray Seales of Tacoma won America's only gold in boxing as Cuba captured three crowns, including heavyweight honors as Teofilio Stevenson knocked out the touted American, Duane Bobick. Americans John Williams and Doreen Wilber swept archery laurels, while John Writer and Lones Wigger won golds in rifle and pistol shooting.

Japan won men's volleyball, while Russia won the women's title. Japan won men's gymnastics, while Russia won the women's title.

A doll-like little Russian, Olga Korbut, won two gold medals and the hearts of the world with a dynamic performance on the balance beam, but she slipped in the individual all-around event and the big prize went to her more experienced and titled teammate, the beautiful Ludmila Tourischeva.

Telecasts of Miss Korbut's spectacular routines have helped popularize the sport of gymnastics in the United States, but in the Soviet Union there is resentment that the more classic accomplishments of Tourischeva have been neglected.

Meanwhile, the highly touted American doll, tiny Cathy Rigby, finished far back in 10th place. She turned pro to tour as "Peter Pan," after marrying football star Tommy Mason.

Russian and West German teams dominated cycling, though a Frenchman, Daniel Morelon, won his second straight gold medal in sprints. Handball was introduced as the latest Olympic sport, and Yugoslavia won. Poland dethroned Hungary's two straight titlists in soccer.

West Germany became the first country other than India or Pakistan ever to win in field hockey. Russians and East Germans dominated canoeing and rowing, but it was New Zealand that won the eight-oared crew crown that most often went to the United States.

The United States was saddest of all at its first-ever loss in basketball. Russians have been catching up in this sport, and the refusal of top American collegians, including Bill Walton, to represent their country in this competition in recent Olympiads has brought the United States back to the pack. Still, it took an extremely controversial ruling by the officials for the Russians to win.

The American team trailed most of the way, but caught up near the finish of the championship game. Jim Forbes hit a jump-shot to bring the United States within 49-48 with 38 seconds to play. Then Jimmy Collins grabbed a bad Russian pass and was fouled as he drove for the basket with 3 seconds to play. He was awarded two free throws and sank both to put the United States team ahead 50-49. The Americans in the roaring crowd were cheering what seemed a certain triumph.

Sapporo and Munich, 1972

The Soviets passed the ball in to midcourt, but their coach was given a time-out with one second showing on the clock. He protested that his request for time should have been granted before the ball was thrown in. Officials upheld the protest and 2 seconds were restored to the time. The Soviets threw the ball in, shot, missed, and time ran out. The buzzer sounded and the Americans jumped for joy as their countrymen flooded the floor.

However, an argument ensued and officials declared the game had been restarted prematurely. The Soviets had their 3 seconds once again. United States coach Hank Iba protested to no avail. The court was cleared. Given yet another chance, the Russians tossed the ball in to their towering center beneath the basket. He threw aside defenders as he dropped the ball in at the buzzer, Russia winning 51-50.

The controversy carried over into the night, but the Soviet team got the gold medal, while the United States team refused the silver.

Swimming and diving was something else. Americans dominated this, though the star among the women was Shane Gould, a big fifteen-year-old from Australia, who won three events in world record time. Still, she was rated a disappointment because she had not lost a race in 18 months and was expected to win five in Munich, but she lost two.

"The pressure almost tears you apart," she sighed. "If I didn't do what some expected of me, I'm proud of what I did do."

As usual, American girls did well in the water. Keena Rothammer, just fifteen, outswam Shane in one race, while Sandy Neilson, sixteen, outswam Shane in another. Cathy Carr won one race, Karen Moe another, and Melissa Belote won two. Shirley Babashoff won silver medals in two races. Additional gold medals were won by Americans in two relays. Neilson, Babashoff, Jane Barkman, and Jennifer Kemp teamed to win one relay, while Neilson, Carr, Belote, and Deena Deardruff teamed to win the other.

A dramatic American winner was Maxine "Micki" King, an air force officer and the first female administrator and coach at the Air Force Academy. A former University of Michigan competitor, she went into service so she could support herself while pursuing her passion for diving.

She was leading in the springboard event in 1964 in Mexico City when she cracked her arm on the board during her next-to-last dive. Despite severe pain, she executed her last dive, but did not do well and fell from first to fourth place, failing to win any medal at all. Then she was examined and was found to have broken her arm.

Disappointed, she retired for a year, then she returned to competition. In 1972 in Munich at the advanced age of twenty-nine she was magnificent, performing spectacularly her twists and spins to gain the gold. "It was worth the wait," she sighed later.

The men's springboard honors escaped America for the first time since 1912, as the Russian Vladimir Vasin prevailed. An Italian, Klaus Dibiasi, won the platform event to give Europe a sweep of the dives. An East German, Roland Matthes, won both backstroke events. A Swede, Gunnar Larsson, won both four-stroke medley events. Nobutaka Tagushi of Japan won a breaststroke event. Otherwise, Americans won all the rest. Mark Spitz won most of them. John Hencken won one. Mike Burton won another. Rick DeMont won still another, but was disqualified for having used a medical drug. Spitz was the star of the Munich Olympics. No Olympic star ever shone more brightly.

Mark Spitz was born on February 10, 1950, in Modesto, California, the first child of Lenore and Arnold Spitz. Sisters followed. Mark was two when the family moved to Honolulu. They lived there four years, during which time Mark learned to swim. He loved the ocean more than anything else and begged his mother to take him to swim in the surf almost every day. When the family returned to the mainland, settling in Sacramento, Mark's father enrolled him in a YMCA swimming program.

Soon Mark was setting records for his age group. Recognizing his son's potential, Arnold Spitz took Mark to the Arden Hills Swim Club, where Sherm Chavoor presided over a fabulous facility. Chavoor, who coached Debbie Meyer and many other champions, saw that he had a coming champ in Spitz and took him in hand.

Mark Spitz had the perfect physique for a swimmer—he was fairly tall and slender, he had broad shoulders and slim hips, exceptionally long arms and large hands, and unusually flexible legs. Chavoor worked with Mark on both his butterfly and freestyle strokes and got them synchronized with his leg and kicking action. He pushed the lad hard and developed his stamina.

Arnold Spitz pushed his son, too. He used to tell him, "Remember, swimming isn't everything; winning is." As Mark began to win, he became cocky. No one close to his age could come close to him. He worked hard, but he didn't like to work. He rebelled at Chavoor's tough tactics and complained to his father. Arnold moved his family to Walnut Creek and put his son in the Santa Clara Swimming Club under the coaching of George Haines.

That was when Haines's prize pupil, Don Schollander, won four gold medals at Tokyo. Spitz credits Haines with truly polishing his strokes and techniques. Haines helped him become a complete swimmer, the most touted young prospect in the country. But the rebellious, sometimes sullen Spitz wanted everything his own way, bristled under his new coach's disciplined system, broke with him, too, and returned to the Arden Hills Club and Chavoor. Spitz predicted he would accomplish more than Haines's top product, Schollander, ever had done. He very much wanted to show Haines he could surpass Schollander.

By 1968 Spitz had won a host of national championships and international tests, surpassed a score of world records, and was recognized as probably the best swimmer in the world. He qualified for the Olympics in Mexico City in three individual and three relay races and openly predicted he would sweep all six to top Schollander and all other swimmers and Olympic athletes of all history. He was arrogant and alienated the other swimmers. Schollander was swimming there in just two events, concluding his career. He was no longer what he had been, but he was "one of the boys," while Spitz was alone in his arrogance, a loner. Nastily, as kids will, and they were mostly just kids, they called the Jewish Spitz anti-Semitic names.

Angered, Spitz wanted to push records in their face. He tried hard, maybe too hard. He lost his looseness and tightened up. His relaxed rhythm disappeared. He was the best, but he was not at his best. He was not prepared properly. Others had worked harder and were ready to give the most they had here when it meant the most. Spitz finished second in one race, third in another, dead last in the third. He got gold medals in all three of his relays, but the others could kid him that they had carried him. While they had won individual races, he had not won a one. He was humiliated, it not humbled. He left Mexico deeply disappointed, but more determined than ever. Now he would do anything to win.

He had been offered many scholarships to colleges and decided to take one he had been reluctant to accept. He went to Indiana University, which consistently recruited and developed the top collegiate swimming team in the country but which also had the toughest coach, Dr. James (Doc) Counsilman. Doc's definition of swimming was "hurt, pain, and agony." He said, "The only way to win is to work until you can't be beat." He got the best and made them better. But he also was something of a psychologist. He befriended Mark and asked his swimmers to befriend him. He took them aside and told them, "Forget any feelings you may have had about Mark in the past. That was yesterday. This is today and today we start fresh."

Burning for revenge, swimming while studying to be a dentist, Mark worked harder than any of them, and he became one of them. In time, they even elected him captain of their talented team as they extended a long string of dual meet victories and national titles. He won five gold medals in swimming at the Pan-Am Games in Winnipeg as he peaked.

By the time of the new Olympiad in Munich, Mark Spitz was twenty-two and much more mature than he had been in Mexico. He had at one time or another surpassed 28 world records in his two strokes and had qualified for no fewer than four individual and three relay races in Germany. He did not now nor did anyone else predict he would sweep all his races. If possible, it was not probable. The pressure on him would be enormous. Other outstanding swimmers were close to him in some events. He could be less than physically fit, he could have a bad day, he certainly could tire. But he was the best and he knew it and now he wanted to prove it.

He was still an egotist and something of a loner. He had grown into a handsome man, who looked a lot like the movie star Omar Sharif. Where others shaved the hair off their bodies and even their heads to increase their speed, Mark had grown a full mustache and let his hair grow long. Still something of a loner among the other lads, he preferred the company of the ladies and dated different girl swimmers in Munich. He said he wanted to be "the Joe Namath of swimming," but he was not quite as abrasive as he'd been in his younger years. And he was better prepared psychologically and physically for the Olympic ordeal.

"I remember what happened in Mexico City," he said as he went into his first event, the 200-meter butterfly. He breasted through the water brilliantly and won by more than two seconds in world record time. Observed U.S. swimming coach Peter Daland, "If Mark had lost his first race, he'd have remembered Mexico too much and might have become discouraged. I think he'll be all right now." Confirmed Mark, "I feel like this is going to be just fine, now." Later that night, he anchored teammates Dave Edgar, John Murphy, and Jerry Heidenreich to triumph in the 400-meter freestyle relay in world record time.

The next night, Spitz swam the 200-meter freestyle, and his toughest foe was teammate Steve Genter. Earlier, when he heard Genter had been taken to the hospital with a collapsed lung, Spitz had said, "Well, at least now I don't have to worry about him." But he did. While others resented what seemed to them a wisecrack in the worst taste, Genter got out of his sick bed to swim magnificently. He led Spitz through the first three turns of the four-lap event. But Spitz sped through the final 50 meters with a furious surge to catch and conquer the tiring Genter by almost a second in still another world record. It was, as it turned out, his toughest test.

Two days later, Spitz splashed to triumph in the 100-meter butterfly by more than a second in yet another world record. Later, he anchored John Kinsella, Fred Tyler, and Genter to victory in the 800-meter freestyle relay to set another world mark. By then he had tied the all-time record of five gold medals in a single Olympiad won by Italian fencer Nedo Nadi at Antwerp in 1920. He had surpassed Schollander and Debbie Meyer and Johnny Weissmuller. He was acclaimed across the world, for the moment the greatest international television star, sought for interviews by thousands of writers and broadcasters, besieged by fans wherever he went. "Hey, it's great," he grinned, "but it's getting a little heavy. I got two races to go."

The 6-foot, 170-pound young man suddenly was a sports superstar who at this time made the top pros pale by comparison. He had done what he wanted to do, and now he wanted to get the rest over with so he could start to enjoy the rest of his life. He admitted, "All of a sudden I was tired of swimming. I never really wanted to be the best swimmer. I just wanted to be the best something. Now I'm that and I want to be the best something else." It turned out, he no longer wanted to be a dentist, he wanted to be a movie star.

With the world watching, he went into his final two races. In the 100-meter freestyle final, teammate Heidenrich pushed him almost to a point of collapse, came close to upsetting him, but could not keep up with him as Spitz splashed powerfully through the stretch to touch with less than half a second to spare. Another world record? Of course. And then a tired but stimulated Spitz went back to the butterfly to help Heidenreich, breaststroker Tom Bruce, and backstroker Mike Stamm win the 400-meter medley relay. The time, once again, was a world record. "All the way the last lap all I could think of was that in a few more strokes it finally would be all over," Mark Spitz sighed.

It was. World records had fallen in all of his races, and as he posed for photographs with the seven gold medals, unequaled by any athlete of the past, draped around his neck, a great grin spread over his handsome face. "God loves a winner," his father said proudly. If not well loved by his fellow swimmers, Mark Spitz now was enormously respected. He had conquered charges he "choked" in the clutch, had worked hard with dedication to prepare himself for revenge, and bounced back to put on a performance unsurpassed in sports history. The Olympics had beaten him. Now he had beaten them. Now he would retire, turn professional, cut television commercials, endorse products, begin to make money, and attempt to act.

He went home before the Games concluded with their traditional and colorful closing ceremonies. He was the star of stars, but he also was a Jew, and there was fear for his safety here where anti-Semitic terrorists had struck. It was ironic that here in Germany, where the American black Jesse Owens had outraged Hitler's Nazi philosophy of Aryan supremacy in an earlier Olympiad, an American Jew now shone as the star of stars amidst reminders of racial and religious persecutions in these still-troubled times. Sometimes, however, the stars of sports can illuminate the darkest of days, relieve the worst of tensions, and show anew the strength of the human spirit.

15
INNSBRUCK AND MONTREAL, 1976
Stars to Be Born

THE INTERNATIONAL OLYMPIC Committee preferred not to play politics when countries of opposing philosophies, the United States and the Soviet Union, bid for the 1976 Summer Olympics. Canada became the compromise choice for the Olympiad. Montreal has mounted a massive effort to prepare its 330-year-old city for the celebration of these ancient Games, including construction of a new 70,000-seat stadium. Moscow will get the Games, as will Los Angeles, but for the moment it is Montreal's turn, as the athletes return to North America for the 21st Olympics.

Meanwhile, Denver was awarded the Winter Olympics for 1976, but citizens of the Colorado city voted against the sort of expense and physical alteration necessary to stage the Games, so they were shifted to Innsbruck in Austria, where the 1964 Games were conducted. Ever since the end of the last Olympics in Japan and Germany in 1972, journalists have been preparing to cover the new contests, television interests have been planning the most extensive sports coverage of any event yet, and fans have been making applications and reservations for travel and housing accommodations and tickets to the hundreds of events in both the winter and summer spectacles.

And of course, above all, the athletes have been practicing, competing, preparing themselves for their efforts to qualify for their national teams and the Olympic competition itself. Four years seems a long time, especially to young people, and the average athlete in the Olympics is in the middle twenties, but this time between Games seems to fly. Will there be another Mark Spitz or

Debbie Meyer in 1976? Another Bill Toomey or Wilma Rudolph? Another Jesse Owens or Babe Didrickson? Another Johnny Weissmuller or Sonja Henie? Another Paavo Nurmi or Emil Zatopek? Another George Foreman? Another Peggy Fleming or Dick Button? Can Olga Korbut gain the gold that eluded her the last time? Will Frank Shorter return to win again?

Let's look briefly at some who may win medals in Montreal:

Marty Liquori: America's ranking runner and a contender to bring the gold medal back from the glamorous metric mile in Munich before he hurt his heel, Liquori says, "Americans haven't had much luck at 1,500 meters in the Olympics and it has become a sort of an obsession with us. Our greatest milers right through to Jim Ryun have failed in the Olympics. Although I always wanted to beat Jim, I felt terrible when he fell in Munich, but no one ever will know if he would have won anyway. And I don't know what's worse, having it over with in seconds or having to wonder and worry for months and years. I was tempted to turn pro, but I kept thinking I should hang on to try for one more Olympics. I'll be twenty-six. I don't know if I'll make it back to my best form. I don't know if I'll make it to Montreal. If I do, I don't know if I'll win. Others have run faster, but when I'm right, I don't run for records, I run to win, and if I'm right, I'll have a chance. It's a dream, anyway. The Olympics are a dream."

Tony Waldrop: As Montreal's Olympics approached, Waldrop suddenly became the hottest runner in the country, running a string of miles below four minutes, running the fastest miles since Ryun ran records. The blond North Carolinian will be twenty-four in 1976, but he says he's not even sure he'll try for the Montreal Olympics. He says, "Everyone has different goals. Mine isn't to get a gold medal. I run because I like it. I tried to make the Munich Olympics and didn't like it. I missed out, but it wasn't that, it was the terrible pressure I hated. I wasn't mature and I wasn't ready. I'm much more ready now, but I don't need the spotlight and I sure don't need the pressure, so right now I'm not aiming for Montreal."

Filbert Bayi: The latest African sensation, the twenty-year-old member of the Tanzanian Air Force ran 1,500 meters in 3:32.2 at the British Commonwealth Games in Christchurch, New Zealand, in 1974 to shatter Jim Ryun's world record of 3:33.1. Bayi's run, 120 yards short of a mile, was comparable to a world record 3:50 mile. Through a translator, he observed, "African countries take pride in the performance of their great athletes in recent years, and it is a natural goal for me to want to follow Kipchoge Keino of Kenya and others in seeking Olympic success. We run not alone for ourselves, but also for our nations and I would dearly like to bring the gold medal home. However, the metric mile is a famous event that draws great competitors and so nothing can be certain."

Emiel Puttemans: The tiny Belgian towers above other distance runners of the world at the moment, but like his predecessor at the top, Australia's Ron Clarke, Olympic gold has eluded him. He has six world records, but only a single silver medal to show for two prior Olympiads. He says, "Great runners return to try for Olympic laurels, but unknown runners at every distance arrive suddenly every Olympic year and you never know what will happen. You can't count on Olympic success no matter how outstanding your record. An Olympic race is one day, one hour. You can't compare it to a lifetime's accomplishments. You can't let defeat on one day in four years frustrate you. If I make it to Montreal, I will give it my best. I will be in my late twenties and may be at my peak. But it has to be only one thing to look forward to in life. It is nothing to stake your life on."

Steve Prefontaine: A cocky, colorful, capable young athlete, Prefontaine has inspired an almost fanatical following around Oregon and is a rare American who may triumph in an Olympic long-distance race. He ran a marvelous race at 5,000 meters in Munich, finishing fourth, barely beaten out for a medal, but at twenty-five will be just approaching his prime in 1976. He admits, "I'm aiming for Montreal. I was tempted by pro offers, but I couldn't give up on the Olympics without giving it my best shot. The gold medal may not be worth much in money, but it's symbolic of what we suffer for. I'm considered cocky, but if you don't think you're the best, you'll never be the best. I've beaten the best in America, but I won't be satisfied until I beat the world. Maybe I will in Montreal."

Dan Gable: The brilliant wrestler from America's Midwest says, "Sometimes people seem to think the Olympics is track and field. And maybe swimming. Or, in the winter, figure skating. It is a lot more. It is a lot of athletes in a lot of different sports. My gold medal means as much to me as a sprinter's means to him. There are a lot of wrestlers and weight lifters and volleyball players, a lot of skiers and gymnasts and field hockey players who sacrifice a lot of their lives and work very hard and suffer a lot to get good at what they do, and maybe they don't get much out of it, maybe not any publicity even in an Olympic year, no attention, no money, no fancy offers, probably not even a medal. They are really what the Olympics is all about. And if I continued to compete as an amateur it would not be for fame, but for a sense of accomplishment, which is why we do what we do when no one much seems to care."

Terry Kubicka: The most brilliant figure-skating prospect to come along in this country in years, this agile lad from Orange County, California, is extremely young, but extremely promising and a long shot for laurels in Innsbruck. He says: "You have to have goals. A gold medal is as good a one as any. I don't know if I can be ready for the Winter Games in Austria, but I sure can try. Some win Olympic medals when they are very young, and some when they are very old. There're a lot of skaters and skiers working hard right now who will be working even harder as 1976 comes closer."

Kubicka skates two hours to six in the morning, two hours after school to three in the afternoon, then two hours to seven at night at Westbrook Ice Arena, which provides facilities for an "army" of figure-skating hopefuls more readily than most rinks, though the youngsters must pay for the use of the surface, plus $25 an hour or more for instruction. He got hooked on skating after seeing the Ice Follies eight years ago and hopes, himself, to skate in shows later. He has had an amazing record and at eighteen finished second in the senior men's national championships in 1974. He says, "I am used to finishing first, but I am moving up among older and more experienced skaters now and have to put in hard work to get to the top." The Winter Olympics in Montreal in 1976 represents the peak, of course.

Mary Decker: Another outstanding young athlete from Orange County, this little lady of less than 100 pounds was developed in the Blue Angels Track Club in Garden Grove, was breaking records at the age of fourteen, and may be the world record holder in the metric half-mile by the time she is seventeen and the Montreal Games arrive. She says: "I'm young, but I'm getting experience early. Beating the Russians in Moscow boosted my confidence. I'm attracting a lot of attention and I'm not at all comfortable with that, but I like to run so I'm aiming at the Olympics. I may run track, but I'm a typical teen-ager. I ride bikes and swim and sew just like any normal girl. I have something I do better than most, maybe, so I want to take advantage of it and I put a lot of time and effort into it. I'm aiming for Montreal, sure."

Francie Larrieu: Winner of three events in the new women's NCAA track championships, this brilliant distance runner from UCLA observes: "Women's track in this country is so far behind the times that I have to work out with the men to bring out the best in myself. Only occasionally does a girl like Mary Decker come along and then she gets almost all the publicity given to women in this sport because she's so young. She's treated like a novelty, as if she was a cute little mechanical doll, not a great runner. Well, you earn an Olympic gold medal and if she gets one, she'll earn hers, and if I get one I'll earn mine. I'll be twenty-three, so I'm not exactly an old lady, even if I'm not a teen-ager any more. They're having a metric mile for women in Montreal, and I want to win it. I'd like them to have a 3,000-meter race I could run in 1980. Women can do anything men can do. It's a matter of being equally dedicated and working as hard. I'm dedicated and I work hard, and I'm aiming for the Olympics because it's an opportunity to get something out of all I've put into this. My brother Ron was in the 1964 Olympics at 10,000 meters. He didn't do well, so no one remembers. I expect to do well in my race."

Rick Wohluter: Disappointed in the Munich Olympics, Wohluter rebounded to run the fastest half-miles in history in preparation for the Montreal competition. A Chicagoan who practices with runs around Lake Michigan, he says, "Like Jim Ryun, I tripped and fell in the trials at Munich. Ryun felt he had run out of chances, but I feel I have to give myself another one. Setting world records is thrilling, but secondary to winning, and winning the Olympics is first above all things in track. I work in insurance as a claims adjustor. And I run. And my main aim in life now is the gold medal I missed in Munich."

Ivory Crockett: Early in 1974 this Tennessee sprinter became the first man to run 100 yards in nine seconds flat. The new world record holder observed, "I've had an up-and-down career. I'm up now and I hope the lift will carry me right through to an Olympic gold medal. I'll be twenty-six in 1976, which is supposed to be old for a sprinter, but I may have matured late. I think I can do 8.9, and maybe in Montreal. Hey, wouldn't that be something!"

Steve Williams: This tall, lean lad from San Diego had emerged as the "world's fastest human" until Crockett rocketed to a world record. He sighed and said, "Just when you think you've gotten to the top, a cat like this Crockett shoves you off. But setting a record one night is one thing and winning the big race on the big day is another. I was injured in 1972 and it was a big, big disappointment when I missed the trip to Munich. I hope to make it to Montreal and if I'm fit the gold medal will fit just fine."

George Woods: A controversial measurement left him a fraction of an inch short of the gold medal in the shot put in Munich. The 6 foot 290-pounder says, "I proved to myself I was the best, even if I didn't get the gold. But I still have to prove it to the world. Which is why I haven't turned pro. I'll be thirty-three by 1976, but I expect to be in Montreal. I may have lost speed, but added strength and improved my technique. The tough thing is to keep going. At my age I found myself working 40 hours to support my family and get a master's degree. It's tough to take the time to train. But I set myself a goal early and I owe it to myself to try one more time to reach it."

Al Feuerbach: The 6-foot-1, 245-pounder is considered small for a shot putter, but he is superb and he, Woods, and Randy Matson are the only 70-footers ever. He says, "Just when I had become the best in the world, Woods comes along to threaten me. We swap the world record back and forth. And then someone else wins the Olympics. I finished fifth and that wasn't good enough. I had a bad day. But, better days are ahead. I'm dedicated to it. The hard thing to realize is you can be great and have a great day, and a guy like George can be greater on that given day. But if you want to be the best, you've got to do it when it means the most. That means Montreal."

Rick DeMont: An asthmatic, this strong, swift northern Californian won the 400-meter freestyle swimming race in Munich and was favored to win the 1,500, in which he held the world record, when he was informed he was disqualified, had to return his gold medal for the first race and could not compete in the second. A postrace test had revealed that ephedrine was in his system when he won, and that was regarded as an illegal drug. DeMont and his coach were suprised because the ingredient had been prescribed by a doctor as part of the swimmer's asthma medication and listed on his Olympic entry blank. He was sixteen at the time, and he is trying not to be bitter.

He says: "I've tried to forget the incident. Every day it gets further away. I don't think Olympic officials always are fair. The thing that bothered me most was that many assumed I was a dope addict or some such thing. This particular drug makes you drowsy and sure doesn't speed up a swimmer. Anyway, I'm going on. I've started college, I'm continuing to compete and I'm improving. I'll be twenty in 1976 and there always are a lot of outstanding swimmers coming to the top young, but I'm hoping I can make the team to Montreal and do well there. I'm not the first guy who didn't get a gold medal, but I'm one of the few who won and still lost. I have a lot to make up for."

Ray Charles "Sugar" Leonard: Named for the brilliant black jazz singer, but nicknamed for the former ring great, "Sugar Ray" Robinson, "Sugar Ray" Leonard from Palmer Park, Maryland, is regarded as the most exciting boxer-puncher to emerge in amateur ring ranks in a decade. Winner of the National AAU welterweight title in 1974, he admitted he was trying to resist lucrative pro offers so he could go for an Olympic crown at the age of 20. "I started boxing with my brother in my backyard, then took up the sport serious at our local rec center down the street," he says. "Pro dough is tempting, but I'm taking the advice of my coach, Jerry Jacobs, and looking for a gold medal. If it was good enough for Muhammad Ali, it's good enough for me. I guess it's a good way to go."

Dwight Stones: After Pat Matzdorf topped 7 feet 6¼ inches in 1971, Dwight Stones came along to raise the record in the high jump by three-eighths of an inch. An injury ruined Matzdorf's 1972 Olympic hopes, but Stones at nineteen became the youngest medalist in track and field, finishing third, and in 1976 he expects to finish first. "I'm called cocky, but I prefer to be considered supremely self-confident," smiles the tall, lanky, southern Californian, who uses the "Fosbury Flop."

"Someone will jump 8 feet some day and I don't see why it can't be me. And someone will win the gold medal in Montreal and I expect it to be me. There's a lot that's wrong with the Olympics, but there's a lot that's wrong in life, too. The thing to do is to make the best of things and try to make them better."

He sighs and says, "I'm not a conventional sort of character. I do things my way. I'm a rebel. But I do want at least one thing a lot of other athletes want, and that's to win in the Olympics. Hey, they put your name in the book and it lasts like for eternity." Smiling, but serious, he concludes, "The beautiful thing about being a star in the Olympics is that it endures forever."

OLYMPICS GAMES SUMMARIES

SUMMER SITES

1896	Athens		1932	Los Angeles
1900	Paris		1936	Berlin
1904	St. Louis		1948	London
1906	Athens		1952	Helsinki
1908	London		1956	Melbourne
1912	Stockholm		1960	Rome
1920	Antwerp		1964	Tokyo
1924	Paris		1968	Mexico City
1928	Amsterdam		1972	Munich

MEN'S TRACK AND FIELD WINNERS

100-METER DASH — Sec.
1896	Tom Burke, United States	12.0
1900	Frank Jarvis, United States	10.8
1904	Archie Hahn, United States	11.0
1908	Reg Walker, South Africa	10.8
1912	Ralph Craig, United States	10.8
1920	Charlie Paddock, United States	10.8
1924	H.M. Abrahams, Great Britain	10.6
1928	Percy Williams, Canada	10.8
1932	Eddie Tolan, United States	10.3
1936	Jesse Owens, United States	10.3
1948	Harrison Dillard, United States	10.3
1952	Lindy Remigino, United States	10.4
1956	Bobby Morrow, United States	10.5
1960	Armin Hary, Germany	10.2
1964	Bob Hayes, United States	10.0
1968	Jim Hines, United States	9.9
1972	Valery Borzov, USSR	10.1

200-METER DASH — Sec.
1900	J W. Tewksbury, United States	22.2
1904	Archie Hahn, United States	21.6
1908	Bob Kerr, Canada	22.6
1912	Ralph Craig, United States	21.7
1920	Allan Woodring, United States	22.0
1924	Jackson Scholz, United States	21.6
1928	Percy Williams, Canada	21.8
1932	Eddie Tolan, United States	21.2
1936	Jesse Owens, United States	20.7
1948	Mel Patton, United States	21.1
1952	Andy Stanfield, United States	20.7
1956	Bobby Morrow, United States	20.6
1960	Livio Berutti, Italy	20.5
1964	Henry Carr, United States	20.3
1968	Tommie Smith, United States	19.8
1972	Valery Borzov, USSR	20.0

400-METER DASH — Sec.
1896	Thomas Burke, United States	54.2
1900	Maxey Long, United States	49.4
1904	Harry Hillman, United States	49.2
1908	Wyndham Halswelle, Great Britain	50.0
1912	Charles Reidpath, United States	48.2
1920	Bevil Rudd, South Africa	49.6
1924	Eric Liddell, Great Britain	47.6
1928	Ray Barbuti, United States	47.8
1932	William Carr, United States	46.2
1936	Archie Williams, United States	46.5
1948	Arthur Wint, Jamaica	46.2
1952	George Rhoden, Jamaica	45.9
1956	Charles Jenkins, United States	46.7
1960	Otis Davis, United States	44.9
1964	Mike Larrabee, United States	45.1
1968	Lee Evans, United States	43.8
1972	Vince Matthews, United States	44.1

800-METER RUN — Min./Sec.
1896	Edwin Flack, Great Britain	2:11.0
1900	Alfred Tysoe, Great Britain	2:10.4
1904	James Lightbody, United States	1:56.0
1908	Melvin Sheppard, United States	1:52.8
1912	James Meredith, United States	1:51.9
1920	Albert Hill, Great Britain	1:53.4
1924	Douglas Lowe, Great Britain	1:52.4
1928	Douglas Lowe, Great Britain	1:51.8
1932	Thompson Hampson, Great Britain	1:49.8

1936	John Woodruff, United States	1:52.9
1948	Mal Whitfield, United States	1:49.2
1952	Mal Whitfield, United States	1:49.2
1956	Thomas Courtney, United States	1:47.7
1960	Peter Snell, New Zealand	1:46.3
1964	Peter Snell, New Zealand	1:45.1
1968	Ralph Doubell, Australia	1:44.3
1972	Dave Wottle, United States	1:45.9

1,500-METER RUN — *Min./Sec.*

1896	Edwin Flack, Great Britain	4:33.2
1900	Charles Bennett, Great Britain	4:06.2
1904	James Lightbody, United States	4:05.4
1908	Melvin Sheppard, United States	4:03.4
1912	Arnold Jackson, Great Britain	3:56.8
1920	Albert Hill, Great Britain	4:01.8
1924	Paavo Nurmi, Finland	3:53.6
1928	Harry Larva, Finland	3:53.2
1932	Luigi Beccali, Italy	3:51.2
1948	Henry Ericksson, Sweden	3:49.8
1952	Joseph Barthel, Luxembourg	3:45.2
1956	Ron Delany, Ireland	3:41.2
1960	Herb Elliott, Australia	3:35.6
1964	Peter Snell, New Zealand	3:38.1
1968	Kip Keino, Kenya	3:34.9
1972	Pekka Vasala, Finland	3:36.3

5,000-METER RUN — *Min./Sec.*

1912	Hannes Kolehmainen, Finland	14:36.6
1920	Joseph Guillemot, France	14:55.6
1924	Paavo Nurmi, Finland	14:31.2
1928	Willie Ritola, Finland	14:38.0
1932	Lauri Lehtinen, Finland	14:30.0
1936	Gunnar Hockert, Finland	14:22.2
1948	Gaston Reiff, Belgium	14:17.6
1952	Emil Zatopek, Czechoslovakia	14:06.6
1956	Vladimir Kuts, USSR	13:39.6
1960	Murray Halberg, New Zealand	13:43.4
1964	Bob Schul, United States	13:48.8
1968	Mohamed Gammoudi, Tunisia	14:00.0
1972	Lasse Viren, Finland	13:26.4

10,000-METER RUN — *Min./Sec.*

1912	Hannes Kolehmainen, Finland	31:20.8
1920	Paavo Nurmi, Finland	31:45.8
1924	Willie Ritola, Finland	30:23.2
1928	Paavo Nurmi, Finland	30:18.8
1932	Janusz Kusocinski, Poland	30:11.4
1948	Emil Zatopek, Czechoslovakia	29:59.6
1952	Emil Zatopek, Czechoslovakia	29:17.0
1956	Vladimir Kuts, USSR	28:45.6
1960	Petr Bolotnikov, USSR	28:32.2
1964	Billy Mills, United States	28:24.4
1968	Naftali Temu, Kenya	29:27.4
1972	Lasse Viren, Finland	27:38.4

MARATHON — *Hr./Min./Sec.*

1896	Spiros Loues, Greece	2:55:20.0
1900	Michael Teato, France	2:59:00.0
1904	Tom Hicks, United States	3:28:53.0
1908	John Hayes, United States	2:55:18.4
1912	Ken MacArthur, South Africa	2:36:54.8
1920	Hannes Kolehmainen, Finland	2:32:35.8
1924	Albin Stenroos, Finland	2:41:22.6
1928	El Ouafi, France	2:32:57.0
1932	Juan Zabala, Argentina	2:31:36.0
1936	Kitei Son, Japan	2:29:19.2
1948	Dolf Cabrera, Argentina	2:34:51.6
1952	Emil Zatopek, Czechoslovakia	2:23:03.2
1956	Alain Mimoun, France	2:25:00.0
1960	Abebe Bikila, Ethiopia	2:15:15.2
1964	Abebe Bikila, Ethiopia	2:12:11.2
1968	Mamo Wolde, Ethiopia	2:20:26.4
1972	Frank Shorter, United States	2:12:19.8

110-METER HIGH HURDLES — *Sec.*

1896	Thomas Curtis, United States	17.6
1900	Alvin Kraenzlein, United States	15.4
1904	Frederick Schule, United States	16.0
1908	Forrest Smithson, United States	15.0
1912	Frederick Kelley, United States	15.1
1920	Earl Thomson, Canada	14.8
1924	Daniel Kinsey, United States	15.0
1928	Sydney Atkinson, South Africa	14.8
1932	George Saling, United States	14.6
1936	Forrest Towns, United States	14.2
1948	William Porter, United States	13.9
1952	Harrison Dillard, United States	13.7
1956	Lee Calhoun, United States	13.5
1960	Lee Calhoun, United States	13.8
1964	Hayes Jones, United States	13.6
1968	Willie Davenport, United States	13.3
1972	Rod Milburn, United States	13.2

400-METER LOW HURDLES — *Sec.*

1900	John Tewksbury, United States	57.6
1904	Harry Hillman, United States	53.0
1908	Charles Bacon, United States	55.0
1920	Frank Loomis, United States	54.0
1924	F. Morgan Taylor, United States	52.6
1928	Lord David Burghley, Great Britain	53.4
1932	Robert Tisdall, Ireland	51.8
1936	Glenn Hardin, United States	52.4
1948	Roy Cochran, United States	51.1
1952	Charles Moore, United States	50.8
1956	Glenn Davis, United States	50.1
1960	Glenn Davis, United States	49.3
1964	Rex Cawley, United States	49.6
1968	Dave Hemery, Great Britain	48.1
1972	John Akii-Bua, Uganda	47.8

3,000-METER STEEPLECHASE — *Min./Sec.*

1920	Percy Hodge, Great Britain	10:00.4
1924	Willie Ritola, Finland	9:33.6
1928	Toivo Loukola, Finland	9:21.8
1932	Volmari Iso-Hollo, Finland	10:33.4
	(3,460-meters—extra lap run by error)	
1936	Volmari Iso-Hollo, Finland	9:03.8
1948	Thore Sjostrand, Sweden	9:04.6
1952	Horace Ashenfelter, United States	8:45.4
1956	Chris Brasher, Great Britain	8:41.2

1960	Zdzislaw Krzyszkowiak, Poland	8:34.2
1964	Gaston Roelants, Belgium	8:30.8
1968	Amos Biwott, Kenya	8:51.0
1972	Kip Keino, Kenya	8:23.6

20,000-METER WALK		*Hr./Min./Sec.*
1956	Leonid Spirine, USSR	1:31:27.0
1960	Vladimir Golubnichy, USSR	1:34:07.2
1964	Ken Matthews, Great Britain	1:29:34.0
1968	Vladimir Golubnichy, USSR	1:33:58.4
1972	Peter Frenkel, East Germany	1:26:42.4

50,000-METER WALK		*Hr./Min./Sec.*
1932	Thomas Green, Great Britain	4:50:10.0
1936	Harold Whitlock, Great Britain	4:30:41.4
1948	John Ljunggren, Sweden	4:41:52.0
1952	Guiseppe Dordoni, Italy	4:28:07.8
1956	Norman Read, New Zealand	4:30:42.8
1960	Donald Thompson, Great Britain	4:25:30.0
1964	Abdon Pamich, Italy	4:11:12.4
1968	Chris Hohne, East Germany	4:20:13.6
1972	Bernd Kannenberg, West Germany	3:56:11.0

400-METER RELAY		*Sec.*
1912	Great Britain (Jacobs, Macintosh, d'Arcy, Applegarth)	42.4
1920	United States (Charles Paddock, Jackson Scholz, Morris Kirksey, Loren Murchison)	42.2
1924	United States (Louis Clarke, Francis Hussey, Loren Murchison, Alfred Leconey)	41.0
1928	United States (Frank Wycoff, James Quinn, Charles Borah, Henry Russell)	41.0
1932	United States (Robert Kiesel, Emmett Toppino, Hector Dyer, Frank Wykoff)	40.0
1936	United States (Jesse Owens, Ralph Metcalfe, Foy Draper, Frank Wykoff)	39.8
1948	United States (Barney Ewell, Lorenzo Wright, Harrison Dillard, Mel Patton)	40.3
1952	United States (Dean Smith, Harrison Dillard, Lindy Remigino, Andy Stanfield)	40.1
1956	United States (Ira Murchison, Leamon King, Thane Baker, Bobby Morrow)	39.5
1964	United States (Paul Drayton, Garry Ashworth, Dick Stebbins, Bob Hayes)	39.0
1968	United States (Charlie Green, Mel Pender, Ronnie Smith, Jim Hines)	38.2
1972	United States (Larry Black, Robert Taylor, Gerald Tinker, Ed Hart)	38.2

1,600-METER RELAY		*Min./Sec.*
1912	United States (Mel Sheppard, Frank Lindberg, James Meredith, Charles D. Reidpath)	3:16.6
1920	Great Britain (Robert Lindsay, Guy Butler, John Ainsworth, Cecil Griffiths)	3:22.2
1924	United States (Charles Cochran, Bill Stevenson, James McDonald, Allen Helffrich)	3:16.0
1928	United States (George Baird, Fred Alderman, Emerson Spencer, Ray Barbuti)	3:14.2
1932	United States (Ivan Fuqua, Edgar Ablowich, Karl Warner, William Carr)	3:08.2
1936	Great Britain (Frederick Wolff, Godfrey Rampling, William Roberts, Arthur Brown)	3:09.0
1948	United States (Cliff Bourland, Art Harnden, Roy Cochran, Mal Whitfield)	3:10.4
1952	Jamaica (Herbert McKenley, Leslie Laing, Arthur Wint, George Rhoden)	3:03.9
1956	United States (Charley Jenkins, Lou Jones, Jesse Mashburn, Tom Courtney)	3:04.8
1960	United States (Jack Yerman, Earl Young, Glenn Davis, Otis Davis)	3:02.2
1964	United States (Ollan Cassell, Mike Larrabee, Ulis Williams, Henry Carr)	3:00.7
1968	United States (Vince Matthews, Ron Freeman, Larry James, Lee Evans)	2:56.1
1972	Kenya (Asati, Nyamu, Ouko, Sang)	2:59.8

POLE VAULT		*Height*
1896	William Hoyt, United States	10'9¾"
1900	Irving Baxter, United States	10'9 9/10"
1904	Charles Dvorak, United States	11'6"
1908	Albert Gilbert, United States	12'2"
	Edward Cook, Jr., United States	12'2"
1912	Harry Babcock, United States	12'11½"
1920	Frank Foss, United States	12'5 9/16"
1924	Lee Barnes, United States	12'11½"
1928	Sabin Carr, United States	13'9⅜"
1932	William Miller, United States	14'1⅞"
1936	Earle Meadows, United States	14'3¼"
1948	O. Qinn Smith, United States	14'1¼"
1952	Robert Richards, United States	14'11¼"
1956	Robert Richards, United States	14'11½"
1960	Don Bragg, United States	15'5⅛"
1964	Fred Hansen, United States	16'9"
1968	Bob Seagren, United States	17'8½"
1972	Wolgang Nordwig, East Germany	18'0½"

HIGH JUMP		*Height*
1896	Ellery Clark, United States	5'11¼"
1900	Irving Baxter, United States	6'2⅘"
1904	Samuel Jones, United States	5'11"
1908	Harry Porter, United States	6'3"
1912	Alma Richards, United States	6'4"
1920	Richard Landon, United States	6'4¼"
1924	Harold Osborn, United States	6'5 15/16"
1928	Robert King, United States	6'4⅜"
1932	Duncan McNaughton, Canada	6'5⅝"
1936	Cornelius Johnson, United States	6'7 15/16"
1948	John Winter, Australia	6'6"
1952	Walter Davis, United States	6'8¼"
1956	Charles Dumas, United States	6'11¼"
1960	Robert Shavlakadze, USSR	7'1"
1964	Valery Brumel, USSR	7'1¾"
1968	Dick Fosbury, United States	7'4¼"
1972	Yuri Tarmak, USSR	7'3¾"

LONG JUMP		*Distance*
1896	Ellery Clark, United States	20'10"
1900	Alvin Kraenzlein, United States	23'6⅞"
1904	Myer Prinstein, United States	24'1"
1908	Frank Irons, United States	24'6½"
1912	Albert Gutterson, United States	24'11¼"

1920	William Patterson, Sweden	23'5½"
1924	DeHart Hubbard, United States	24'5⅛"
1928	Edward Hamm, United States	25'4¾"
1932	Edward Gordon, United States	25'0¾"
1936	Jesse Owens, United States	26'5⅜"
1948	Willie Steele, United States	25'8"
1952	Jerome Biffle, United States	24'10"
1956	Gregory Bell, United States	25'8¼"
1960	Ralph Boston, United States	26'7¾"
1964	Lynn Davies, Great Britain	26'5½"
1968	Bob Beamon, United States	29'2½"
1972	Randy Williams, United States	27'0½"

TRIPLE JUMP (Hop-Step-Jump)		*Distance*
1896	James Connolly, United States	45'0"
1900	Myer Prinstein, United States	47'4¼"
1904	Myer Prinstein, United States	47'0"
1908	Timothy Ahearne, Great Britain	48'11¼"
1912	Gustof Lindblom, Sweden	48'5⅛"
1920	Vilho Tuulos, Finland	47'6⅞"
1924	Archibald Winter, Australia	50'11⅛"
1928	Mikio Oda, Japan	49'10 13/16"
1932	Chuhei Nambu, Japan	51'7"
1936	Naoto Tajima, Japan	52'5⅞"
1948	Arne Ahman, Sweden	50'6¼"
1952	Adhemar da Silva, Brazil	53'2½"
1956	Adhemar da Silva, Brazil	53'7½"
1960	Jozef Schmidt, Poland	55'1¾"
1964	Jozef Schmidt, Poland	55'3¼"
1968	Victor Saneyev, USSR	57'0¾"
1972	Viktor Saneyev, USSR	56'11"

16-POUND SHOT PUT		*Distance*
1896	Robert Garrett, United States	36'9¾"
1900	Richard Sheldon, United States	46'3⅛"
1904	Ralph Rose, United States	48'7"
1908	Ralph Rose, United States	46'7½"
1912	Patrick McDonald, United States	50'4"
1920	Ville Porhola, Finland	48'7⅛"
1924	Clarence Houser, United States	49'2½"
1928	John Kuck, United States	52'0 11/16"
1932	Leo Sexton, United States	52'6 3/16"
1936	Hans Woellke, Germany	53'1¾"
1948	Wilbur Thompson, United States	56'2"
1952	Parry O'Brien, United States	57'1½"
1956	Parry O'Brien, United States	60'11"
1960	Bill Nieder, United States	64'6¾"
1964	Dallas Long, United States	66'8½"
1968	Randy Matson, United States	67'4¾"
1972	Wladyslaw Komar, USSR	69'6"

DISCUS THROW		*Distance*
1896	Robert Garrett, United States	95'7½"
1900	Rudolf Bauer, Hungary	118'2 9/10"
1904	Martin Sheridan, United States	128'10½"
1908	Martin Sheridan, United States	134'2"
1912	Armas Taiple, Finland	145'0 9/16"
1920	Elmer Ninklander, Finland	146'7"
1924	Clarence Houser, United States	151'5¼"
1928	Clarence Houser, United States	155'2⅘"
1932	John Anderson, United States	162'4⅞"
1936	Kenneth Carpenter, United States	165'7½"
1948	Adolfo Consolini, Italy	173'2"
1952	Sim Iness, United States	180'6½"
1956	Al Oerter, United States	184'10½"
1960	Al Oerter, United States	194'2"
1064	Al Oerter, United States	200'1½"
1968	Al Oerter, United States	212'6½"
1972	Ludvik Danek, Czechoslovakia	211'3½"

16-POUND HAMMER THROW		*Distance*
1900	John Flanagan, United States	167'4"
1904	John Flanagan, United States	168'1"
1908	John Flanagan, United States	170'4¼"
1912	Matthew McGrath, United States	179'7⅛"
1920	Patrick Ryan, United States	173'5⅝"
1924	Frederick Tootell, United States	174'10¼"
1928	Patrick O'Callaghan, Ireland	168'7½"
1932	Patrick O'Callaghan, Ireland	176'11⅛"
1936	Karl Hein, Germany	185'4¼"
1948	Imre Nemeth, Hungary	183'11½"
1952	Jozsef Csermak, Hungary	197'11¾"
1956	Harold Connolly, United States	207'3½"
1960	Vasiliy Rudenkov, USSR	220'1⅝"
1964	Romuald Klim, USSR	228'10½"
1968	Gyula Zsivotzky, Hungary	240'8"
1972	Anatoliy Bondarchuk, USSR	247'8½"

JAVELIN THROW		*Distance*
1908	Erik Lemming, Sweden	179'10½"
1912	Erik Lemming, Sweden	198'11¼"
1920	Jonni Myra, Finland	215'9¾"
1924	Jonni Myra, Finland	206'6¾"
1928	Erik Lundquist, Sweden	218'6⅛"
1932	Matti Jarvinen, Finland	238'7"
1936	Gerhard Stock, Germany	235'8 5/16"
1948	Tapio Rautavaara, Finland	228'10½"
1952	Cy Young, United States	242'0¾"
1956	Egil Danielson, Norway	281'2¼"
1960	Viktor Cybulenko, USSR	277'8⅜"
1964	Pauli Nevala, Finland	271'2¼"
1968	Janis Lusis, USSR	295'7¼"
1972	Klaus Wolfermann, West Germany	296'10"

DECATHLON		*Points*
1912	Hugo Weislander, Sweden	7724.49
1920	Helge Lovland, Norway	6804.35
1924	Harold Osborn, United States	7710.77
1928	Paavo Yrjola, Finland	8053.29
1932	James Bausch, United States	8462.23
1936	Glenn Morris, United States (New Point System)	7900.00
1948	Bob Mathias, United States	7193.00
1952	Bob Mathias, United States	7887.00
1956	Milt Campbell, United States	7937.00
1960	Rafer Johnson, United States	8392.00
1964	Willi Holdorf, Germany (New Point System)	7887.00
1968	Bill Toomey, United States	8193.00
1972	Nikolay Avilov, USSR	8454.00

DISCONTINUED EVENTS

STANDING HIGH JUMP		*Height*
1900	Ray Ewry, United States	5'5"

Olympic Games Summaries

1904	Ray Ewry, United States	4'11"
1908	Ray Ewry, United States	5'2"
1912	P. Adams, United States	5'4"

STANDING BROAD JUMP		Distance
1900	Ray Ewry, United States	10'6¼"
1904	Ray Ewry, United States	11'4⅞"
1908	Ray Ewry, United States	10'11¼"
1912	C. Tsiclitiras, Greece	11'0"

STANDING TRIPLE JUMP		Distance
1900	Ray Ewry, United States	34'8½"
1904	Ray Ewry, United States	34'7¼"

PENTATHLON		
1912	F. R. Bie, Norway	
1920	R. Lehtonen, Finland	
1924	R. Lehtonen, Finland	

GREEK STYLE DISCUS THROW		Distance
1908	Martin Sheridan, United States	124'8"

GREEK STYLE HAMMER THROW		Distance
1912	John Flanagan, United States	170'4"

GREEK STYLE JAVELIN THROW		Distance
1908	Eric Lemming, Sweden	179'10½"

TWO-HANDED JAVELIN THROW		Distance
1912	J. Saaristo, Finland	358'10"

TWO-HANDED SHOT PUT		Distance
1912	Ralph Rose, United States	90'5½"

TWO-HANDED DISCUS THROW		Distance
1912	A. Taipole, Finland	274'0"

56-POUND WEIGHT THROW		Distance
1920	Pat McDonald, United States	36'11¾"

CROSS-COUNTRY RUN		
1912	Hannes Kolehmainen, Finland	
1920	Paavo Nurmi, Finland	
1924	Paavo Nurmi, Finland	

WOMEN'S TRACK AND FIELD WINNERS

100-METER DASH		Sec
1928	Elizabeth Robinson, United States	12.2
1932	Stella Walsh Walasiewiz, Poland	11.9
1936	Helen Stephens, United States	11.5
1948	Fanny Blankers-Koen, Netherlands	11.9
1952	Marjorie Jackson, Australia	11.5
1956	Betty Cuthbert, Australia	11.5
1960	Wilma Rudolph, United States	11.0
1964	Wyomia Tyus, United States	11.4
1968	Wyomia Tyus, United States	11.0
1972	Renata Stecher, Easy Germany	11.1

200-METER DASH		Sec.
1948	Fanny Blankers-Koen, Netherlands	24.4
1952	Marjorie Jackson, Australia	23.7
1956	Betty Cuthbert, Australia	23.4
1960	Wilma Rudolph, United States	24.0
1964	Edith McGuire, United States	23.0
1968	Irene Szewinska, Poland	22.5
1972	Renata Stecher, East Germany	22.4

400-METER DASH		Sec.
1964	Betty Cuthbert, Australia	52.0
1968	Colette Besson, France	52.0
1972	Monika Zehrt, East Germany	51.1

800-METER RUN		Min./Sec.
1928	Linda Radke, Germany	2:16.8
1960	Ludmila Shevtsova, USSR	2:04.4
1964	Ann Packer, Great Britain	2:01.1
1968	Madeline Manning, United States	2:00.9
1972	Hildegard Falck, West Germany	1:58.6

1,500-METER RUN		Min./Sec.
1972	Lyudmila Bragina, USSR	4:01.4

400-METER RELAY		Sec.
1928	Canada (Cook, Smith, Rosenfeld, Bell)	48.4
1932	United States (Mary Carew, Evelyn Furtsch, Annette Rogers, Willy von Bremen)	47.0
1936	United States (Hariette Bland, Annette Rogers, Elizabeth Robinson, Helen Stephens)	46.9
1948	Netherlands (deJongh, Timmers, Koudijs, Blankers-Koen)	47.5
1952	United States (May Faggs, Barbara Jones, Janet Moreau, Cathy Hardy)	45.9
1956	Australia (Strickland, Crocker, Mellor, Cuthbert)	44.5
1960	United States (Martha Hudson, Lucinda Williams, Barbara Jones, Wilma Rudolph)	44.5
1964	Poland (Ciepela, Kirzenstein, Gorecka, Klobukowska)	43.6
1968	United States (Barbara Ferrell, Margaret Bailes, Mildrette Netter, Wyomia Tyus)	42.8
1972	West Germany (Krause, Mickler, Richter, Rosendahl)	42.8

1,600-METER RELAY		Min./Sec.
1972	East Germany (Kasling, Kuhne, Seidler, Zehrt)	3:23.0

80-METER HURDLES		Sec.
1932	Mildred Didrikson, United States	11.7
1936	Trebisonda Villa, Italy	11.7
1948	Fanny Blankers-Koen, Netherlands	11.2
1952	Shirley Strickland de la Hunty, Australia	10.9
1956	Shirley Strickland de la Hunty, Australia	10.7
1960	Irina Press, USSR	10.8
1964	Karin Balzer, Germany	10.5
1968	Maureen Caird, Australia	10.3

100-METER HURDLES		Sec.
1972	Annelie Ehrhardt, East Germany	12.6

HIGH JUMP		Height
1928	Ethel Catherwood, Canada	5'3"
1932	Jean Shiley, United States	5'5¼"

1936	Ibolya Csak, Hungary	5'3"
1948	Alice Coachman, United States	5'6⅛"
1952	Esther Brand, South Africa	5'5¾"
1956	Mildred McDaniel, United States	5'9¼"
1960	Ioland Balas, Roumania	6'0¾"
1964	Ioland Balas, Roumania	6'2¾"
1968	Miloslava Rezkova, Czechoslovakia	5'11¾"
1972	Ulrike Meyfarth, West Germany	6'3⅝"

LONG JUMP		*Distance*
1948	Olga Gyarmati, Hungary	18'8¼"
1952	Yvette Williams, New Zealand	20'5¾"
1956	Elzbieta Krzeskinka, Poland	20'10"
1960	Vyera Krepina, USSR	20'10⅞"
1964	Mary Rand, Great Britain	22'2¼"
1968	Viorica Viscopoleanu, Roumania	22'4½"
1972	Heide Rosendahl, West Germany	22'3"

8-LB./13 4/5oz. SHOT PUT		*Distance*
1948	Micheline Ostermeyer, France	45'1½"
1952	Galina Zybina, USSR	50'1½"
1956	Tamara Tishkyvich, USSR	54'5"
1960	Tamara Press, USSR	56'9⅞"
1964	Tamara Press, USSR	59'6¼"
1968	Margitta Gummel, East Germany	64'4"
1972	Nadezhda Chizhova, USSR	69'0"

DISCUS THROW		*Distance*
1928	Helena Konopacka, Poland	129'11⅞"
1932	Lilian Copeland, United States	133'2"
1936	Gisela Mauermayer, Germany	156'0 3/16"
1948	Micheline Ostermayer, France	137'6½"
1952	Nina Romaschkova, USSR	168'8½"
1956	Olga Fikotova, Czechoslovakia	176'1½"
1960	Nina Ponomaryeva, USSR	180'8¼"
1964	Tamara Press, USSR	187'10¾"
1968	Lia Manoliu, Roumania	191'2½"
1972	Faina Melnik, USSR	218'7"

JAVELIN THROW		*Distance*
1932	Mildred Didrikson, United States	143'4"
1936	Tilly Fleischer, Germany	148'2¾"
1948	Hermine Bauma, Austria	149'6"
1952	Dana Zatopek, Czechoslovakia	165'7"
1956	Inese Janzeme, USSR	176'8"
1960	Elvira Ozolina, USSR	183'8"
1964	Mihaela Penes, Roumania	198'7½"
1968	Angela Nemeth, Hungary	198'0½"
1972	Ruth Fuchs, East Germany	209'7"

PENTATHLON		*Points*
1904	Irina Press, USSR	5246
1968	Ingrid Becker, West Germany	5098
1972	Mary Peters, Great Britain	4801

MEN'S SWIMMING AND DIVING WINNERS

100-METER FREESTYLE		*Min./Sec.*
1896	Alfred Hajos, Hungary (100 yards)	1:22.2
1904	Zoltan de Halmay, Hungary	1:02.8
1908	Charles Daniels, United States	1:05.6
1912	Duke Kahanamoku, United States	1:03.4
1920	Duke Kahanamoku, United States	1:01.4
1924	John Weissmuller, United States	59.0
1928	John Weissmuller, United States	58.2
1932	Yasuji Miyazaki, Japan	58.6
1936	Ferenec Csik, Hungary	57.6
1948	Walter Ris, United States	57.3
1952	Clarke Scholes, United States	57.4
1956	Jon Henricks, Australia	55.4
1960	John Devitt, Australia	55.2
1964	Don Schollander, United States	53.4
1968	Mike Wenden, Australia	52.2
1972	Mark Spitz, United States	51.2

200-METER FREESTYLE		*Min./Sec.*
1900	Fred Lane, Australia	2:25.2
1968	Mike Wenden, Australia	1:55.2
1972	Mark Spitz, United States	1:52.7

400-METER FREESTYLE		*Min./Sec.*
1896	Paul Neumann, Austria (500 meters)	8:12.6
1904	Charles Daniels, United States (440 yards)	6:16.2
1908	Henry Taylor, Great Britain	5:36.8
1912	George Hodgson, Canada	5:24.4
1920	Norman Ross, United States	5:26.8
1924	John Weissmuller, United States	5:04.2
1928	Albert Zorilla, Argentina	5:01.6
1932	Clarence Crabbe, United States	4:48.4
1936	Jack Medica, United States	4:44.5
1948	William Smith, United States	4:41.0
1952	Jean Boiteaux, France	4:30.7
1956	Murray Rose, Australia	4:27.3
1960	Murray Rose, Australia	4:18.3
1964	Don Schollander, United States	4:12.2
1968	Mike Burton, United States	4:09.0
1972	Brad Cooper, Australia	4:00.2

1,500-METER FREESTYLE		*Min./Sec.*
1896	Alfred Hajos, Hungary (1,200 meters)	18:22.2
1900	John Jarvis, Great Britain (1,000 meters)	13:40.2
1904	Emil Rausch, Germany (1,609 meters)	27:18.2
1908	Henry Taylor, Great Britain	22:48.4
1912	George Hodgson, Canada	22:00.0
1920	Norman Ross, United States	22:23.2
1924	Andrew Charlton, Australia	20:06.6
1928	Arne Borg, Sweden	19:51.8
1932	Kusuo Kitamura, Japan	19:12.4
1936	Noburo Terada, Japan	19:13.7
1948	James McLane, United States	19:18.5
1952	Ford Konno, United States	18:30.0
1956	Murray Rose, Australia	17:58.9
1960	Jon Konrads, Australia	17:19.6
1964	Robert Windle, Australia	17:01.7
1968	Mike Burton, United States	16:38.9
1972	Mike Burton, United States	15:52.5

Olympic Games Summaries

100-METER BACKSTROKE		Min./Sec.
1900	Ernst Hoppenberg, Germany (200 meters)	2:47.0
1904	Walter Brack, Germany (100 yards)	1:16.8
1908	Arno Bieberstein, Germany	1:24.6
1912	Harry Hebner, United States	1:21.2
1920	Warren Kealoha, United States	1:15.2
1924	Warren Kealoha, United States	1:13.2
1928	George Kojac, United States	1:08.2
1932	Masaji Kiyokawa, Japan	1:08.6
1936	Adolph Kiefer, United States	1:05.9
1948	Allen Stack, United States	1:06.4
1952	Yoshinobu Oyakawa, United States	1:05.4
1956	David Thiele, Australia	1:02.2
1960	David Thiele, Australia	1:01.9
1964	Not held	
1968	Roland Matthes, East Germany	58.7
1972	Roland Matthes, East Germany	56.5

200-METER BACKSTROKE		Min./Sec.
1900	Ernest Hoppenberg, Germany	2:47.0
1964	Jed Graef, United States	2:10.3
1968	Roland Matthes, East Germany	2:09.6
1972	Roland Matthes, East Germany	2:02.8

100-METER BREASTSTROKE		Min./Sec.
1968	Don McKenzie, United States	1:07.7
1972	Nobutaka Tagushi, Japan	1:04.9

200-METER BREASTSTROKE		Min./Sec.
1908	Frederick Holman, Great Britain	3:09.2
1912	Walter Bathe, Germany	3:01.8
1920	Haken Malmroth, Sweden	3:04.4
1924	Robert Skelton, United States	3:56.6
1928	Yoshiyuki Tsuruta, Japan	2:48.8
1932	Yoshiyuki Tsuruta, Japan	2:45.4
1936	Tetsuo Hamuro, Japan	2:41.5
1948	Joseph Verdeur, United States	2:39.3
1952	John Davies, Australia	2:34.4
1956	Masura Furukawa, Japan	2:34.7
1960	William Mulliken, United States	2:37.4
1964	Ian O'Brien, Australia	2:27.8
1968	Felipe Munoz, Mexico	2:28.7
1972	John Hencken, United States	2:21.5

100-METER BUTTERFLY		Sec.
1968	Doug Russell, United States	55.9
1972	Mark Spitz, United States	54.2

200-METER BUTTERFLY		Min./Sec.
1956	William Yorzyk, United States	2:19.3
1960	Michael Troy, United States	2:12.8
1964	Kevin Berry, Australia	2:06.6
1968	Carl Robie, United States	2:08.7
1972	Mark Spitz, United States	2:00.7

200-METER MEDLEY		Min./Sec.
1968	Charles Hickcox, United States	2:12.0
1972	Gunnar Larsson, Sweden	2:07.1

400-METER MEDLEY		Min./Sec.
1964	Richard Roth, United States	4:45.4
1968	Charles Hickcox, United States	4:48.4
1972	Gunnar Larsson, Sweden	4:31.9

400-METER FREESTYLE RELAY		Min./Sec.
1964	United States (Steve Clark, Mike Austin, Gary Ilman, Don Schollander)	3:33.2
1968	United States (Zach Zorn, Steve Rerych, Mark Spitz, Ken Walsh)	3:31.7
1972	United States (Dave Edgar, John Murphy, Jerry Heidenreich, Mark Spitz)	3:26.4

800-METER FREESTYLE RELAY		Min./Sec.
1908	Great Britain (Derbyshire, Radmilovic, Foster, Taylor)	10:55.6
1912	Australia (Healy, Champion, Boardman, Hardwick)	10:11.2
1920	United States (Perry McGillivray, Pua Kealoha, Norman Ross, Duke Kahanamoku)	10:04.4
1924	United States (Wally O'Connor, Harry Glancy, Ralph Breyer, John Weissmuller)	9:53.4
1928	United States (Austin Clapp, Walter Laufer, George Kojac, John Weissmuller)	9:36.2
1932	Japan (Miyazaki, Yokoyama, Yusa, Toyoda)	8:58.4
1936	Japan (Yusa, Sugiura, Taguchi, Arai)	8:51.5
1948	United States (Wally Ris, Wally Wolf, Jimmy McLane, Bill Smith)	8:46.0
1952	United States (Wayne Moore, Bill Woolsey, Ford Konno, Jimmy McLane)	8:31.1
1956	Australia (O'Halloran, Devitt, Rose, Hendricks)	8:23.6
1960	United States (George Harrison, Richard Blick, Mike Troy, Jeff Farrell)	8:10.2
1964	United States (Steve Clark, Roy Saari, Gary Ilman, Don Schollander)	7:52.1
1968	United States (John Nelson, Steve Rerych, Mark Spitz, Don Schollander)	7:52.3
1972	United States (John Kinsella, Fred Tyler, Steve Genter, Mark Spitz)	7:35.7

400-METER MEDLEY RELAY		Min./Sec.
1960	United States (Frank McKinney, Paul Hait, Lance Larson, Jeff Farrell)	4:05.4
1964	United States (Harold Mann, Bill Craig, Fred Schmidt, Steve Clark)	3:58.4
1968	United States (Charles Hickcox, Don McKenzie, Doug Russell, Ken Walsh)	3:54.9
1972	United States (Mike Stamm, Tom Bruce, Mark Spitz, Jerry Heidenreich)	3:48.1

SPRINGBOARD DIVING
1908 Albert Zurner, Germany
1912 Paul Guenther, Germany
1920 Louis Kuehn, United States
1924 Albert White, United States
1928 Pete Desjardins, United States
1932 Michael Galitzen, United States
1936 Richard Degener, United States
1948 Bruce Harlan, United States
1952 David Browning, United States

1956	Robert Clotworthy, United States	
1960	Gary Tobian, United States	
1964	Ken Sitzberger, United States	
1968	Bernie Wrightson, United States	
1972	Vladimir Vasin, USSR	

PLATFORM (HIGH) DIVING

1904	Dr. G. E. Sheldon, United States
1908	Hjalmar Johannson, Sweden
1912	Erik Adlerz, Sweden
1920	Clarence Pinkston, United States
1924	Albert White, United States
1928	Pete Desjardins, United States
1932	Harold Smith, United States
1936	Marshall Wayne, United States
1948	Dr. Samuel Lee, United States
1952	Dr. Samuel Lee, United States
1956	Joaquin Capilla, Mexico
1960	Robert Webster, United States
1964	Robert Webster, United States
1968	Klaus Dibiase, Italy
1972	Klaus Dibiase, Italy

WOMEN'S SWIMMING AND DIVING WINNERS

100-METER FREESTYLE		Min./Sec.
1912	Fanny Durack, Australia	1:22.2
1920	Ethelda Bleibtrey, United States	1:13.6
1924	Ethel Lackie, United States	1:12.4
1928	Albina Osipowich, United States	1:11.0
1932	Helene Madison, United States	1:06.8
1936	Hendrika Mastenbroek, Holland	1:06.8
1948	Greta Andersen, Denmark	1:06.3
1952	Katalin Szoke, Hungary	1:06.8
1956	Dawn Fraser, Australia	1:02.0
1960	Dawn Fraser, Australia	1:01.2
1964	Dawn Fraser, Australia	59.5
1968	Jan Henne, United States	1:00.0
1972	Sandra Neilson, United States	58.5

200-METER FREESTYLE		Min./Sec.
1968	Debbie Meyer, United States	2:10.5
1972	Shane Gould, Australia	2:03.5

400-METER FREESTYLE		Min./Sec.
1920	Ethelda Bleibtrey, United States (300 meters)	4:34.0
1924	Martha Norelius, United States	6:02.2
1928	Martha Norelius, United States	5:26.4
1932	Helene Madison, United States	5:28.5
1936	Hendrika Mastenbroek, Holland	5:26.4
1948	Ann Curtis, United States	5:17.8
1952	Valeria Gyenge, Hungary	5:12.1
1956	Lauraine Crapp, Australia	4:54.6
1960	Chris Von Saltza, United States	4:50.6
1964	Virginia Duenkel, United States	4:43.3
1968	Debbie Meyer, United States	4:31.8
1972	Shane Gould, Australia	4:19.0

800-METER FREESTYLE		Min./Sec.
1968	Debbie Meyer, United States	9:24.0
1972	Keena Rothhammer, United States	8:53.6

100-METER BACKSTROKE		
1924	Sybil Bauer, United States	1:23.2
1928	Marie Braun, Holland	1:22.0
1932	Eleanor Holm, United States	1:19.4
1936	Dina Senff, Holland	1:18.9
1948	Karen Harup, Denmark	1:14.4
1952	Joan Harrison, South Africa	1:14.3
1956	J. Grinham, Great Britain	1:12.9
1960	Lynn Burke, United States	1:09.3
1964	Cathy Ferguson, United States	1:07.7
1968	Kaye Hall, United States	1:06.2
1972	Melissa Belote, United States	1:05.7

200-METER BACKSTROKE		Min./Sec.
1968	Pokey Watson, United States	2:24.8
1972	Melissa Belote, United States	2:19.1

100-METER BREASTSTROKE		Min./Sec.
1968	Djurdjica Bedov, Yugoslavia	1:15.8
1972	Cathy Carr, United States	1:13.5

200-METER BREASTSTROKE		Min./Sec.
1924	Lucy Morton, Great Britain	3:33.2
1928	Hilde Schrader, Germany	3:12.6
1932	Clare Dennis, Australia	3:06.3
1936	Hideko Maehata, Japan	3:03.6
1948	Nel Van Vliet, Netherlands	2:57.2
1952	Eva Szekely, Hungary	2:51.7
1956	U. Happe, Germany	2:53.1
1960	Anita Lonsbrough, Great Britain	2:49.5
1964	Galina Prozumenshirova, USSR	2:46.4
1968	Sharon Wichman, United States	2:44.4
1972	Bev Whitfield, Australia	2:41.7

100-METER BUTTERFLY		Min./Sec.
1956	Shelly Mann, United States	1:11.0
1960	Carolyn Schuler, United States	1:09.5
1964	Sharon Stouder, United States	1:04.7
1968	Lyn McClements, Australia	1:05.5
1972	Mayumi Aoki, Japan	1:03.3

200-METER BUTTERFLY		Min./Sec.
1968	Aaoje Kok, Netherlands	2:24.7
1972	Karen Moe, United States	2:15.5

400-METER FREESTYLE RELAY		Min./Sec.
1912	Great Britain (Moore, Steer, Speirs, Fletcher)	5:52.8
1920	United States (Ethelda Bleibtrey, Frances Schroth, Irene Guest, Margaret Woodbridge)	5:11.6
1924	United States (Gertrude Ederle, Mariechen Wehselau, Ethel Lackie, Euphrasia Donelly)	4:58.8
1928	United States (Adelaide Lambert, Albina Osipowich, Eleanora Garatti, Martha Norelius)	4:47.6
1932	United States (Josephine McKim, Eleonare Saville, Helen Johns, Helene Madison)	4:38.0
1936	Netherlands (Selbach, Wagner, den Ouden, Mastenbroek)	4:36.0
1948	United States (Marie Corridon, Thelma Kalama, Brenda Helser, Ann Curtis)	4:29.2

Olympic Games Summaries

1952	Hungary (I. Novak, Temes, E. Novak, Szoke)	4:24.4
1956	Australia (Fraser, Leech, Morgan, Crapp)	4:17.1
1960	United States (Joan Spillane, Shirley Stobs, Carolyn Wood, Chris Von Saltza)	4:08.9
1964	United States (Kathy Ferguson, Cynthia Goyette, Sharon Stouder, Kathy Ellis)	4:03.8
1968	United States (Jane Barkman, Linda Gustavson, Sue Pedersen, Jan Henne)	4:02.5
1972	United States (Sandra Neilson, Jennifer Kemp, Jane Barkman, Shirley Babashoff)	3:55.1

400-METER MEDLEY RELAY Min./Sec.

1960	United States (Lynn Burke, Patty Kempner, Carolyn Schuler, Chris Von Saltza)	4:41.1
1964	United States (Sharon Stouder, Donna de Varona, Lilian Watson, Kathy Ellis)	4:33.9
1968	United States (Kaye Hall, Catie Ball, Ellie Daniel, Sue Pedersen)	4:28.3
1972	United States (Melissa Belote, Sandra Neilson, Cathy Carr, Deena Deardruff)	4:20.7

SPRINGBOARD DIVING
- 1920 Aileen Riggin, United States
- 1924 Elizabeth Becker, United States
- 1928 Helen Meany, United States
- 1932 Georgia Coleman, United States
- 1936 Marjorie Gestring, United States
- 1948 Victoria Draves, United States
- 1952 Pat McCormick, United States
- 1956 Pat McCormick, United States
- 1960 Ingrid Kramer, Germany
- 1964 Ingrid Engel, Germany
- 1968 Sue Gossick, United States
- 1972 Micki King, United States

PLATFORM (HIGH) DIVING
- 1912 Greta Johansson, Sweden
- 1920 Stefani Fryland-Clausen, Denmark
- 1924 Caroline Smith, United States
- 1928 Elizabeth Pinkston, United States
- 1932 Dorothy Poynton, United States
- 1936 Dorothy Poynton, United States
- 1948 Victoria Draves, United States
- 1952 Pat McCormick, United States
- 1956 Pat McCormick, United States
- 1960 Ingrid Kramer, Germany
- 1964 Lesley Bush, United States
- 1968 Milena Duchkova, Czechoslovakia
- 1972 Ulrika Knape, Sweden

OTHER AMERICAN AND SELECTED SUMMER WINNERS

ARCHERY
- 1972 Men: John Williams, United States
- 1972 Women: Doreen Wilber, United States

BOXING (MEN)
- 1904 O.L. Kirk, bantamweight, United States
  O.L. Kirk, featherweight, United States
  George Finnegan, flyweight, United States
  H. J. Spangler, lightweight, United States
  Albert Young, welterweight, United States
  Charles Mayer, middleweight, United States
  Sammy Berger, heavyweight, United States
- 1920 Frank de Genaro, flyweight, United States
  Sammy Mosbert, lightweight, United States
  Harry Mallin, middleweight, Great Britain
  Eddie Eagen, light heavyweight, United States
- 1924 Fidel LaBarba, flyweight, United States
  Jackie Fields, featherweight, United States
  Harry Mallin, middleweight, Great Britain
- 1932 Ed Flynn, welterweight, United States
  Carmen Barth, middleweight, United States
- 1948 Pascal Perez, flyweight, Argentina
  Laszlo Papp, middleweight, Hungary
- 1952 Nathan Brooks, flyweight, United States
  Charles Adkins, light welterweight, United States
  Floyd Patterson, middleweight, United States
  Laszlo Papp, light middleweight, Hungary
  Norvel Lee, light heavyweight, United States
  Ed Sanders, heavyweight, United States
- 1956 Laszlo Papp, light middleweight, Hungary
  James Boyd, light heavyweight, United States
  Pete Rademacher, heavyweight, United States
- 1960 Nino Benvenuti, welterweight, Italy
  Wilbert McClure, light middleweight, United States
  Ed Crook, middleweight, United States
  Cassius Clay, light heavyweight, United States
- 1964 Jerzy Kulej, light welterweight, Poland
  Boris Lagutin, light middleweight, USSR
  Joe Frazier, heavyweight, United States
- 1968 Ronnie Harris, lightweight, United States
  Jerzy Kulej, light middleweight, Poland
  Boris Lagutin, light middleweight, USSR
  George Foreman, heavyweight, United States
- 1972 Ray Seales, light welterweight, United States
  Teofilio Stevenson, heavyweight, Cuba

CYCLING *Gold Medals*

1896	Emile Masson, France	3
1904	Marcus Hurley, United States	4
	B. Downing, United States	2
	C. Schlee, United States	1
1960	Sante Gaiardoni, Italy	2
1968	Daniel Morelon, France	2
1972	Niels Fredborg, Denmark	1
	Knut Kundsen, Norway	1
	Hennie Kulper, Netherlands	1

EQUESTRIAN
- 1928 Lt. C. F. Pahud de Mortanges, Holland 3-day event
- 1932 Lt. C. F. Pahud de Mortanges, Holland 3-day event
- 1952 Pierre d'Oriola, France, grand prix
  Henri St. Cyr, Sweden, dressage
- 1956 Henri St. Cyr, Sweden, dressage
- 1964 Pierre d'Oriola, France, grand prix
- 1968 Billy Steinkraus, United States, grand prix
- 1972 Richard Meade, Great Britain, 1 gold
  Grazinao Mancinelli, Italy, 1 gold
  Liselott Linsenhoff, West Germany, 1 gold

FENCING
- 1900 Ramon Fonst, Cuba, epee
- 1904 Ramon Fonst, Cuba, epee

1908 Emil Fuchs, Hungary, saber
1912 Emil Fuchs, Hungary, saber
    Nedo Nadi, Italy, foil
1920 Nedo Nadi, Italy, saber
    Nedo Nadi, Italy, foil
1936 Ilona Elek, Hungary, women's foil
1948 Ilona Elek, Hungary, women's foil
1952 Christian d'Oriola, France, foil
1956 Christian d'Oriola, France, foil
    Rudolf Karpati, Hungary, saber
1960 Rudolf Karpati, Hungary, saber
1972 Witold Woyda, Poland, gold
    Victor Sidiak, Soviet Union, gold
    Casaba Fenyvesi, Hungary, gold
    Antonella Lonzo Rango, Italy, gold

MEN'S GYMNASTICS

All-Around Individual
1908 Alberto Braglia, Italy
1912 Alberto Braglia, Italy
1952 Viktor Tchoukarine, USSR
1956 Viktor Tchoukarine, USSR
1968 Sawao Kato, Japan
1972 Sawao Kato, Japan

WOMEN'S GYMNASTICS

All-Around Individual
1956 Larisa Latynina, USSR
1960 Larisa Latynina, USSR
1964 Vera Caslavska, Czechoslovakia
1968 Vera Caslavska, Czechoslovakia
1972 Ludmila Tourischeva, USSR
    Also:
    Olga Korbut, USSR, 2 golds
    Karin Janz, East Germany, 2 golds

JUDO
1972 Willem Ruska, Netherlands, open class

MILITARY PENTATHLON
1952 Lars Hall, Sweden
1956 Lars Hall, Sweden
1972 Andres Balczo, Hungary

ROWING
1904 Frank Greer, United States, single sculls
1920 John Kelly, United States, single sculls
1928 Henry Pearce, Australia, single sculls
1932 Henry Pearce, Australia, single sculls
1948 Gert Frederiksson, Sweden, kayak singles, 1,000 and 10,000
    Josef Holocek, Czechoslovakia, canoe singles, 1,000
1952 Gert Frederiksson, Sweden, kayak singles, 1,000
    Josef Holocek, Czechoslovakia, canoe singles, 1,000
1956 Gert Frederiksson, Sweden, kayak singles, 1,000 and 10,000
    Vyacheslav Ivanov, USSR, single sculls
1960 Vyacheslav Ivanov, USSR, single sculls
1964 Vyacheslav Ivanov, USSR, single sculls
1972 Yuri Malishev, USSR, single sculls
    Aleksandr Shaparenko, USSR, kayak singles
    Siegbert Horn, East Germany, kayak slalom
    Ivan Patzaichiu, Rumania, canoe singles
    Reinhard Eiben, East Germany, canoe slalom

SHOOTING
1896 Sommer Paine, United States, free pistol
1912 Alfred Lane, United States, free pistol
    James Graham, United States, trap
1920 Karl Frederick, United States, free pistol
    Carl Osburn, United States, free rifle
    Lawrence Nusslein, United States, small rifle, prone
    Mark Arie, United States, trap
1924 Morris Fisher, United States, free rifle
    H. M. Bailey, United States, revolver
1948 Arthur Cook, United States, small rifle, prone
    Karoly Takacs, Hungary, rapid pistol
1952 Karoly Takacs, Hungary, rapid pistol
    Huelet Banner, United States, free pistol
1960 Bill McMillan, United States, free pistol
1964 Lones Wigger, United States, small rifle triple
    Gary Anderson, United States, free rifle
1968 Gary Anderson, United States, free rifle
    Josef Zepedski, Poland, rapid pistol
1972 Lones Wigger, United States, free rifle
    John Writer, United States, small rifle triple
    Josef Zepedski, Poland, rapid pistol
    Roger Shanaker, Sweden, free pistol
    Angelo Scalzone, Italy, trap
    Konrad Wirnheir, West Germany, skeet

WEIGHT LIFTING
1932 Louis Hostin, France, light heavyweight
1936 Louis Hostin, France, light heavyweight
    Anthony Terlazzo, United States, featherweight
1948 Joseph de Pietro, United States, bantamweight
    Frank Spellman, United States, middleweight
    John Davis, United States, heavyweight
1952 John Davis, United States, heavyweight
    Norbert Schemansky, United States, middle heavyweight
    Peter George, United States, middleweight
1956 Paul Anderson, United States, heavyweight
    Tommy Kono, United States, light heavyweight
    Arkadi Vorobiev, USSR, middle heavyweight
    Charles Vinci, United States, bantamweight
1960 Charles Vinci, United States, bantamweight
    Arkadi Vorobiev, USSR, middle heavyweight
1964 W. Baszanowski, Poland, lightweight
    Leonid Jabotinski, USSR, heavyweight
    W. Baszanowski, Poland, lightweight
1968 Leonid Jabotinski, USSR, heavyweight
1972 Vasily Alekseyev, USSR, super heavyweight

FREESTYLE WRESTLING
1904 George Mehnert, United States, bantamweight
    (All other classes also won by United States)
1908 George Mehnert, United States, bantamweight
    George Dole, United States, featherweight
1920 Charles Ackerly, United States, featherweight
1924 Robin Reed, United States, featherweight
    Russell Vis, United States, lightweight
    Harry Steele, United States, heavyweight
1928 Allie Morrison, United States, featherweight
    Johan Richtoff, Sweden, heavyweight
1932 Johan Richtoff, Sweden, heavyweight
    Pete Mehringer, United States, light heavyweight
    Jack Van Bebber, United States, welterweight
1936 Frank Lewis, United States, welterweight
1948 Glenn Brand, United States, middleweight
    Henry Wittenberg, United States, light heavyweight
1952 Bill Smith, United States, welterweight

Olympic Games Summaries

1960 Shelby Wilson, United States, lightweight
D. Blubaugh, United States, welterweight
Terry McCann, United States, bantamweight
1964 Yojiro Uetake, Japan, bantamweight
Alexander Medved, USSR, light heavyweight
1968 Alexander Medved, USSR, heavyweight
Yojiro Uetake, Japan, bantamweight
1972 Alexander Medved, USSR, super heavyweight
Dan Gable, United States, lightweight
Wayne Wells, United States, welterweight
Ben Peterson, United States, light heavyweight

GRECO-ROMAN WRESTLING
1912 Eemil Vare, Finland, lightweight
1920 Eemil Vare, Finland, lightweight
1928 Vaino Kokkinen, Finland, middleweight
1932 Vaino Kokkinen, Finland, middleweight
1956 Mitha Bayrak, Turkey, welterweight
1960 Mitha Bayrak, Turkey, welterweight
1964 Istvan Kozma, Hungary, heavyweight
1968 Istvan Kozma, Hungary, heavyweight
Peter Kirov, Bulgaria, flyweight
1972 Peter Kirov, Bulgaria, flyweight
Anatoly Roshin, USSR, super heavyweight

YACHTING
1948-1960 Paul Elvstrom, Denmark, 4 straight golds, finns class
1968-1972 Valentin Mankin, USSR, 2 straight golds, finns class

TENNIS (*discontinued*)
1904 Beals Wright, United States, men's
1924 Vinnie Richards, United States, men's
Helen Wills, United States, women's

DIVING FOR DISTANCE (*discontinued*)
1904 W. E. Dickey, United States, 62'6"

FANCY DIVING (*discontinued*)
1904 G. E. Sheldon, United States
1920 C. E. Pinkston, United States
1924 A. C. White, United States

ONE-HAND WEIGHT LIFTING (*discontinued*)
1904 O. C. Osthoff, United States

SUMMER TEAM CHAMPIONS

Year	Basketball	Soccer	Field Hockey	Rowing (8-Oar Shell)
1896				
1900		Great Britain		United States (Vespers BC)
1904		Great Britain		United States (Vespers BC)
1908		Great Britain	Great Britain	Great Britain
1912		Great Britain	None	Great Britain
1920		Belgium	Great Britain	United States (Naval Academy)
1924		Uruguay	None	United States (Yale)
1928		Uruguay	India	United States (California)
1932		None	India	United States (California)
1936	United States	Italy	India	United States (Washington)
1948	United States	Sweden	India	United States (California)
1952	United States	Hungary	India	United States (Navy)
1956	United States	USSR	India	United States (Yale)
1960	United States	Yugoslavia	Pakistan	West Germany
1964	United States	Hungary	India	United States (Vespers BC)
1968	United States	Hungary	Pakistan	East Germany
1972	USSR	Poland	West Germany	New Zealand

Year	Water Polo	Fencing (unofficial)	Men's Gym	Women's Gym
1896		France	Germany	
1900	Great Britain	France	None	
1904	United States	Cuba	United States	
1908	Great Britain	France	Sweden	
1912	Great Britain	Hungary	None	
1920	Great Britain	Italy	Italy	
1924	France	France	Italy	
1928	Germany	France	Switzerland	Holland
1932	Hungary	Italy	Italy	None
1936	Hungary	Italy	Germany	Germany
1948	Italy	Italy	Finland	Czechoslovakia
1952	Hungary	Italy	USSR	USSR
1956	Hungary	Italy	USSR	USSR
1960	Italy	USSR	Japan	USSR
1964	Hungary	USSR	Japan	USSR
1968	Yugoslavia	USSR	Japan	USSR
1972	USSR	USSR	Japan	USSR

Olympic Games Summaries

Year	Men's Volleyball	Women's Volleyball	Handball
1964	USSR	Japan	
1968	USSR	USSR	
1972	Japan	USSR	Yugoslavia

WINTER SITES

1924	Chamonix, France		1956	Cortina, Italy
1928	St. Moritz, Switzerland		1960	Squaw Valley, California, United States
1932	Lake Placid, N.Y., United States		1964	Innsbruck, Austria
1936	Garmisch-Partenkirchen, Germany		1968	Grenoble, France
1948	St. Moritz, Switzerland		1972	Sapporo, Japan
1952	Oslo, Norway			

ALPINE SKIING (MEN)

DOWNHILL RACE
1948 Henri Oreiller, France
1952 Zeno Colo, Italy
1956 Toni Sailer, Austria
1960 Jean Vuarnet, France
1964 Egon Zimmerman, Austria
1968 Jean-Claude Killy, France
1972 Bernhard Russi, Switzerland

GIANT SLALOM
1952 Stein Eriksen, Norway
1956 Toni Sailer, Austria
1960 Roger Staub, Switzerland
1964 Francois Bonlieu, France
1968 Jean-Claude Killy, France
1972 Gustavo Thoeni, Italy

SLALOM
1948 Edi Reinalter, Switzerland
1952 Othmar Schneider, Austria
1956 Toni Sailer, Austria
1960 Ernst Hinterseer, Austria
1964 Pepi Stiegler, Austria
1968 Jean-Claude Killy, France
1972 Francisco Fernandez-Ochoa, Spain

ALPINE SKIING (WOMEN)

DOWNHILL RACE
1948 Hedi Schlunegger, Switzerland
1952 Trudi Jochum-Beiser, Austria
1956 Madeleine Berthod, Switzerland
1960 Heidi Biebl, Germany
1964 Christi Haas, Austria
1968 Olga Pall, Austria
1972 Marie-Therese Nadig, Switzerland

SLALOM
1948 Gretchen Fraser, United States
1952 Andrea Mead Lawrence, United States
1956 Renee Colliard, Switzerland
1960 Anne Heggtveit, Canada
1964 Christine Goitschel, France
1968 Marielle Goitschel, France
1972 Barbara Cochran, United States

GIANT SLALOM
1952 Andrea Mead Lawrence, United States
1956 Ossi Reichert, Germany
1960 Yvonne Ruegg, Switzerland
1964 Marielle Goitschel, France
1968 Nancy Greene, Canada
1972 Marie-Therese Nadig, Switzerland

SKI JUMP

ONE-HILL JUMP
1924 Jacob Thams, Norway
1928 Alfred Andersen, Norway
1932 Birger Ruud, Norway
1936 Birger Ruud, Norway
1948 Peter Hugsted, Norway
1952 Arnfinn Bergman, Norway
1956 Antti Hyvarinen, Finland
1960 Helmut Recknagel, Germany

90-METER JUMP
1964 Toralf Engan, Norway
1968 Vladimir Beloussov, USSR
1972 Wojciech Fortuna, Poland

70-METER JUMP
1964 V. Kankkonen, Finland
1968 J. Raska, Czechoslovakia
1972 Yoko Kasaya, Japan

SPEED SKATING (MEN)

500 METERS		Sec.
1924	Charles Jewtraw, United States	44.0
1928	Clas Thunberg, Finland and	
	Bernt Evensen, Norway	43.4
1932	John A. Shea, United States	43.4
1936	Ivar Ballangrud, Norway	43.4
1948	Finn Helgesen, Norway	43.1
1952	Ken Henry, United States	43.2

Olympic Games Summaries

1956	Evgenij Grishin, USSR	40.2
1960	Evgenij Grishin, USSR	40.2
1964	Terry McDermott, United States	40.1
1968	Erhard Keller, West Germany	40.3
1972	Erhard Keller, West Germany	39.4

1,500 METERS		Min./Sec.
1924	Clas Thunberg, Finland	2:20.8
1928	Clas Thunberg, Finland	2:21.1
1932	John Shea, United States	2:57.5
1936	Charles Mathisen, Norway	2:19.2
1948	Sverre Farstad, Norway	2:17.6
1952	H. Andersen, Norway	2:20.4
1956	Evgenij Grishin, USSR	2:08.6
1960	Evgenij Grishin, USSR Roald Aas	2:11.5
1964	Ants Antson, USSR	2:10.3
1968	Kees Verkerk, Netherlands	2:03.4
1972	Ard Schenk, Netherlands	2:02.9

5,000 METERS		Min./Sec.
1924	Clas Thunberg, Finland	8:39
1928	Ivar Ballangrud, Norway	8:50.5
1932	Irving Jaffee, United States	9:40.8
1936	Ivar Ballangrud, Norway	8:19.6
1948	Reidar Liaklev, Norway	8:29.4
1952	H. Andersen, Norway	8:10.6
1956	Boris Shilkov, USSR	7:48.7
1960	Viktor Kosichkin, USSR	7:51.3
1964	Knut Johannesen, Norway	7:38.4
1968	Fred Anton Maier, Norway	7:22.4
1972	Ard Schenk, Netherlands	7:23.6

10,000 METERS		Min./Sec.
1924	Julien Skutnabb, Finland	18:04.8
1928	Irving Jaffee, United States	18:36.5
1932	Irving Jaffee, United States	19:13.6
1936	Ivar Ballangrud, Norway	17:24.3
1948	Ake Seyffarth, Sweden	17:26.3
1952	H. Andersen, Norway	16:45.8
1956	Sigvard Ericsson, Sweden	16:35.9
1960	Knut Johannesen, Norway	15:46.6
1964	Johnny Nilson, Sweden	15:50.1
1968	Johnny Hoeglin, Sweden	15:23.6
1972	Ard Schenk, Netherlands	15:01.3

SPEED SKATING (WOMEN)

500 METERS		Sec.
1960	Helga Haase, Germany	45.9
1964	Lydia Skoblikova, USSR	45.0
1968	Ludmilla Titova, USSR	46.1
1972	Anne Henning, United States	43.3

1,000 METERS		Min./Sec.
1960	Klara Guseva, USSR	1:34.1
1964	Lydia Skoblikova, USSR	1:33.2
1968	Carolina Geijssen, Netherlands	1:32.6
1972	Monika Pflug, West Germany	1:31.4

1,500 METERS		Min./Sec.
1960	Lydia Skoblikova, USSR	2:25.2
1964	Lydia Skoblikova, USSR	2:22.6
1968	Kaija Mustonen, Finland	2:22.4
1972	Dianne Holum, United States	2:20.8

3,000 METERS		Min./Sec.
1960	Lydia Skoblikova, USSR	5:14.3
1964	Lydia Skoblikova, USSR	5:14.9
1968	Johanna Schut, Netherlands	4:56.2
1972	Stien Baas-Kaiser, Netherlands	4:52.1

ICE HOCKEY

1920	Canada
1924	Canada
1928	Canada
1932	Canada
1936	Great Britain
1948	Canada
1952	Canada
1956	USSR
1960	United States
1964	USSR
1968	USSR
1972	USSR

FIGURE SKATING (MEN'S)

1908	Salchow, Sweden
1920	Gillis Grafstrom, Sweden
1924	Gillis Grafstrom, Sweden
1928	Gillis Grafstrom, Sweden
1932	Karl Schaefer, Austria
1936	Karl Schaefer, Austria
1948	Dick Button, United States
1952	Dick Button, United States
1956	Hayes Alan Jenkins, United States
1960	David Jenkins, United States
1964	Manfred Schnelldorfer, Germany
1968	Wolfgang Schwarz, Austria
1972	Ondrej Nepela, Czechoslovakia

FIGURE SKATING (WOMEN'S)

1908	Syers, Great Britain
1920	Julin, Sweden
1924	Herma Szabo-Planck, Austria
1928	Sonja Henie, Norway
1932	Sonja Henie, Norway
1936	Sonja Henie, Norway
1948	Barbara Ann Scott, Canada
1952	Jeanette Altwegg, Great Britain
1956	Tenley E. Albright, United States
1960	Carol Heiss, United States
1964	Sjoukje Dijkstra, Netherlands
1968	Peggy Fleming, United States
1972	Beatrix Schuba, Austria

FIGURE SKATING (PAIRS)

1908	Anna Hubler and Heinrich Burger, Germany
1920	Ludovika and Walter Jacobsson, Finland

1924	Helene Engelmann and Alfred Berger, Austria	
1928	Andree Joly and Pierre Brunet, France	
1932	Andree and Pierre Brunet, France	
1936	Maxie Herber and Ernst Baier, Germany	
1948	Micheline Lannoy and Pierre Baugniet, Belgium	
1952	Ria and Paul Falk, Germany	
1956	Elizabeth Schwarz and Kurt Oppelt, Austria	
1960	Barbara Wagner and Robert Paul, Canada	
1964	Ludmilla Beloussova and Oleg Protopopov, USSR	
1968	Ludmilla Beloussova and Oleg Protopopov, USSR	
1972	Irina Rodnina and Aleksei Vlanov, USSR	

BOBSLED

4-MAN BOB (DRIVER) — *Min./Sec.*
1924	Switzerland, Scherrer	5:45.54
1928	United States, Fiske	3:20.50
1932	United States, Fiske	7:53.68
1936	Switzerland, Musy	5:19.85
1948	United States, Tyler	5:20.10
1952	Germany, Ostler	5:07.84
1956	Switzerland, Kapus	5:10.44
1960	Not held	
1964	Canada, Emery	4:14.46
1968	Italy, Monti	2:17.39
1972	Switzerland, Wicki	4:43.07

2-MAN BOB (DRIVER) — *Min./Sec.*
1932	United States, Stevens	8:14.74
1936	United States, Brown	5:29.29
1948	Switzerland, Endrich	5:29.20
1952	Germany, Ostler	5:24.54
1956	Italy, Costa	
1960	Not held	
1964	Great Britain, Nash	4:21.90
1968	Italy, Monti	4:41.54
1972	West Germany, Zimmerer	4:57.07

LUGE (SMALL SLED)

MEN'S SINGLES — *Min./Sec.*
1964	Thomas Koehler, Germany	3:26.77
1968	Manfred Schmid, Austria	2:52.48
1972	Wolfgang Scheidel, East Germany	3:27.58

MEN'S DOUBLES — *Min./Sec.*
1964	Pfiestmantl and Stengl, Austria	1:41.62
1968	Bonsack and Koehler, Easy Germany	1:35.85
1972	Hildgartner and Plaikner, Italy	1:28.35

WOMEN'S SINGLES — *Min./Sec.*
1964	Ortrun Enderlein, Germany	3:24.67
1968	Erica Lechner, Italy	2:28.66
1972	Anne Marie Muller, East Germany	2:59.18

OTHER AMERICAN AND SELECTED WINTER WINNERS

MEN'S NORDIC SKIING
1928		J. Grottumsbraaten, Norway	combined race-jump
1932		J. Grottumsbraaten, Norway	combined race-jump
1952		Hallgeir Brenden, Norway	15 km. cross-country
1956		Hallgeir Brenden, Norway	15 km. cross-country
		Sexten Jernberg, Sweden	50 km. cross-country
		Veikko Hakulinen, Finland	30 km. cross-country
1960		Veikko Hakulinen, Finland	50 km. cross-country
		Sexten Jernberg, Sweden	30 km. cross-country
1964		Sexten Jernberg, Sweden	50 km. cross-country
		Eero Meantyranta, Finland	15 km. cross-country
		Eero Meantyranta, Finland	30 km. cross-country
1968		Magnar Solberg, Norway	biathlon
1972		Sven-Ake Lundback, Sweden	15 km. cross-country
		Vyacheslav Vedenin, USSR	30 km. cross-country
		Paal Tyldum, Norway	50 km. cross-country
		Ulrich Wehling, East Germany	combined race-jump
		Magnar Solberg, Norway	biathlon
		USSR	team relay

WOMEN'S NORDIC SKIING
1964	Claudia Boyarskich, USSR	5 and 10 km. cross-country
1968	Toini Gustafsson, Sweden	5 and 10 km. cross-country
1972	Galina Koulacova, USSR	5 and 10 km. cross-country

INDEX

Abrahams, Harold, 41
Acker, Carl, 92
African pygmies, 23-24
Akii-Bua, John, 148
Albright, Tenley, 91, 101
Alekseyeve, Vasily, 151
Alexandra, 26
Allen, Scott, 125
Altwegg, Jeanette, 91
Amateurism, concept of, 14, 33
American Indians, 23-24, 28-29
American Olympic Committee, 64
Andersen, Hjalmar, 91
Anderson, Gary, 131
Anderson, Paul, 100
Andersson, Arne, 78
Anspach, Paul, 26
Anthropology Day games, 23-24
Aochi, Seiji, 143
Arab terrorists, 15, 144
Arden Hills Swim Club, 137, 154, 155
Arzhanov, Yevgeniy, 147
Ashenfelter, Horace, 88
Avilov, Nikolay, 2, 8, 149

Babashoff, Shirley, 153
Babe Didrickson All-Americans, 53
Babka, Rink, 95
Bachrach, Bill, 44, 45, 46
Balas, Iolanda, 121
Ballangrud, Ivar, 60
Bannister, Roger, 90, 121
Barbuti, Ray, 41
Barkman, Jane, 153
Barthel, Josey, 90
Basilio, Norma Enriqueta, 130
Baszanowski, Waldemar, 131

Bathe, Walter, 27
Bauer, David, 123
Bausch, Jim, 58
Baxter, Irving, 22
Bayi, Filbert, 160-161
Bayrak, Turki Mihat, 111
Beamon, Bob, 135-136
Beccali, Luigi, 58
Becker, Elizabeth, 43
Bellamy, Walt, 112
Belote, Melissa, 153
Belousova, Ludmila, 123
Beloussov, Vladimir, 128
Ben Abdesselem, Mhadi, 107
Bendlin, Kurt, 2, 8, 10, 136
Bennett, Bruce, 46
Benvenuti, Nino, 87
Berlin, Irving, 26
Berrutti, Livio, 105-106
Bie, Ferdinand, 32, 34
Biffle, Jerry, 89
Bikila, Abebe, 107-108
Biwott, Amos, 133
Black, Larry, 145
Black Hawk, Chief, 28-29
Black power salute, 15, 132
Blanders-Koen, Fanny, 75
Bleibtrey, Ethelda, 43
Blue Angels Track Club, 162
Bobick, Duane, 85, 151
Boit, Mike, 147
Bolotnikov, Pyotr, 107
Bondarchuk, Aatoliy, 149
Boozer, Bob, 112
Borg, Arne, 45
Borzov, Valery, 145
Boston, Ralph, 106, 121
Boston Athletic Association, 16

181

Index

Boston Braves, 34
Boyerskikh, Klaudia, 123
Boysen, Auden, 97, 98
Bradley, Bill, 122
Bragg, Don "Tarzan," 47, 106
Braglia, Alberto, 28
Braumuller, Ellen, 49
Brenden, Hallgeir, 101
Brix, Herman, 46
Brown, Earlene, 105
Brown, Larry, 122
Browning, David "Skippy," 87
Bruce, Harold, 31
Bruce, Tom, 158
Brumel, Valery, 105
Brundage, Avery, 14, 32, 55, 63-64, 129, 130, 132, 144
Brunet, Pierre, 57
Buek, Dick, 101
Burghley, David, 74, 132
Burka, Sylvia, 140-141
Burke, Lynn, 111
Burke, Thomas, 17
Burton, Mike, 154
Bush, Lesley, 118
Button, Dick, 70-73, 91, 160

Caldwell, Joe, 122
Calhoun, Lee, 96-97, 106
Camp, Walter, 31
Campbell, Milt, 97, 109
Canton Bulldogs, 34
Capilla, Juan, 99
Carlisle Indian School, 30, 31, 33
Carlos, John, 15, 86, 132, 145
Carpenter, Ken, 66
Carr, Cathy, 153
Carr, Henry, 120
Carr, Sabin, 25
Carr, William, 58
Carrock, Susan, 142
Carvajal, Felix, 23
Caslavska, Vera, 122, 131
Cawley, Rex, 120
Chavoor, Sherm, 137, 154, 155
Chepulis, Iones, 85-86
Chicago Athletic Club, 44
Chicago Cardinals, 34
Christian, Bill, 113-114
Christian, Roger, 113-114
Cincinnati Reds, 34

"Citius, Altius, Fortius," 14
Clark, Ellery, 17
Clarke, Ron, 119, 135, 161
Cleary, Bob, 113-114
Coakes, Marion, 131
Cochran, Barbara, 142
Cochran, Gordon "Mickey," 142
Cochran, Lindy, 142
Cochran, Marilyn, 142
Collett, Wayne, 145
Collins, Jimmy, 152
Connelly, Jim, 113
Connolly, Harold, 24, 98, 105
Connolly, James, 16
Consolini, Adolfo, 94
Cook, Ed, 25
Corbett, Jim, 86
Coubertin, Pierre de, 13, 14, 19
Counsilman, James (Doc), 155-156
Courtney, Tom, 97-98
Crabbe, Buster, 46, 47, 58
Craig, Ralph, 28
Crockett, Ivory, 163
Cromwell, Dean, 63-64
Crothers, Bill, 120
Cunningham, Glenn, 58, 66
Curtis, Ann, 75
Curtis, Charles, 34
Curtis, Tommy, 17, 57-58
Cuthbert, Betty, 99, 121,

Dagistanli, Mustafa, 100
Daland, Peter, 156-157
Danek, Ludvik, 95, 96, 149
Daniels, Charles, 23, 26
Davies, Lynn, 121
Davis, Glenn, 96-97, 106
Davis, Jack, 77
Davis, John, 74, 87
Davis, Otis, 106
Davis, Walt, 89
Deardruff, Deena, 153
Decker, Mary, 162-163
DeGenaro, Frank, 86
Delany, Ron, 98
Delgado, Ricardo, 131
DeMont, Rick, 154, 164-165
DePietro, Joe, 74
Desjardins, Ulysses J. "Pete," 43
Desmarteau, Etienne, 22
Dibiasi, Klaus, 154

Index

Didrickson, Mildren "Babe," 49-55, 58, 59, 160
Didrickson, Ole, 50-51
Dijkstra, Sjoukje, 123
Dillard, Harrison, 76-78, 89
Dischinger, Terry, 112
Dixon, Jeff, 57
Dodds, Gil, 78
Dodson, Murl, 109
"Dorando," 26
D'Oriola, Christian, 100
Doubell, Ralph, 133
Doyle, Arthur Conan, 26
Draper, Foy, 63, 65
Draves, Vicki, 75
Durocher, Leo, 54

Eagen, Eddie, 59, 82
Ederle, Gertrude, 43
Edgar, Dave, 157
Edward VII, 24
Eisenhower, Dwight David, 33, 58
Elliott, Herb, 106-107, 121
Ellis, Jimmy, 84
Elvstrom, Paul, 112
Employers Casualty Insurance Company, 51, 52
Engan, Toralf, 123
Eriksson, Henri, 78
Evans, Lee, 132
Ewell, Barney, 76, 77
Ewry, Ray, 20-25, 26

Farrell, Jeff, 111
Farrow, Mia, 116
Ferguson, Cathy, 118
Feuerbach, Al, 164
Figg, James, 86
Fikotova, Olga, 98, 105
Fish, Jenny, 128
Flack, Teddy, 17
Flanagan, John J., 21-22
Fleischer, Tilly, 61
Fleming, Peggy, 125-127, 128, 137
Fonst, Ramon, 23
Fonville, Charles, 76
Forbes, Jim, 152
Foreman, George, 84, 85-86, 131, 160
Fort Worth Women's Invitational (1934), 54

Fosbury, Dick, 136
Fraser, Dawn, 99, 111
Fraser, Don, 73
Fraser, Gretchen, 73-74
Frazier, Joe, 83, 85, 86
Fredriksson, Gert, 99
Frigerio, Ugo, 41
Fuchs, Jeno, 28

Gable, Clark, 57
Gable, Dan, 151, 161-162
Gammoudi, Mohamed, 119, 133, 135
Garrett, Bob, 17
Genter, Steve, 157
George, Pete, 87
Gestring, Marjorie, 65
Gilbert, A. C., 25
Glickman, Marty, 64, 65
Goebbels, Josef, 64
Goitschel, Christine, 123
Goitschel, Marielle, 123, 128
Golubnichy, Vladimir, 130
Gordien, Fortune, 94
Göring, Herman, 61
Gould, Shane, 153
Gouscos, Miltiades, 17
Graef, Jed, 118
Grafstrom, Gillis, 42, 57
Gray, Clinton, 103-104
Greene, Charlie, 132
Greene, Nancy, 128
Grelle, Jim, 134
Grischin, Yevgeniu, 101
Grischin, Yuri, 112
Gronberg, Axel, 87
Grottumsbraaten, Johan, 42
Guillemot, Joseph, 37, 38
Gustav V, 32

Hagg, Gunder, 78
Hahn, Archie, 22
Haile Selassie, 108
Haines, George, 116-117, 155
Hakulinen, Veikko, 101
Halberg, Murray, 107
Hall, Evelyn, 49
Hanneman, Larry, 35
Hans Brinker, 72
Hansen, Fred, 121
Hardin, Glen, 66

Harlan, Bruce, 75
Harrison, Dillard, 148
Hart, Eddie, 145
Hary, Armin, 105, 106
Haugen, Anders, 42
Havens, Frank, 87
Hayes, Johnny, 25, 26
Haywood, Spencer, 131
Hazzard, Walt, 122
Head, Don, 113
Hefferon, Charles, 25
Heidenreich, Jerry, 157, 158
Heinrich, Ignace, 79, 80, 81
Heiss, Carol, 101, 112, 126
Hemery, Dave, 148
Hencken, John, 154
Henie, Sonja, 42, 56–57, 60, 125, 160
Henning, Annie, 140–141, 142
Henry, Ken, 91
Hicks, Thomas, 23
Hill, Albert, 41
Hill, Ralph, 58
Hillman, Harry, 22
Hines, Jim, 132
Hirohito, 99
Hitler, Adolf, 60, 61, 62, 63, 64, 110, 158
Hodge, Russ, 5, 6, 7, 8
Hodgson, George, 27
Holdorf, Willi, 4, 121
Holecek, Josef, 87
Holm, Eleanor, 47, 55–56
Holum Dianne, 128, 141–142
Hoover, Herbert, 57
House of David (baseball team), 53
Houser, Bud, 41
Huber, Hans, 85
Huega, Jimmy, 123
Hustiu, Beatrice, 128
Hyvarinen, Antti, 101

Iba, Hank, 153
Illinois Athletic Club, 44
Imhoff, Darrall, 112
Iness, Sim, 89
Ingrid, Kramer, 111
International Olympic Committee (IOC), 14, 32, 34, 35, 39, 61, 63, 129, 144, 148, 159
International Meet of Champions, 19
Irish-American Athletic Club, 21
Iso-Rollo, Volmari, 40
Ivanov, Vyacheslav, 122

Jabbar, Kareem Abdul, 129
Jackson, Arnold, 28
Jackson, Luke, 122
Jackson, Marjorie, 88
Jackson, Virgil, 79
Jaervinen, Akilles, 58
Jaffee, Irving, 42, 57
Jarvinen, Mati, 40
Jarvis, Johnny, 22
Jenkins, Charley, 97
Jenkins, David, 101, 112
Jenkins, Hayes Alan, 101, 112
Jensen, Jackie, 75
Jernberg, Sixten, 101, 123
Jewtraw, Charles, 42
Jipcho, Ben, 134, 148
Jochum-Beiser, Trude, 73, 91
Johansson, Ingemar, 84
Johansson, Ivar, 58–59
Johnson, Cornelius, 61
Johnson, Derek, 97–98
Johnson, Paul, 113
Johnson, Rafer, 97, 108–110, 111
Joly, Andrée, 57
Jones, Hayes, 120

Kahanamoku, Duke, 27–28, 43, 45
Kamp Olympik, 47
Karpati, Rudolf, 111
Kasaya, Yukio, 143
Kazantsev, Vladmir, 88
Kealoha, Warren, 43
Keily, Ken, 107
Keino, Kipchoge "Kip,", 133, 134, 135, 146–147, 148, 161
Keller, Erhard, 128, 143
Kelly, Grace, 42
Kelly, Jack, 42
Kelly, Jack, Jr., 74–75, 99
Kemp, Jennifer, 153
Kennedy, Robert, 110
Kidd, Billy, 123
Killanin, Lord, 14
Killy, Jean Claude, 127–128
King, Maxine "Micki," 153–154
Kinmont, Jill, 101
Kinsella, John, 157
Kiprugut, Wilson, 133
Kirk, O. L., 86
Kirov, Petar, 151
Kirst, Joachim, 2, 8, 9

Index

Kistenmacher, Enrique, 79, 80
Kogo, Ben, 133
Kolb, Claudia, 138
Kolehmainen, Hannes, 28, 37, 40
Komar, Wladyslaw, 148
Konno, Akitsugo, 143
Konno, Ford, 87
Kono, Tommy, 87
Korbut, Olga, 152, 160
Kosinsky, Vladimir, 130
Koulacova, Galina, 143
Kraenzlein, Alvin, 20, 21, 39
Kraenzlein, Ralph, 75
Kruger, Luise, 61
Kubicka, Terry, 162
Kuehn, Louis, 43
Kunigk, William, 73
Kurland, Bob, 74
Kuts, Vladimir, 98
Kuzma, Istevan, 131
Kuznetsov, Vasily, 97, 109
Kysner, Kathy, 122

LaBarba, Fidel, 86
Lake Tahoe Ski Club, 42
Landy, John, 98
Larrabee, Mike, 119
Larrieu, Francie, 163
Larrieu, Ron, 163
Larsson, Gunnar, 154
Latour, Count Baillet, 61
Latyinina, Larisa, 100
Lawrence, Andrea Mead, 91-92, 142
Lee, Sammy, 75, 87
Lehtinen, Lauri, 58
Lehtonen, Eric, 40
Lemming, Eric, 25
Leonard, Ray Charles "Sugar," 165
Lightbody, James, 22
Lindgren, Gerry, 120
Liquori, Marty, 146, 160
Lismont, Karl, 149
Liston, Sonny, 84
Long, Dallas, 121
Long, Luz, 62-63
Lorz, Fred, 23
Loues, Spiridion, 17-18
Loukola, Toivo, 39
Lovell, Alberto, 86-87
Lovell, Pedro, 87
Lovelock, Jack, 58, 66

Lucas, Jerry, 112
Lusis, Janis, 136, 149
Lydiard, Arthur, 120
Lynn, Janet, 143

McCarten, Jack, 113
McCombs, M. J., 51, 52
McCormick, Pat, 87-88, 99
McDaniel, Mildred, 99
McDermott, Terry, 123, 128
McDonald, Pat, 28
McGrath, Matty, 28
McGregor, Don, 115
McGuire, Edith, 121
McKenley, Herb, 88
McLane, Jimmy, 75
McMillen, Bob, 90
Madison, Helen, 55
Maentyranta, Eero, 123
Magee, Barry, 107
Magnusson, Karen, 143
Mann, Ralph, 148
Manning, Madeline, 137
Marciano, Rocky, 84
Mariles, Humberto, 75
Maskova, Hana, 127
Mason, Tommy, 152
Masson, 18
Mastenbroek, Hendrika, 65
Mathias, Bob, 78-82, 89, 109
Mathis, Buster, 85
Matson, Randy, 121, 136, 164
Matthes, Rollie, 138, 154
Matthews, Vince, 145
Matzdorf, Pat, 165
Mayer, Helene, 64
Meadows, Earle, 66
Medved, Alexander, 151
Meredith, Teddy, 28
Metcalfe, Ralph, 58, 63, 64, 65, 68
Meyer, Debbie, 128, 137-138, 154, 157, 160
Meyers, Mary, 128
Milburn, Rod, 148
Miller, Bill, 58
Mills, Billy, 119-120
Mimoun, Alain, 98
Mimoun, Olympe, 98
Miyake, Yoshinobu, 131
Mjoen, Haakon, 127
Moe, Karen, 153

Moens, Roger, 106, 120
Monti, Eugenio, 128
Moore, Archie, 83-84
Moore, Charlie, 88
Moore, Ken, 150
Morelon, Daniel, 131, 152
Morris, Glenn, 46, 56, 66, 81
Morrow, Bobby Joe, 97
Mottley, Wendell, 119
Muhammad Ali (Cassius Clay), 38, 84, 85
Mukhin, Lev, 85
Munoz, Felipe, 130-131
Murphy, John, 157
Myrrha, Jon, 40

Nadi, Nedo, 157
Nadig, Marie-Therese, 143
National Amateur Athletic Union, 33
National anthems, playing of, 14, 15, 63, 120, 131, 145
National Collegiate Championships, 67-68
National Football League, 34
National Hockey League All-Stars, 143
Nazi salute, 64
Neilson, Sandy, 153
Nepela, Ondrej, 143
Nero, Emperor, 12
New York Athletic Club, 19
New York Evening Mail, 33
New York Giants, 34
New York State Athletic Commission, 59
New York World's Fair (1939), 56
Newell, Pete, 112
Nieder, Bill, 106
Nixon, Richard M., 58
Nones, Franco, 128
Noorlander, Eduard de, 9
Nordwig, Wolfgang, 136, 148
Norelius, Martha, 43
Norpoth, Harold, 119, 134
Norton, Ray, 105
Nurmi, Paavo, 36-40, 75, 91, 160

Oberg, Karl, 123
O'Brien, Parry, 89-90, 96, 106
O'Callaghan, Patrick, 22
Odlozil, Josef, 120, 131
Oerter, Al, 21, 93-96, 106, 121, 136
Olsen, Zoe Ann, 75
Olympic flag, 13-14

Olympic Games
  first Olympiad, 12
  number of competing nations (by 1970s), vii
  oath of, 13
  origin of, 12
  participation of women in, vii, 15, 27
  politics and, 14-15
Olympic Games of 1896, vii, 16, 17-18, 19
Olympic Games of 1900, 16, 19-20, 21-22, 24, 27, 39
Olympic Games of 1904, 21, 22-24, 86
Olympic Games of 1906 (unofficial), 15, 21, 23, 24
Olympic Games of 1908, 13, 21, 24-26, 27, 28
Olympic Games of 1912, 15, 27-28, 31-32
Olympic Games of 1916 (cancelled), 36, 70
Olympic Games of 1920, 23, 27, 36, 37-38, 41, 86
Olympic Games of 1924, vii, 15, 28, 36, 38-39, 40, 41, 42, 43, 45, 137
  division of (into Winter and Summer games), 42
Olympic Games of 1928, vii, 36, 39, 40, 42, 43, 46, 55, 64, 74
Olympic Games of 1932, 34, 39, 40, 42, 46, 49-50, 51, 55, 56, 57-59, 86-87, 92
Olympic Games of 1936, 14, 40, 42, 46, 55, 56, 58, 60-69, 73, 144
  racial and religious issues, 63-64, 65
Olympic Games of 1940 (cancelled), 70, 73
Olympic Games of 1944 (cancelled), 70
Olympic Games of 1948, 70-82, 86, 90, 94, 99
Olympic Games of 1952, 40, 72, 79, 81, 83-92, 94, 97, 99, 101, 102
Olympic Games of 1956, 84, 85, 89, 93-102, 105, 109, 122, 128
Olympic Games of 1960, 58, 84, 85, 89, 95, 103-114, 120, 122
Olympic Games of 1964, 4, 84, 89, 99, 105, 106, 115-124, 128, 136, 153, 163
Olympic Games of 1968, 1-3, 8-10, 75, 84, 91, 106, 108, 118, 125-130, 155
  barring of South Africa, 129
  protests by black Americans, 15, 131-132
  random tests for drug taking, 8
  riots against, 129
Olympic Games of 1972, 138, 140-158
  Arab terrorists, 15, 144
  black-power protests, 145

Index

Olympic Games of 1976, vii
   future stars of, 159-165
Oorang Indians, 34
Osborn, Harold, 41
Ostermeyer, Micheline, 75-76
O'Sullivan, Maureen, 116
Owen, Laurence, 125
Owen, Maribel Vinson, 125
Owens, Jesse, 60-69, 75, 76, 104, 106, 110, 158, 160
Ozolina, Elvira, 121-122

Paddock, Charlie, 41, 66
Pal Joey, 72
Pan-American Games, 5-6, 95, 109, 150, 156
Papp, Laszlo, 86, 87
Paraskevopoulos, Panagiotis, 17
Paris Exposition of 1900, 19
Patterson, Floyd, 83-84, 87
Patton, George, 27
Patton, Mel, 76, 77
Peacock, Eulace, 68
Pedraza, Jose, 130
Pender, Paul, 132
Perrillat, Guy, 127
Peters, Mary, 151
Petersen, Dane Anders, 86
Peterson, Ben, 151
Philadelphia Athletics, 53
Philippides, 17
Pietri, Dorando, 25-26
Pietrzykowski, Anton, 85
Pitou, Penny, 123
Plato, 12
Pollard, Fritz, 66
Ponomaryeva, Nina, 105
Poynton-Hill, Dorothy, 65
Prefontaine, Steve, 161
Press, Irina, 105, 121
Press, Tamara, 105, 121
Prinstein, Myer, 21, 23
Proell, Annemarie, 142
Protopopov, Oleg, 123
Puttemans, Emiel, 161

Racing Club de France, 19-20
Rademacher, Pete, 84, 85
Ramirez Vasquez, Pedro, 130

Rand, Mary (Mrs. Bill Toomey), 4, 6, 11, 121
Raska, Jiri, 128
Rausch, Emil, 23
Ray, Joie, 41
Reidpath, Chuck, 28
Reiff, Gaston, 78
Remigino, Lindy, 88
Rhoden, George, 88
Rice, Grantland, 53
Rice, Greg, 78
Richards, Bob, 89, 96, 109
Richards, Vinnie, 53
Richtoff, John, 59
Rigby, Cathy, 152
Riggin, Aileen, 42
Riley, Charlie, 66
Ris, Wally, 75
Ritola, Willie, 38-39, 40
Robertson, Lawrence, 64
Robertson, Oscar, 112
Robertson, Ronnie, 101
Robinson, Bill "Bojangles," 68
Robinson, Elizabeth, 43
Robinson, Jackie, 63
Robinson, Mack, 63
Robinson, Rey, 145
Robinson, "Sugar Ray," 165
Rodnina, Irina, 143
Roldon, Antonio, 131
Rom, Dagmar, 91
Roosevelt, Alice, 23
Rose, Billy, 56
Rose, Murray, 99, 177
Rose, Ralph, 23
Ross, Norman, 43
Roth, Dick, 117-118
Rothammer, Keena, 153
Rudd, Birger, 60
Rudolph, Wilma, 103-105, 106, 111, 121, 160
Ruth, Babe, 51
Ryun, Jim, 121, 133-135, 146-147, 160, 163

Saari, Roy, 117
Sailer, Anton "Toni," 102
Salas, Joe, 86
Saltza, Chris von, 111
San Romani, Archie, 66
Sanders, Ed, 84

Index

Saneyev, Viktor, 136, 149
Santa Clara Swimming Club, 155
Saubert, Jeannie, 123
Schafer, Karl, 57, 60
Schemansky, Norbert, 74
Schenck, Ard, 143-144
Schiprowski, Claus, 136
Schirmer, Friedel, 4
Schnelldorfer, Manfred, 123
Schollander, Don, 44, 115-124, 155, 157
Schranz, Karl, 127-128, 144
Schuba, Trixi, 143
Schul, Bob, 119
Schwarz, Wolfgang, 125
Scott, Barbara Ann, 73
Scott, Randoph, 46
Seagren, Bob, 136, 148
Seales, Ray, 151
Selvetti, Humberto, 100
Seyfert, Gabriele, 127
Shakhlin, Boris, 111
Shavlakadze, Robert, 105
Shea, Jack, 57
Sheldon, Richard, 21
Sheppard, Mel, 24
Sheridan, Martin, 23, 24, 25
Shiley, Jean, 50
Shorter, Frank, 149-151, 160
Silvester, Jay, 96, 149
Sime, Dave, 105
Simmons, Floyd, 80
Sinden, Harry, 113
Sitzberger, Ken, 118
Skoblikova, Lydia, 112, 123
Smith, Bill, 75
Smith, Guinn, 76
Smith, Tommie, 15, 86, 132, 145
Smithson, Foster, 25
Snell, Peter, 106, 107, 120, 121
Snyder, Larry, 67
Socrates, 12
Solberg, Magnar, 143
South Pacific, 72
South Pacific tribesmen, 23-24
Sowell, Arnie, 97, 98
Spitz, Lenore and Arnold, 154
Spitz, Mark, 138, 154-158, 159
Spock, Benjamin, 41-42
St. Louis Cardinals, 53
St. Louis Exposition of 1904, 22
Stagg, Amos Alonzo, 19
Stamm, Mike, 158

Stanfield, Andy, 89
Statkevich, Nina, 141
Stecher, Renate, 151
Steinkraus, Billy, 131
Stephens, Helen, 65
Stevenson, Theofilio, 84-85, 151
Stinnes, Matias, 128
Stoller, Sam, 64, 65
Stones, Dwight, 148-149, 165
Stouder, Sharon, 118
Strand, Lennart, 78
Strickland, Shirley, 99
Sullivan, James, 32
Sullivan, John L., 86
Sullivan Award, 75, 78, 88, 104, 137

Taft, William Howard, 33
Tarmak, Yuri, 148
Taylor, Bob, 145
Taylor, Chris, 151
Taylor, Henry, 26
Tchoukarine, Viktor, 100
Teato, Michel, 22
Temple, Ed, 104
Temple, Shirley, 57
Temu, Naftali, 133
Ter-Ovanesyan, Igor, 106, 121
Tewanima, 31
Tewksbury, John, 22
Thams, Jacob, 42
Theodosius, Emperor, 12-13
Third Reich Sports Field, 61
Thoeni, Gustavo, 143
Thomas, John, 105, 121
Thomas, Lowell, 74
Thompson, Wilbur, 76
Thoreson, Dave, 6
Thorpe, Charles, 29
Thorpe, Hiram, 29
Thorpe, Jim, 10, 28-35
Thunberg, Clas, 42
Tinker, Gerald, 145
Tita, Vasile, 83
Titova, Ludmilla, 128
Tobian, Gary, 99
Tolan, Eddie, 58
Toomey, Bill, 1-11, 80, 121, 136, 160
Toomey, Samantha, 11
Torres, Jose, 87
Tourischeva, Ludmila, 152
Towns, Forrest, 66

Index

Trentin, Pierre, 131
Trusenyov, Vladimir, 95
Tummler, Bodo, 134
Tyler, Fred, 157
Tyus, Wyomia, 121, 136–137

Uetake, Yojiro, 131
Ulanov, Alexei, 143

Varoff, George, 66
Varona, Donna de, 118
Vasin, Vladimir, 154
Vasla, Pekka, 147–148
Verdeur, Joe, 75
View, Charlotte, 29
Vinci, Charles, 111
Viren, Lasse, 147–148
Viscopoleanu, Viorica, 136
Vorobiev, Arkadi, 111

Walde, Hans-Joachim, 2, 9, 10, 136
Waldrop, Tony, 160
Walsh, Stella (Stanislawa Walasiewicz), 52, 55, 65–66
Walton, Bill, 152
Warmerdam, Cornelius "Dutch," 76
Warner, "Pop," 31, 33
Webster, Bob, 118
Weissmuller, Johnny, 27, 43–48, 59, 115, 137, 157, 160
Werner, Buddy, 101
West, Jerry, 112
Whitfield, Mal, 78, 88–89, 133
Wieslander, Hugo, 32, 34
Wigger, Lones, 152
Wilber, Doreen, 151–152
Williams, Archie, 66

Williams, Gardner, 18
Williams, John, 151–152
Williams, Percy, 41
Williams, Randy, 148
Williams, Steve, 163–164
Williams, Tom, 113
Wilson, Jackie, 87
Wint, Arthur, 88
Wittenberg, Henry, 74
Woellke, Hans, 61
Wohluter, Rick, 163
Wolde, Mamo, 133, 149
Wolferman, Klaus, 149
Wood, Tim, 125
Woodruff, John, 66
Woods, George, 148, 164
World War I, 20, 36
World War II, 27, 64
Wottle, Dave, 145–146
Wright, Stan, 145
Writer, John, 152
Wykoff, Frank, 63, 65, 67

Yale crew, 100
Yang, C. K., 109, 110, 121
Young, Cy, 89

Zaharias, George, 54–55
Zappas, Evangelios, 13
Zatopek, Dana, 90
Zatopek, Emil, 78, 90–91, 98, 108, 149, 160
Zhabotinski, Leonid, 131
Zivic, Fritzie, 86
Zivic, Jack, 86
Zivic, Pete, 86
Zsivotzky, Gyula, 136

GV
697
.A1
L53
1975

GV
697
.A1
L53
1975